Our Magnif...
Are
Mirac...

Unspoiled and wondrous, the National Parks System offers over 77,000,000 acres of rich, natural land for all to share. Thrilling scenic beauty, glistening lakes below the earth, sculptured snowcapped mountains, and abundant plant life and wildlife make our bountiful world of parks a vacationer's paradise.

Generous guidance and unlimited information was provided by:

> The National Parks Service—U.S. Department of the Interior
> The U.S. Travel Service—U.S. Department of Agriculture
> The U.S. Coast Guard
> The National Wildlife Federation
> The National Audubon Society

POCKET BOOKS GUIDE
TO NATIONAL PARKS

Pocket Books Guide To National Parks

William Wallace Rhodes

PUBLISHED BY POCKET BOOKS NEW YORK

Another *Original* publication of POCKET BOOKS

POCKET BOOKS, a division of Simon & Schuster, Inc.
1230 Avenue of the Americas, New York, N.Y. 10020

ISBN: 0-671-50382-0

First Pocket Books printing April, 1984

10 9 8 7 6 5 4 3 2 1

ACKNOWLEDGMENTS

Far more than is usual, this book has been a collaboration. Creative Editorial Productions and the editor have been the beneficiaries of the generous courtesy of many individuals and institutions throughout America.

Among the organizations that assisted by providing guidance and information are: the National Park Service, U.S. Department of the Interior; the U.S. Travel Service, Department of Agriculture; the U.S. Coast Guard; the National Wildlife Federation; the National Audubon Society; and Rhodes Geographic Library.

I especially would like to thank journalist Sally Barker and assistant editor Jean Butt for their help with the manuscript.

—WILLIAM WALLACE RHODES
EDITOR

CONTENTS

FOREWORD

As with millions of other Americans, I don't suppose I gave too much thought to the natural wonders of this country, much less its national parks, until one fateful day. That was the day my wife, Jean, and I quite accidentally stumbled into the Acadia National Park in Maine. That first glimpse of Mount Desert Island and I was convinced I'd finally found my piece of paradise.

Over the years my enthusiasm for that breathtaking bastion of natural beauty has remained undiminished. If anything, it has steadily grown to where it now encompasses not only Acadia but also the awesome grandeur of all the national parks from one end of the country to the other.

If, perhaps, my adjectives seem a bit too effusive on the subject of these parks, it's most likely because I came to discover these incomparable natural resources rather late and regret the wasted years when I did not know about the joys and excitement waiting for me out there.

Many of you may have already experienced some of these miracles of nature and have picked up this volume seeking information about new areas to explore, new vistas to enjoy. That information is here indeed, in abundance. Others of you, however, will be discovering the national parks for the first time, and what a discovery it will be! The thrill of actually watching the dramatic, constantly changing color of the Grand Canyon at sunset or marveling at a cool, shimmering lake deep below the earth in Mammoth Cave are beyond any words of description I could possibly use.

Americans are notorious for spending millions of dollars a year to travel abroad in order to visit natural wonders that are not half as spectacular as the ones we have right here at home, literally in our own backyards. This is as true today as it was at the beginning of the century when Gilbert H. Grosvenor, the esteemed, longtime Director of the National Geographic Society, wrote:

Switzerland, the playground of Europe . . . cannot compare in attractiveness with the High Sierra of central California. Nothing in the Alps can rival the famous Yosemite Valley, which is as unique as the Grand Canyon. The view from the summit of Mount Whitney surpasses that from any of the peaks of Switzerland. There are no canyons in Switzerland equal to those of the Kern and the King rivers, which contain scores of waterfalls and roaring streams, any one of which in Europe would draw thousands of visitors annually. Many of the big yellow and red pines, of the juniper and cedar, eclipse the trees of Switzerland as completely as the pines are eclipsed by the giant red-woods.

And then, as to birds and flowers, the High Sierra so excels the Alps that there is no comparison. Never will the writer forget the melodies of the birds and luxuriance of the meadows . . . the fields of blue, red, yellow, orange, white and purple flowers, all graceful and fragrant, or the divine dignity of the great Siberian Plateau, nearly eleven thousand feet above the sea, and yet carpeted from end to end with blue lupine and tiny flowers.

All this unspoiled beauty remains today much as it was when Grosvenor first saw it. Indeed, it may be even more awe inspiring since we've lost so much of our virgin wilderness to development over the intervening years. Those areas which are preserved forever through the National Park System, though, stand as superlative monuments to our country's historical, geological, and biological heritage.

What's more, these national parks offer Americans recreational and educational bargains which just cannot be equalled anywhere else. For thousands and thousands of dollars less than it costs to travel to foreign lands, you can enjoy exciting and memorable vacations here inside your own country. Whether you desire plush hotel accommodations or prefer to "rough it" through the backcountry, photographing spectacular mountain scenery or exploring underwater coral reefs, spotting deer in dense northern forests or glimpsing alligators in the subtropical Everglades, there is literally something for everyone.

That these parks can offer so much to everyone is

not terribly surprising when you consider how vast an area the national parks cover. The National Park System envelops over seventy-seven million acres of land, not only within the continental United States but in Alaska, Hawaii, and the Virgin Islands as well.

Deciding on which time of year to visit a particular park is a matter of personal preference. The great majority of people travel to the parks during the summer months, although I've always preferred the spring and fall, when the parks are just as lovely and far less crowded. Winter poses a few additional problems for northern parks which may become snowbound, although quite a few offer excellent skiing and other winter activities. Southern parks, on the other hand, tend to remain in full operation on a year-round basis.

One word of caution, however, before you venture out to explore this bountiful world of unspoiled nature: Don't take on more than you can comfortably manage in the time you have available. By that I mean taking great care in gauging the distances you may have to travel between parks or even within the park itself. It's easy to deceive yourself into thinking a proposed route is much shorter than it really is. For example, both the Redwood National Park and Sequoia National Park are located in California. They are, however, 440 miles apart—not exactly convenient for a one-day sightseeing trip to both. By the same token, Yellowstone National Park is the size of a small country, encompassing 3,400 square miles. A week might not be long enough to see and do everything in that one park alone.

As you read through this book, savoring the kaleidoscope of climates, colors, animals, and plant life to be found in the parks, I'm sure you'll be as impressed by their incredible diversity as I am. Each one is magnificent, so beautiful, so unique.

It would be impossible for any one person to cross every river, scale all the peaks, trek through every rain forest, peer into each canyon, and photograph every plant and animal species in the millions of acres of the parklands. Therefore, I am deeply grateful to the dedicated men and women of the National Park Service who were able to provide the information needed to bridge the gaps in my own personal experience.

Some of the following material is the product of years of work by archeologists, naturalists, historians, and travel writers commissioned by the Park Service and other federal agencies. Thanks to the gracious and unstinting cooperation of the National Park Service, I am able to incorporate their authoritative information here.

No matter whether you have a weekend or three weeks to spend exploring the parks, there's no better place to "get away from it all" while having fun and saving money at the same time.

Whether you are looking for the wonders of unspoiled nature, a stroll through America's heritage, or simply relaxation, the National Park System was designed for your enjoyment. There is something for everyone: hiking, boating, camping, even scaling a glacier or bouncing over golden waves of windswept sand in a dune buggy. Whatever you're looking for—sports, recreation, history lesson, or just an escape from the workaday routines—you can find it in the national parks.

And who knows? You may find your own personal piece of paradise too.

GRAND CANYON NATIONAL PARK

ARIZONA

The incomparable Grand Canyon is, without doubt, the most famous natural landmark on this continent—and justifiably so. This 1-mile-deep mammoth gorge is so overwhelming that, as John Muir wrote in 1898, it seems like something out of another world:

> The Grand Canyon of the Colorado will seem as novel to you, as unearthly in the color and grandeur and quantity of its architecture, as if you had found it after death on some other star . . .

The Grand Canyon is aptly acclaimed as one of the seven natural wonders of the world. In form, glowing

1

color, and geological significance, nothing compares
with the Grand Canyon of the Colorado River. For
centuries, the canyon walls have weathered and
crumbled, giving the river tools for scouring and goug-
ing. The canyon has widened and changed. It is never
twice the same from one day to the next. Its appearance varies with the hour of the day. The vistas and
changing colors caused by the changing angles of the
sun's rays striking against the canyon walls are spectacular to behold. The visitor at the brink of the mighty
abyss feels himself humbled and swept up by the spirit
of this wonderful spectacle, alive with a million
moods.

After more than one hundred years of studies,
significant parts of the geological story are still obscure. We do know, however, that the Grand Canyon
is a product of the conflict between two great forces:
mountain building on the one hand and gravity on the
other. This portion of the earth's crust has been
elevated 1.5 miles above sea level, and water, powered
by gravity, is carrying this place to the sea. The vehicle is the mighty Colorado River.

Today, the Grand Canyon is about 1 mile deep; it
ranges in width from about 600 feet to 18 miles; and
measured along the river, it is 217 miles long. From the
rims of the canyon, we look down on the tops of mountains that measure 2,000 feet or more from their bases
within the canyon.

The Colorado River below Grand Canyon Village is
only 2,400 feet above sea level. The vast inner canyon
is a hot, dry desert with summer temperatures exceeding 40°C (104°F). Above the rims, the surface of the
land slopes from north to south. Water falling on the
South Rim flows away from the canyon; water falling

on the North Rim flows toward the canyon. Thus the
North Rim has been eroded farther back from the river
because of this extra water.

One result of the conflict here is that perhaps nowhere else on earth has such a geological record been
so clearly exposed. Within the walls of the Grand Canyon we have a view of geological time—a view that
stretches back at least 2 billion years.

Besides providing insights into geological history,
the Grand Canyon is a vast biological museum. The
"grand" canyon and its innumerable side canyons are
bounded by high plateaus that have cool north-facing
slopes and hot south-facing slopes, year-round and intermittent streams, and seasonal climatic variations.
These various environments support life in abundance—from desert life-forms at the lower elevations
near the river and on the canyon walls to the conifer
forest communities on the rims.

In the Grand Canyon, geological and biological
processes are combined in one awesome spectacle. An
appreciation and an understanding of this spectacle
come with a recognition that creation of the canyon is
a continuing process that is happening today and every
day.

The Colorado River divides the park in half. The
North Rim and South Rim are only 9 miles apart, but
they are two different worlds. The North Rim is about
1,200 feet higher than the South Rim and is similar to
Canada in climate, vegetation, and plant life, while the
South Rim is more typical of the arid Southwest.

Maj. John Wesley Powell, a one-armed veteran of
the Civil War, led the first expedition down the Colorado River through the Grand Canyon. He rode the
river in a chair strapped to one of the group's wooden

boats and searched the river ahead for hidden rocks and rapids. This adventuresome geologist was also responsible for naming the "Grand Canyon," as he referred to it in his diary of that 1869 trip.

The inner canyon desert may be explored on foot or by boat. On such trips, you will see more closely the canyon's rich natural beauty and sense even more sharply its immense size.

Hiking is popular during summer and autumn at both North and South Rims, but visitors are required to obtain a hikers bulletin from the visitor center before beginning any canyon hikes. Nature walks, lectures, and films are provided at the North Rim and South Rim visitor centers. Canyon trips by muleback are available for half-day to two-day trips. Reservations well in advance are required through: Fred Harvey, Inc., P.O. Box 699, Grand Canyon, AZ 86023 for the South Rim; or through: Grand Canyon Scenic Rides, North Rim, AZ 86022 (summer) and Box S, Kanab, UT 84741 (winter) for the North Rim.

Grand Canyon River Float Trips depart from Lee's Ferry, Arizona, outside the park. Trips may vary from three to eighteen days, and reservations are required six months in advance. Write to the park superintendent for information on float trip outfitters.

Scenic air tours and sightseeing tours to museums, Indian villages, ruins, and the Painted Desert are available at the North and South rims. Reservations are not required, and information regarding schedules and fees is available at the visitor centers.

Because of heavy snowfalls, the North Rim is closed every year from about mid-October to mid-May. The South Rim remains open, but temperatures average between 43°F and 20°F (6°C to -7°C), so dress appropriately and have your car equipped with snow tires or chains. Summer temperatures are generally mild on both rims, but down within the inner canyon the mercury can soar as high as 120°F (49°C).

Those persons with heart conditions should bear in mind that the two rims are 7,000 feet or more above sea level and the air is extremely thin. Overexertion at this altitude could be dangerous.

LODGING—SOUTH RIM: Lodging is available within the park at Bright Angel Lodge, El Tovar Hotel, Yavapai Lodge, Phantom Ranch, Thunderbird and Kachina lodges. Reservations are required through: Fred Harvey, Inc., Grand Canyon, AZ 86023. Additional lodging and facilities are available at Tusayan, 5 miles from the park; in Williams, 60 miles away, and Flagstaff, 80 miles away. Groceries, meats, supplies, souvenirs, camper services, laundry, service station, garage, and transportation are also available within the park.

LODGING—NORTH RIM: Lodging is available within the park at Grand Canyon Lodge in the summer. For reservations, write: TWA Services, Inc., Box 400, Cedar City, UT 84720. Lodging is also available at Jacob Lake, 30 miles from the park. Meals, transportation, curios, barber, a service station, and medical services are also available within the park.

Camping on the South Rim is provided at Mather Campground (open all year), Desert View Campground (open May to October 1), and Trailer Village (open all year). Stays at the drive-in campgrounds are limited to fifteen days at Trailer Village and seven days elsewhere. At the five hike-in campgrounds, stays are limited to seven days at Havasu and two days elsewhere. All campsites provide parking, picnic tables, fire grates, water outlets, and rest rooms.

On the North Rim camping is encouraged (summer only) in designated areas near the ranger station and lodge. Stays are limited to seven days. All campsites provide parking, picnic tables, fire grates, water outlets, rest rooms, showers, and a supply store, but no utility connections. Within the national forest, 5 miles from the park boundaries, DeMotte Park Campground is open to the public. There are also campgrounds available at Jacob Lake. Reservations required for backcountry camping.

SOUTH RIM—HOW TO GET THERE: From the nearest principal cities of Phoenix, Arizona; Las Vegas, Nevada; and Salt Lake City, Utah, Hughes Airwest and/or Scenic Airlines schedule flights into Grand Canyon Airport within the park boundaries. From nearby Flagstaff, Frontier Airlines also schedules daily flights to Grand Canyon Airport. Ground transportation service to and from the hotel/motel area meets all regularly scheduled flights for a nominal fee. Taxis and rental cars are available at the park airport or in other nearby towns. By bus, Continental Trailways and Greyhound schedule daily service to both Flagstaff and Williams. From either point, Nava Hopi tour buses continue the trip to Grand Canyon. By car, State Route 64 from Cameron and U.S. Highway 180 from Flagstaff lead directly to the South Rim.

NORTH RIM—HOW TO GET THERE: Cedar City, Utah, is served by Hughes Airwest. Rental cars are available, and there is bus service directly to the North Rim from Cedar City from mid-June through August. By car, State Road 67 from Jacob Lake, Arizona, is the only highway entrance to the North Rim.

PETRIFIED FOREST NATIONAL PARK

ARIZONA

The eerie and alien landscape of the Petrified Forest is far more than a mere collection of oddly shaped mesas and fossilized trees; it's an experience in appreciating how the forces of time and nature can transform even the most unlikely materials into creations of great beauty.

Scattered around this park in the Arizona badlands are thousands of great logs, their very fibers preserved forever in glittering crystals of quartz. A close examination of broken sections and chips will reveal even the smallest details of the original wood now converted into lumps of jasper, agate, and amethyst. But even more amazing is to realize that these were once living trees, not unlike those we see today, flourishing long before the first man set foot upon the earth.

During the 20 million years of the late Triassic period of geological time (200 to 180 million years ago), this area was part of a vast floodplain crossed by many streams. On well-drained sites, near the headwaters of these streams, grew stately pinelike trees. Some of these trees fell and were soon buried in mud, sand, and volcanic ash carried by flooding streams. The scarcity of oxygen deep under these stream deposits arrested the processes of decay and rot, while the surrounding deposits hardened into sandstones and shales of the Chinle Formation.

This set the stage for petrifaction, a process not completely understood. Apparently the ancient Triassic streams contained chemicals that allowed the mineral silica to dissolve in their waters. This silica-bearing water penetrated the buried logs' wood cells and holes created by rot and insects. The water evaporated, leaving only the silica in the cell interiors and the holes. The wood tissues remained intact, and the silica turned into quartz.

Over millions of years, this area sank below sea level, was flooded, and then covered by layers of new sediments. Later it was uplifted far above sea level. The petrified trees, entombed in layers of rock, heaved under these great pressures and cracked and broke into the large and small pieces you see today. In recent times, wind and water have carved away the sandstones and shales surrounding the logs, leaving them on the surface as you see them today.

Prehistoric Indians lived here and built their homes with the petrified wood. Surviving are ruins of these dwellings, as well as their petroglyphs (drawings and signs etched on stone).

Wayside exhibits at major points of interest along the twenty-seven-mile park road will increase your enjoyment and understanding of this area. Interesting drives to several places off the road increase the distance of the complete trip through the park to about twenty-nine miles. If you enter the park from the north, your first stop will be 1; if you enter from the south, it is 13:

1. Painted Desert Visitor Center and Headquarters: U.S. 66 entrance. Information. Orientation to this and other units of the National Park System. Lunchroom, souvenir shop, and service station.

2. Painted Desert; Sweeping views from several overlooks along the rim and from the observation site on Kachine Point. Picnic area on Chinde Point, just west of Kachine Point observation site.

3. Puerco Indian Ruin: Remains of walls at this site, which was occupied about 600 years ago, indicate a rectangular village of perhaps 150 rooms enclosing a large courtyard. A few rooms have been excavated.

4. Newspaper Rock: Petroglyphs (prehistoric Indian rock art) pecked into the surface of a massive sandstone block.

5. The Tepees: Small peaks resembling tepees or haystacks showing erosion of soft, layered clay deposits.

6. Blue Mesa: Illustrates the way petrified logs play a part in the constant renewal of the sculptured landscape. The soft earth is eroded away, leaving a gradually narrowing ridge beneath the length of each log. Eventually, sections of the log roll off the ridge; ero-

sion then reduces the ridge to a series of rounded pinnacles. When a section of a fossil log remains as a
protecting cap atop one of these ridges, erosion often
produces a pedestal-like formation capped by the log
section. Sections of logs that come to rest at new locations on the soft clay after tumbling from their perches
start the erosional cycle all over again. An excellent
short trail takes you into this interesting area.

7. Agate Bridge: More than one hundred feet of this
famous log are exposed, but both ends are still encased
in the sandstone in which the log was buried. A forty-
foot-wide ravine has gradually been carved into the
sandstone, with the log spanning the narrow draw. A
concrete-beam support was placed under the heavy
log in 1917 as a precaution against collapse.

8. Jasper Forest Overlook: The spur road leads to
the edge of Jasper Forest Mesa. Great masses of log
sections litter the valley floor and clog the gullies that
cut into the edge of the mesa.

9. Crystal Forest: Here were once many fossil logs
in which beautiful clear and amethyst quartz crystals
filled the cracks and hollows. Before federal protection
of the area, collectors and souvenir hunters blasted
many of the logs in search of these gems. This type of
activity and commercial exploitation prompted the
citizens of the Arizona Territory to petition Congress
for the preservation of Petrified Forest.

10. The Flattops: Massive remnants of a once-
continuous layer of durable sandstone protecting a
series of layered deposits that have elsewhere been
removed by erosion. The road passes through a cleft
separating the two main bodies of this surviving table-
land.

11. The Long Logs and Agate House: The eastern

part of Rainbow Forest is most notable for the number of exceptionally long logs, which are only partly uncovered. A partially restored pueblo, now called Agate House, is at the end of a foot trail from the parking area. A paved self-guiding trail serves the area.

12. Rainbow Forest Museum and Giant Logs: Exhibits here are designed to answer pertinent questions that visitors may have when arriving at or leaving the park. Behind the exhibit hall are Old Faithful Log and many other exceedingly large logs. Picnic area nearby. Lunchroom, souvenir shop, and service station.

13. Rainbow Forest Entrance Station: Park boundary on U.S. 180.

14. Wilderness Area: Entry into the wilderness area by permit only. Apply at ranger station.

HIKING. Walking trails will take you to additional points of interest. If you plan to hike away from established trails, be sure to carry an adequate supply of water, for there is *no water* in the desert. Before such hiking, you are required to register with a park ranger at the visitor center or at one of the entrance stations.

Picnicking is permitted only at Chinde Point and in Rainbow Forest, where there are tables, water, and rest rooms.

LODGING: There are no overnight facilities within the park. Motels and facilities are available within a moderate distance on U.S. 66/I-40. For reservations, write to the Chamber of Commerce of St. Johns and Springerville, Arizona. Painted Desert Oasis and Rainbow Forest Lodge provide refreshments, lunches, souvenirs, and auto service. Both are open all year.

Camping is not permitted within the park. The nearest public campground is at Lyman Lake State Park, about fifty miles southeast of Petrified Forest. Two private campgrounds, Red Arrow Campground in Joseph City and KOA Campground in east Holbrook, provide camping facilities, including electricity and sewer hookups.

HOW TO GET THERE: U.S. Highway 66 connects the park with Gallup, New Mexico, on the east and Winslow, Arizona, on the west. Both towns are served by Frontier Airlines from Albuquerque, New Mexico, and Phoenix, Arizona. The nearest private airport is in Holbrook, Arizona, twenty-five miles west of the park's north entrance. Bus connections and rental cars are available at all airline points, and bus tours are available through the park.

CHANNEL ISLANDS NATIONAL PARK

CALIFORNIA

Everyone needs a special place where he can take temporary refuge from the pressures inherent in everyday life, a place where he can regain a closeness with nature and renourish his spirit. And what better place for such a personal renewal than an island? Particularly an island inhabited only by wildlife and cleansed by the diurnal cycles of sea, sun, and wind.

Just off the coast of Southern California, the eight California Channel Islands beckon the world-weary. Three of these islands, Anacapa, San Miguel, and Santa Barbara, constitute Channel Islands National Park, where you are invited to land and explore, swim, dive, fish, camp, and picnic.

Anacapa is the closest island to the mainland, being approximately eleven miles south of Oxnard. In reality, it is a chain of three separate islets almost five miles in length and about 700 acres in area. West Anacapa Island rises directly out of the sea to form two small peaks, the highest of which is approximately 930 feet. East and Middle Anacapa islands are smaller and consist of rolling plateaus almost entirely surrounded by 90- to 300-foot cliffs. There are few beaches on Anacapa Island; only one, at Frenchy's Cove, is not regularly submerged at high tide.

For much of the year, Anacapa looks brown and lifeless, but with the advent of the winter rains, the island's plants emerge from their summer dormancy and again turn green. The most unusual plant on Anacapa also grows on the other Channel Islands. This grotesque-looking plant, called giant coreopsis or tree sunflower, may grow up to 10 feet high in some favorable locations. In early spring, each plant grows several large yellow flowers. On a clear day, Anacapa can look like a green and yellow table from a distance.

Sea mammals are often observed around Anacapa's shores. Though the sea otter has been nearly exterminated from these waters, the California sea lion and the harbor seal are found in park waters. During January, the annual migration of gray whales passes close to Anacapa.

The most easily noticed animals around Anacapa are the birds. Around the cliffs and in the ocean, western gulls, cormorants, scoter ducks, black oyster catchers, and brown pelicans can be seen. The pelicans, nearly exterminated along the California coast just a few years ago, use the slopes of West Anacapa for their only large nesting site on the western coast of the United States. Recent increases in the pelican population are believed to be due to a reduction of DDT in the food chain. Various species of land birds are also found on Anacapa. West Anacapa has been designated a research natural area for the protection of the brown pelican rookery. No landings are permitted without written permission from the superintendent.

Each of Anacapa's three islets has different offerings to visitors. Picnicking is allowed anywhere. Picnic fires at Frenchy's Cove are allowed only on the beach.

A self-guiding nature trail, approximately one and a half miles long, shows visitors some of the features and moods of East Island. Trail booklets are available near the ranger station.

Fishing and diving for game are popular sports; fish commonly caught in reserve waters include rockfish, perch, sand dabs, and sheepshead. Divers enjoy going after abalone, lobster, and scallops. These activities are regulated by California fish and game laws, and a valid fishing license is required. One further stipulation: All the plants and invertebrate life in most of the accessible tide pools on Anacapa and Santa Barbara islands are protected and may not be taken or disturbed. In this way, visitors can continue to enjoy the rich diversity of unmolested tide pools.

Scuba and skin diving for the pleasure of observing and photographing undersea life are very popular, and the islands have a reputation for the beauty and variety of their marine life. There are also interesting caves, coves, and shipwrecks to explore.

Santa Barbara Island is a small, 640-acre triangular island about thirty-eight miles west of San Pedro Harbor in Los Angeles. Like Anacapa, it is almost entirely surrounded by cliffs, some rising to more than 500 feet. From the cliffs, gentle canyon-cut slopes rise to two hilltops, the highest being Signal Peak at 635 feet. Numerous caves, coves, offshore pillars, and blowholes make this small island as dramatic and majestic in its own way as the larger islands.

Because of Santa Barbara's isolation, sea mammals are abundant around the island. Present in large numbers are California sea lions and harbor seals. During winter, elephant seals breed here. These are named for the huge size of the bulls—up to six thousand pounds—whose large proboscis-like noses are inflated during the mating season. One special opportunity here is that of studying marine mammals at close range. Remember that federal law prohibits molesting or disturbing any marine mammal.

San Miguel, the westernmost of the Channel Islands, is an island of extremes. Unprotected by the mainland, the wind and weather sweep across the North Pacific, battering her shores and creating an environment both harsh and yet extremely beautiful.

The island has the most dangerous approach of all the Channel Islands, as evidenced by the many shipwrecks that have occurred on the outlying rocks and reefs. The island's isolation allows three of the five major seabird colonies in Southern California to live relatively undisturbed. Auklets, cormorants, gulls, guillemots, and snowy plovers, as well as others, all breed on San Miguel and nearby Prince Island. Six species of seals and sea lions are found here. At Point Bennett, five species, including elephant seals and northern fur seals, "haul out" on the beaches to breed.

The San Miguel Island fox is the largest land mammal on the island. Barn owls, peregrine falcons, and red-tailed hawks are among the birds of prey sometimes seen.

Several rare plant species, including live-forever, wild buckwheat, and rose mallow, are found on the island. Springtime can be most colorful. And preserved beneath blowing sand are barren forests of wind-carved caliche. These fossils are the encrusted forests of ancient vegetation buried by blowing sands.

LODGING: There are no park facilities. Camping on Anacapa is confined to a campground on East Island, which has fireplaces and tables. Latrines are also located at the East Anacapa campground and Frenchy's Cove. The campground is free on a first-come, first-served basis. There is a limit to the number of persons who may use the campground; therefore, everyone must register in advance with park headquarters in Ventura.

HOW TO GET THERE: Commercial Boat Service: Public transportation to the islands is available from many Southern California ports, though presently there is only one charter operation running on a regular basis. Contact park headquarters in Ventura for up-to-date transportation information.

Using Personally Owned Boats: Visitors planning to take their own boats should study U.S. Coast and Geodetic Survey Charts 18720, 18729, and 18756. The Santa Barbara Channel is subject to sudden rising sea and wind conditions, especially in the afternoons. Anchorage off Santa Barbara Island is usually confined to the landing cove area; Anacapa anchorages include East Fish Camp and Frenchy's Cove. Anchoring at either island can be hazardous; be sure to have adequate tackle aboard. There are loading docks at the landing coves on both East Anacapa and Santa Barbara islands, but neither is acceptable for docking boats. Persons wishing to go ashore will need a skiff or small boat.

Access to San Miguel Island (by permit only) is by private boat and is limited to Cuyler Harbor, usually safe anchorage under normal weather conditions. Another safe anchorage on the south side of the island is Tyler Bight. Sea conditions around the island are usually rough; only experienced boaters with sturdy vessels should contemplate the trip. No public transportation is available.

LASSEN VOLCANIC NATIONAL PARK

CALIFORNIA

Approximately seventy years have passed since Lassen Peak last erupted in a flurry of volcanic activity that lasted, off and on, for seven years, but that doesn't mean the ground beneath this 10,500-foot-high dome-shaped mountain is completely quiet today. Among the park's most popular attractions are the bubbling hot springs, steaming fumaroles, and sulfurous vents which are evidence of continuing underground activity.

The peak, which dominates this park, was created from a plug of stiff, pasty lava forced out of a vent on the north slope of a larger extinct volcano known as Tehama. After its emergence, Lassen Peak was quiet for a long period until May 30, 1914, when the last series of eruptions began. The effects of these eruptions can still be seen in the devastated area where all vegetation was wiped out by the hot mud and lava flows.

Apart from this devastated area, the remainder of the 160-square-mile park is a lush wilderness of coniferous forest, lakes, streams, and smaller mountains accessible only by foot trails. Lassen Park Road is the only paved road in the park, but it does wind around three sides of the volcanic peak and affords many beautiful views of woodlands and meadows, clear brooks and lakes.

In the course of a hike through this sweet-smelling and sparkling land, you may see a variety of conifers—pines, firs, and cedars. Stands of broadleaf trees—aspens and cottonwoods—add color to the autumn landscape. Willows and alders border Lassen's many streams and lakes. Wild flowers are usually abundant from mid-June through September.

Because this national park is so well watered and has such a variety of habitats, it is rich in animal life—some 50 kinds of mammals, 150 kinds of birds, about 12 different kinds of amphibians and reptiles.

To learn as much as possible about the geology, plants, animals, and history of the park, you are invited to participate in the free interpretive programs. During the summer season, park naturalists lead nature walks and hikes to nearby points of interest.

Evening programs are held in the campgrounds at Manzanita Lake, Summit Lake, and Butte Lake. Talks on Indian lore and other special-interest subjects are given at various locations in the park. Schedules are posted and are available at the visitor center and at ranger stations.

More than 150 miles of hiking trails lead to lakes, streams, waterfalls, mountain meadows, thermal areas, old volcanoes, and lava flows. Trails are well marked and easy to follow. Wayside exhibits located at the devastated area and other places in the park explain the natural features.

Several lakes and streams in the park have rainbow, brook, and brown trout. You may fish anywhere except in Emerald Lake, Manzanita Creek, and within 150 feet of the inlet to Manzanita Lake. You'll need a California fishing license.

Rowboats, canoes, and other non-powered craft may be used on any lake except Reflection, Emerald, Helen, and Boiling Springs. Follow the safety rules for boating; large lakes can become quite rough in windy weather.

Lassen Park is open year round, but the trans-park road is closed by heavy snow from the end of October until early June. At a winter-sports area near the southwest entrance, downhill ski facilities are in operation Friday through Sunday and on holidays, from about Thanksgiving until Easter. Hot lunches, refreshments, instruction, and rental ski equipment are available at the Ski Chalet. Two rope tows and a poma lift provide beginning, intermediate, and limited advanced skiing opportunities.

Snow conditions are usually excellent for cross-country skiing; but when deep, heavy snow makes avalanches possible, the backcountry will be closed. The southern section of the park has terrain suitable for beginning and advanced skiers. The road to Manzanita Lake is open in winter. The gentle terrain in the vicinity of the lake is ideally suited for cross-country skiing.

The park's two visitor information centers, at Manzanita Lake (northwest entrance) and Sulphur Works (southwest entrance), are open from early June to late September. Publications about the park are available at both places.

LODGING: Drakesbad Guest Ranch operates from July 1 until early September. Food service and souvenirs are also available at Lassen Chalet near the southwest entrance station from July 1 through early September. For all reservations, write: Lassen National Park, P.O. Box 21, Mineral, CA 96063.

Four campgrounds and five picnic sites are located along Lassen Park Road. The campgrounds at Manzanita Lake, Crags, Summit Lake, and Butte Lake have sanitary facilities and spaces for trailers (no hookups for electricity, water, or sewage). The Southwest Campground also has modern facilities, but you will have to walk about a hundred yards from the parking area to the site. Camping is permitted from mid-May to October—depending on the weather and the location of the campground. All campsites have fireplaces. Wilderness permits are required for all backcountry camping.

HOW TO GET THERE: The nearest principal cities are Sacramento and San Francisco. Nearby Redding is served by Hughes Airwest, by train and bus lines, and rental cars are available there. By car from Redding,

on Interstate 5, State Road 44 leads to the northwest
park entrance at Manzanita Lake. Buses schedule
daily year-round service (except Sunday) from Red
Bluff and Susanville to Mineral, adjoining the south
park entrance at State Road 89.

REDWOOD NATIONAL PARK

CALIFORNIA

Trees. Gorgeous, gargantuan trees. That's what Redwood National Park is all about. Here are found the legendary giants of the plant world, spreading their massive canopies over the primeval forest much as they did in the "age of the dinosaurs."

The coast redwood (*Sequoia sempervirens*) is the tallest living tree on earth, occasionally reaching heights of more than three hundred feet. There are no known diseases which can kill this marvel of nature, leaving only man and fire as the greatest threats to its survival.

Redwoods are more than individual trees. They form a unique and diverse forest. Once found in many parts of the world, the coast redwood now grows as a natural forest only in a narrow strip along the northern California coast and barely into Oregon. Portions of the redwood forest here were cut as long ago as the 1850s, but most were downed within the past twenty-five years.

The forest is dependent on the ocean-created climate of thick summer fogs and moderate year-round temperatures. Torrential winter rains regularly swell the Smith River, Redwood Creek, and the Klamath River. The long, rainy winter season has occasional periods of cool, clear weather.

The coast redwood grows here in pure stands and in mixed forests. The litter from the trees and a cover of ferns conceal the forest floor. The understory is thick with shrubs, such as rosebay rhododendron, salal, and huckleberry. On alluvial flats along streams grow some of the finest stands, such as the Tall Trees Grove on Redwood Creek and Stout Grove on the Smith River. Alder, maple, cedar, and California laurel (bay) thrive along the streams. The rivers are also known for their runs of spawning salmon and steelhead.

At higher inland elevations, the drier, warmer conditions of summer influence the forest. Tan oak, madrone, and Douglas fir increase in numbers, and redwood decreases. In such a ridge forest near Lady Bird Johnson Grove, Jedediah Smith found "noble cedars" in 1828. He saw, too, the abundant wildlife of the open forest: black-tailed deer, black bear, foxes, cougar, bobcats, and elk. The numbers of Roosevelt elk have declined in recent times; their range has decreased so much that they are seen regularly only in the park vicinity. The open grassy area beside U.S. 101 in Prairie Creek Redwood State Park is a good place to look. The elk are wild, so observe them from a distance.

Early explorers also encountered Indians living in villages along streams and in coastal communities. Indian trails were crisscrossed in later years as miners and pack trains moved inland to look for gold in the Trinity and Klamath River drainages. With settlement came improved roads, although as late as the 1920s parts of the Redwood Highway were still under construction. In 1926 the Klamath River, previously crossed by ferry, was first bridged, completing an important link in the road.

Now, people from all over the world visit the redwood forest. They come mostly in summer, the season of fogs that gently encircle and engulf, pierced occasionally by brilliant shafts of sun. With the changing seasons, fall finds the big-leaf and vine maples adding yellow and red to the prevailing green of the forest. Spring decorates the forest floor with a host of small wild flowers. Winter brings stormy winds and rains. The redwoods seem most natural in this dim, wet setting, wrapped in mist and silence, the hush broken only by sounds of the rain and of a nearby creek.

The repeated yearly cycles help us understand the age and dimension of these magnificent trees. Not only does the species date back more than thirty million years, but individual redwoods live as long as two thousand years. In the quietness of a walk in the forest, time seems to slow, and you can appreciate the natural forest living at a pace and rhythm all its own.

The national park which helps to protect these magnificent specimens is only forty-six miles long, and seven miles wide at the point of its greatest width.

Included within this area are three separate parks administered by the state of California: Jedediah Smith Redwoods, Del Norte Coast Redwoods and Prairie Creek Redwoods. In addition to the redwood forest, the total park area also covers thirty miles of coastal zone with its abrupt cliffs, eroding headlands, beaches, lagoons, and tide pools.

Beautiful stands of redwoods can be viewed from U.S. 199 and U.S. 101, both inside and outside the national park. The Avenue of the Giants is a worthwhile scenic drive through redwood groves in several nearby state parks. Hiking trails lead to bluffs overlooking the Pacific Ocean, Tall Trees Grove, and Lady Bird Johnson Grove. Rocky promontories along the coast cannot be skirted even at low tide. Cold water, jagged shoals, strong undertow, and steep descending beaches discourage swimming and surfing. Fishing (by license) for salmon, steelhead, and trout is good. Picnic facilities are provided at a number of locations in the national, state, and county parks.

Park rangers present evening programs and guided walks in summer at the visitor center. Nearby, a sawmill, fish hatchery, and timber companies offer free self-guided tours to the public. In Crescent City several museums are open to the public. For reservations for float trips on the rivers of the north coast, write: Six Rivers Float Trips, P.O. Box 981, Arcata, CA 95521.

LODGING: Overnight facilities are not yet provided within the park, but motels are located at various points along U.S. 199 and U.S. 101 leading to the parks.

The national park does not have operating

campgrounds, although each state park has a developed campground suitable for tents, campers, and trailers up to twenty-six feet long. State park campsites can be reserved in advance through any California State Park office. Additional facilities are available in nearby national forests of Six Rivers, Klamath, and Trinity. There are also facilities available at private campgrounds along U.S. 101, Calif. 299 and 96, and U.S. 199.

HOW TO GET THERE: Along the northern coast of California, U.S. Highway 101 passes through the park, connecting Crescent City, north of the park, with Eureka to the south. Both cities are served by Hughes Airwest, bus lines, and rental car companies.

SEQUOIA AND KINGS CANYON NATIONAL PARKS

CALIFORNIA

Only on the western slopes of the Sierra Nevada can you witness one of nature's most impressive and enduring achievements—massive groves of giant sequoias outlined against the majesty of snowcapped mountains. Here, because of their great age and size, it is possible to literally miss the forest for the trees.

It's also possible to become so wrapped up in these magnificent woody specimens that you miss noticing the spectacular granite mountains, deep canyons, jeweled lakes, and tumbling waterfalls embraced by Sequoia and Kings Canyon national parks.

These two parks, established separately but administered as one, stretch for 65 miles along the crest of the Sierra Nevada range. Within their more than 1,300-square-mile area is Mt. Whitney, the highest peak in the lower forty-eight states.

The features which define the parks are distinctly different. Sequoia, the southernmost, preserves thirty-two groves of giant sequoia trees. Attractions include the Giant Forest where the groves are concentrated; magnificent views of the Great Western Divide from Moro Rock; the beautiful calcite formations of Crystal Cave; the High Sierra Trail leading over Crescent Meadow; spectacular Bearpaw Meadow, Kern Canyon, and Mt. Whitney.

King's Canyon is a region of giant canyons with towering rock walls, countless lakes, waterfalls, and mountain meadows. Here too, are beautiful stands of giant sequoias, as well as Roaring River Falls, Zumwalt Meadow, and the sheer granite cliffs of North Dome and Grand Sentinel.

Tremendous earth upheavals, erosion, the movements of ponderous glaciers and raging rivers, the winds and changing temperatures—all have had a part in sculpturing this vast region. The great Sierra Nevada is a huge block of the earth's crust which has been uplifted and tilted westward in several major stages. Tilting steepened the slopes, thus increasing the speed and the rate of downcutting of the rivers. With the advent of the great Ice Age, about a million years ago, canyons approaching their present depths were formed.

Ice Age glaciers quarried the canyons wider and deeper, great natural amphitheaters called cirques were gouged into the higher crests, and basins were scooped out and later became lakes. Then the glaciers melted back, and the stage was set for renewed plant growth.

The giant sequoias *(Sequoiadendron giganteum)* are survivors of an ancient lineage of huge trees that grew over much of the earth millions of years ago and persisted in places that escaped the last Ice Age. Today, these trees grow nowhere else except in the scattered groves on the western slope of the Sierra Nevada. They have thrived here because of a particular combination of physical characteristics, climate, growth habits, and fire.

Some of the finest examples of giant sequoias are at Giant Forest, Sequoia National Park. Here is the General Sherman Tree, largest and one of the oldest of living things. Its age is estimated at more than three thousand years. Other attractions include Crescent Meadow, Crystal Cave, Tokopah Valley, and Moro Rock. Short climbs up Moro Rock and Little Baldy afford superb views of valley, forest, and high mountain scenery.

You can see the world's second largest tree—the General Grant—in Grant Grove, Kings Canyon National Park. Nearby is another notable giant, the Robert E. Lee. In striking contrast to these living survivors of antiquity stands the weathered Centennial Stump, remnant of a tree cut in 1875 to provide an exhibit for the Philadelphia World's Fair. Big Stump basin, where ancient trees were cut during the logging era, is in the vicinity.

Kings Canyon is a steep-walled valley of the South Fork of the Kings River. Towering peaks rise to heights of one mile or more above the stream. Cedar Grove is the center of activity in Kings Canyon and a

popular base for extensive trail trips into the high
country. Zumwalt Meadow, Roaring River Falls, and
Mist Falls are readily accessible.

The high country is a vast region of mountains, canyons, rivers, lakes and meadows. The Sierra Crest,
ranging in elevation from 11,000 to 14,495 feet at the
summit of Mount Whitney, forms the eastern boundary of the parks. Evolution Basin, Tehipite Valley, and
Kern Canyon are a few of the places where you can
find spectacular and unspoiled scenes. These and
other objectives are accessible only by trail; those in
the higher elevations are generally open from early
July through September.

Generals Highway (open all year) is the main road
that connects Sequoia and Kings Canyon national
parks. It winds through the sequoia belt and covers 46
miles, a two-hour drive from the Ash Mountain entrance to Grant Grove. Branch roads will take you to
other scenic attractions or within short trail distances
of them. From Grant Grove, you travel 30 miles on
Calif. 180 through Sequoia National Forest and along
the South Fork of the Kings River to Cedar Grove.
The road then continues for six miles through the canyon to road's end. Here you are at the foot of solid
granite walls that tower thousands of feet above the
canyon floor. The road to Cedar Grove is closed from
about November 1 to May 1.

Giant Forest, Grant Grove, and Cedar Grove have
self-guiding nature trails. Numerous other trails in
these areas wait to be enjoyed. More than 900 miles of
trails invite you to visit the high country.

In summer you can rent saddle horses and pack animals at corrals near Wolverton (Giant Forest), Grant
Grove, and Cedar Grove; and in Owens Valley, which

is on the eastern side of the Sierra; and at many other places around the parks' borders.

Many lakes and streams in these parks contain brook, brown, rainbow, and golden trout. The most popular fishing spots are along the Kings River and the forks of the Kaweah River. You can buy a California fishing license at the stores. Certain closures and special regulations are in effect from time to time, so before you fish, check at a visitor center, at a bulletin board, or with a park ranger.

For winter-sports enthusiasts, complete rental equipment is available at Wolverton and Giant Forest. Ski runs vary in difficulty. Sledders also enjoy the snowy slopes at Lodgepole, Wolverton, and Grant Grove.

Year-round schedules for naturalist-conducted walks through the big-tree areas and to important scenic points are posted on bulletin boards. Limited tours through Crystal Cave are scheduled weekends during May and September, weather permitting, and on a daily basis from mid-June through Labor Day. There is a steep one-half-mile walk to the cave entrance and wraps are needed. An entrance fee is charged.

LODGING: Lodges and camps are operated by Sequoia and Kings Canyon Hospitality Service, Sequoia National Park, CA 93262. In Sequoia, Giant Forest Lodge, the main lodge, is open from late May to as long as weather permits, usually mid-October. Facilities include motel rooms, rustic cabins, a dining room, cocktail lounge, and gift shop. Bearpaw Meadow Camp, a trail camp for hikers and saddle-horse parties, is open from late June to early September.

In Kings Canyon, Grant Grove Lodge provides cottages with bath, cabins with access to free showers, a coffee shop, cocktail lounge, and gift shop. The lodge is open from May until mid-October. Cedar Grove Camp, open early June to early September, offers sleeping cabins without bath, a snack bar, market, and supply store. For reservations, write: Wilsonia Lodge, Kings Canyon National Park, CA. 93633.

Potwisha, Dorst, and Lodgepole campgrounds in Sequoia National Park; and Canyon View, Moraine, Sentinel, and Sheep Creek in Kings Canyon are best suited for trailer use. Facilities include running water, toilets, fireplaces, and tables. Lodgepole and Canyon View have dumping stations. Sunset has limited trailer services. Lodgepole, Potwisha, and South Fork are open all year. The others open April 15 to June 15 and close September 15 to November 1. Stays are limited to fourteen days. Visalia, 38 miles away, and Fresno, 58 miles away, have campers for rent. A free back-country permit is required. Reservations are accepted.

HOW TO GET THERE: The south end of Kings Canyon National Park adjoins the north end of Sequoia. From Fresno, the nearest principal city, State Road 180 leads to Kings Canyon and Sequoia at Big Stump entrance. From Visalia, State Road 198 leads to Sequoia. Both cities are served by United Airlines. Hughes Airwest also serves Fresno. Both cities are on State Road 99, which connects with Interstate 5, leading to Sacramento to the north and Los Angeles to the south. Rental cars are available in Fresno. By bus, Continental Trailways serves Tulare and Fresno, and Western

Greyhound serves Tulare, Fresno, and Visalia. Sequoia Motor Coach from Tulare and Visalia serve Giant Forest Lodge within the park. Sightseeing motor coach tours to both parks are available from Tulare and Visalia. By rail, Southern Pacific Railway to Tulare, then motor coach service to Sequoia; or Santa Fe Railway to Fresno or Hanford, then rental cars to the park.

YOSEMITE NATIONAL PARK

CALIFORNIA

Yosemite National Park is big, bold, and beautiful—a 1,189-square-mile wonderland of scenic wild lands set in the Sierra Nevada of eastern California. Here, summer or winter, you can revel in the sublime splendor of sculptured mountain peaks and domes, waterfalls tumbling out of hanging valleys across glistening granite cliffs, groves of giant sequoias, and alpine meadows carpeted in masses of brilliant wild flowers.

The Yosemite region, as you see it today, first began to form 500 million years ago when a warm, shallow sea spread across what is now the Sierra Nevada and Great Valley of California. Eventually the thick layers of sea-laid sediment were twisted and thrust above sea level, while molten rock welled up underneath to create a base of granite. As the eons passed, erosion and glaciers worked to strip away the softer layers of sediment and leave the underlying granite exposed.

Elevations within the park range from less than 2,000 to more than 13,000 feet above sea level. In this range are five plant belts, each with its related community of animals. Conifers are the predominant trees, but there are a number of hardwoods, especially black oak and canyon live oak. Flowering trees and shrubs include dogwood and azalea. Seasonal wild flowers color the meadows at almost every elevation. Of 220 bird and 75 mammal species that live in Yosemite, many stay within their accustomed zones. Others, like the mule deer, migrate seasonally between high and low elevations.

More than 200 miles of roadways provide access to the major features of the park either by car or, in some places, by free shuttle bus. Here are some of the highlights you shouldn't miss:

Yosemite Valley and its sheer cliffs, and waterfalls that reach their maximum flow in May and June; some have no water from about mid-August through early autumn. Principal scenic features of the valley, which is open all year, are Yosemite Falls (second highest in the world), Bridalveil Fall, Mirror Lake, Half Dome, Sentinel Rock, El Capitan, The Three Brothers, and Cathedral Rocks.

Happy Isles Trail Center, which is accessible by shuttle bus and has information about traveling in the wildlands. This is the trailhead for the John Muir Trail, Vernal and Nevada falls, and the high country.

Three groves of giant sequoias, the largest of which

is Mariposa Grove. This grove, 35 miles from the valley near the south entrance, includes the Grizzly Giant tree. Private vehicles may be driven only to the edge of this grove. Beyond that point, board the free shuttle bus or hike the trail system through the grove. You will find other giant sequoias at Tuolumne and Merced groves near Crane Flat.

Glacier Point, from which you can get one of the best high views of Yosemite Valley and the crest of the lofty Sierra Nevada. The approach road from the Badger Pass intersection is closed in winter.

Pioneer Yosemite History Center at Wawona, where living history demonstrations, historic buildings, and horse-drawn vehicles tell of man's history in the park.

Tuolumne Meadows (8,600 feet), the largest subalpine meadow in the High Sierra. Closed in winter, this area is 55 miles from the valley by way of highly scenic Big Oak Flat and Tioga roads and is the starting point for hiking and pack trips into the high country. The National Park Service operates a large campground and conducts a full-scale naturalist program here in summer.

Yosemite Travel Museum in El Portal, where exhibits tell the story of early-day railroad and auto transportation in the Yosemite region.

There are more than 700 miles of hiking and climbing trails, ranging from short to overnight trips into the high country. Rock climbing may be done only after registering at the visitor center. In summer, saddle and pack animals are available at stables in Yosemite Valley, White Wolf, Tuolumne Meadows, Wawona, and Mather. Swimming is permitted, but the park waters have no lifeguards. Trout fishing is excellent in most of the park streams and lakes. A California fishing license is required.

The slopes at Badger Pass, where ski equipment is available, challenge beginner and intermediate skiers during the season, mid-December to early April. For details, write: Yosemite Park and Curry Co., Yosemite National Park, CA 95389. More than 50 miles of cross-country ski and snowshoe trails are maintained by the National Park Service.

The visitor center in Yosemite Valley has audiovisual programs and exhibits about the park. Schedules for naturalist-presented walks, talks, youth programs, seminars, living history programs, and arts and skills demonstrations are posted at the visitor center and at campgrounds.

LODGING: There are numerous restaurants, cafeterias, stores, and lodgings in Yosemite Valley and at Wawona, El Portal, and Tuolumne Meadows. Accommodations range from cabins and cottages to modern or Victorian hotels. Reservations are advised at all times for lodging accommodations. Write: Yosemite Park and Curry Co., Yosemite National Park, CA 95389.

Park lodges have swimming pools, tennis courts, pitch and putt courses, bike and horse rentals, lounges and live entertainment, dancing, and movies. Three-, four-, and six-day all-expense saddle trips, seven-day all-expense hiking trips, and daily sightseeing tours are available.

Within the park, campgrounds are plentiful. From June 1 to September 15, camping is limited to seven days in Yosemite Valley and fourteen days in the rest

of the park. From September 16 to May 30, it is limited
to thirty days throughout the park. Sunnyside and
Lower Pines, in the Valley, are open all year. There
are no utility connections for house trailers, but all
campgrounds are near water and rest rooms. Showers
are available for a small fee in Yosemite Valley and at
Tuolomne Meadows. Fresno, 88 miles away, is the
nearest city where campers can be rented. Camping
equipment may be rented at the Housekeeping section
of Curry Village in Yosemite Valley; ski equipment is
available at Badger Pass in winter. All the
campgrounds in Yosemite have flush toilets, tap water, fire grills, picnic tables, and garbage collection.
Campgrounds along Big Oak Flat and Tioga roads are
usually less crowded than those in Yosemite Valley.
Wawona is open all year. Backcountry camping permits are required. Reservations are accepted.

HOW TO GET THERE: Yosemite, in east central California, is accessible by State Road 41 from Fresno on
the south; State Road 140 from Merced on the west;
and State Road 120 from Manteca on the west and Lee
Vining on the east. Fresno, Stockton, Merced, and
Modesto, California, and Reno, Nevada, are served by
United Airlines. Service to the park is scheduled on a
daily basis, between May 1 and September 30, by
Yosemite Trans System, which links Yosemite with
Merced, Fresno, and Lee Vining. Advance reservations are required. Connecting buses and rental cars
are available at all points served by air.

HALEAKALA NATIONAL PARK

MAUI, HAWAII

As the bright sunlight cascades down the slopes of Haleakala, it is easy to see why the ancient Hawaiians named this dormant volcanic mountain the "House of the Sun." Giant webs of lava streak the mountain's sides with red, yellow, gray, and black against a rich, deep green mantle of wild tropical vegetation.

Located on Maui, the second largest island in the Hawaiian chain, Haleakala National Park cuts a 10-mile-long swath from the mountain summit to the southeast coast. Dominating the park is Haleakala Crater, a cool, cone-studded reminder of a once-violent volcano which began as part of the 1,600-mile-long volcanic chain in the Pacific.

Modern geology indicates that the Hawaiian Islands are situated near the middle of the Pacific plate, one of a dozen thin, rigid structures covering our planet like the cracked shell of an egg. Though adjoining each other, these plates are in constant slow motion, the Pacific plate moving northwestward several centimeters per year. Scattered around the world are many weak areas in the earth's crust where magma slowly wells upward to the surface as a "plume." Here volcanoes and volcanic islands, such as Maui, are born.

This constant northwestward movement of the Pacific plate over a local volcanic "hot spot," or plume, has produced a series of islands one after another in assembly line fashion. The result is a chain of volcanic islands stretching from the island of Hawaii along a southeast-northwest line for 2,500 miles toward Japan.

Maui, one of the younger islands in this chain, began as two separate volcanoes on the ocean floor; time and again, eon after eon, they erupted, and thin new sheets of lava spread upon the old, building and building, until the volcano heads emerged from the sea. Lava, wind-blown ash, and alluvium eventually joined the two by an isthmus or valley, forming Maui, "The Valley Isle." Finally, Haleakala, the larger, eastern volcano, reached its greatest height, 12,000 feet above the ocean—some 30,000 feet from its base on the ocean floor.

For a time, volcanic activity ceased, and erosion dominated. The great mountain was high enough to trap the moisture-laden northeast trade winds. Rain fell and streams began to cut channels down its slopes. Two such streams eroding their way headward created large amphitheater-like depressions near the summit.

Ultimately these two valleys met, creating a long erosional "crater." At the same time a series of Ice Age submergences and emergences of the shoreline occurred; the final submergence formed the four islands of Lanai, Molokai, Kahoolawe, and Maui.

Haleakala National Park encompasses, in fact, two distinct park areas: the Haleakala Crater near the summit, and the lush rain forests and abundant waters of the Kipahulu coastal area. No road directly links the two sections of the park, although each can be reached by roads outside the park area.

Unlike the gritty lava ash and cinder cones of the Haleakala Crater, the Kipahulu section of the park abounds in the tropical verdancy so typical of the islands. Here the visitor is greeted by a chain of usually placid sparkling pools, some large, some small, and each connected by a waterfall or short cascade. But 'Ohe'o, the stream joining the pools, has many moods and at times becomes a thundering torrent of whitewater, burying these quiet pools as it churns and plunges headlong toward the ocean. The upper rain forest above the pools receives up to 250 inches of rainfall a year, and flash floods can and do occur here.

A pastoral scene of rolling grasslands and forested valleys surrounds the pools. Ginger and ti form an understory in forests of kukui, mango, guava, and bamboo, while beach naupaka, false kamani, and pandanus abound along the rugged coastal cliffs. Pictographs, painted by long-forgotten artists, and farm plots, once flourishing with cultivated taro and sweet potatoes, remind us of an age when the ali'i—Hawaiian chiefs—ruled this land.

Hawaii is noted for its unique birdlife, and many species are found nowhere else. The golder plover, commonly seen from September to May, is famous for its migratory flights to and from Alaska. You may also see the 'apapane, 'i'iwi, 'amakihi, and nene, which are among those birds native only to the Hawaiian Islands. The 'i'iwi is one of the most beautiful of all Hawaiian birds, with a bright scarlet body, black wings and tail, and inch-long curved bill. The 'apapane is also scarlet, but has a white belly and black legs and bill. The bright green and yellow 'amakihi is known for the speed at which it searches for nectar and insects. However, most of the birds you will see along park roads—pheasants, chukars, skylarks, mockingbirds—are introduced forms.

Park headquarters is 1 mile from the entrance to the park. Here park personnel furnish general information, permits, and publications.

Haleakala Visitor Center, 11 miles from the park entrance, is near the summit of Mt. Haleakala. Besides a magnificent view of the crater, there are exhibits explaining the geology, archeology, and ecology of the park as well as the wilderness protection programs. Periodically during the day, a park ranger is on duty to answer specific questions and to give interpretive talks.

Overlooks with orientation panels and exhibits are located at Leleiwi, Kalahaku, and Puu Ulaula along the park road between park headquarters and the summit. The rare silversword plant can be seen at Kalahaku, and if cloud conditions are right, the "Specter of the Brocken" can be seen at Leleiwi.

Many opportunities for walking and hiking await you in the crater area—and they range from short self-guilding walks to hikes of several days. Ranger-guided crater rim walks are conducted during the summer months. These vary in length from half-hour to two-hour walks covering about 2 miles. Check at park headquarters for current schedules.

Horseback and hiking concessioners sponsor their own trips through the crater—on a one-day or overnight basis.

Picnicking facilities are maintained at Hosmer Grove, near the park entrance. Tables, fireplaces, a cooking shelter with barbeque grills, drinking water, and a short nature trail are provided. Backpack camping in Haleakala Crater is permitted in designated areas by permit only.

LODGING: The island of Maui is designed for resort activity and sightseeing and has numerous accommodations, but there are no overnight facilities within the park grounds. The nearest restaurant and lodge is 12 miles toward Kahului. The National Park Service does maintain three crater cabins, which can be reached by foot or horse. Each cabin accommodates twelve persons, with drinking water, cookstove, firewood, and kerosene lamps. The limit is three nights. For reservations, write to the park superintendent.

HOW TO GET THERE: Air service is frequent from the other islands to the island of Maui. Rental cars are available at the airports. From Kahului Airport to the park, 26 miles, take Hawaii 37 to 377, then to 378, which enters the park at the north.

HAWAII VOLCANOES NATIONAL PARK

HAWAII

According to ancient Hawaiian mythology, Pele, the goddess of fire, the maker of mountains, melter of rocks, eater of forests, and burner of lands, makes her home on the Big Island of Hawaii, some 140 miles southeast of Oahu where Honolulu is situated. By all accounts Pele is a capricious goddess, popping up here and there with little warning, her fiery temper liable to explode at unexpected times.

But whether Pele is responsible, or the molten rock that flows below the surface of the Hawaiian Archipelago, there's little doubt that the island's two impressive shield volcanoes, Mauna Loa and Kilauea, are among the earth's most active today. These two volcanoes form the heart of Hawaii Volcanoes National Park.

The island of Hawaii is also one of the earth's most prodigious volcanic constructions. The ocean floor lies more than 18,000 feet below its sandy beaches, and the highest point, the dormant volcano Mauna Kea, measures 13,796 feet above sea level. The next tallest, Mauna Loa, is 13,667 feet high. Measured from the ocean floor, these volcanoes are considered to be the greatest mountain masses in the world.

Geologists tell us it took Mauna Loa about three million years to attain its present size: two million to reach the surface of the ocean and perhaps another million to make that vast mound of stone now visible above sea level. Although Mauna Loa appears to be so much bigger, Kilauea is an impressive shield volcano in its own right. It rises about 22,000 feet above the ocean floor; its height above sea level is slightly more than 4,000 feet.

Kilauea's activity is evident almost everywhere within the bounds of this park. Recently, its most frequent and spectacular displays have been presented along the east rift zone. Sometimes magma pushes its way through lateral conduits and flows from vents in a volcano's sides instead of in its summit crater—usually along the structural weaknesses in a shield volcano known as rift zones. Kilauea has two such rift zones. One extends from the caldera toward the southwest, through Ka'u. The other, which includes the Chain of Craters, extends east-southeast through the Puna area and into the sea beyond. Several eruptions have occurred in the summit crater of Halemaumau also, and a few have broken out along the southwest rift zone extending into Ka'u.

Since 1969 repeated eruptions have created a new parasitic lava shield in the area known as Mauna Ulu, "Growing Mountain," on the east rift zone. In the first five years of its existence, Mauna Ulu's vents poured out enough lava to fill up two pit craters; to build a new lava shield 400 feet above the level of the surrounding area; to bury or block off 12 miles of park road—burying some sections of it under more than 300 feet of rock; to cover 10,000 acres of parkland; and, where the flows entered the ocean, to add about 200 acres to the island's area.

Active though they are, Hawaii's volcanoes are relatively gentle. Violent outbursts—characterized by tremendous explosions, destructive earthquakes, clouds of poisonous gases, showers of hot mud, and rains of erupted rocks—have occurred only twice in recorded history. Both happened at Kilauea, one about 1790, the other in 1924. In general, however, Kilauea's eruptions are mild, and by far the greatest part of the material it releases appears in the form of slowly moving lava flows. The lava, gases, and cinders issuing from the vents can be dangerous, of course. Lava flows have destroyed forests, crops, houses, and other property, even villages, on occasion.

You can get up-to-date information about ongoing eruptions or potential activity by calling 1-808-967-7977 day or night. The automatic answering service is updated whenever Kilauea or Mauna Loa shows signs of change. Because eruptions are the most exciting events at Hawaii Volcanoes, temporary road signs will also direct you to access or vantage points where you can confront the power of these events when conditions are safe.

Crater Rim Drive, your best orientation to Hawaii

Volcanoes National Park, is an 11-mile drive clock-wise from park headquarters. You will pass lush rain forests, raw craters, and great areas of devastation. Pumice is piled high from recent eruptions, and lava flows only a few years old cover much of the land-scape. Along the road are well-marked trails and over-looks to help you explore this lava-formed world of the not-so-distant past and to understand life in a world that has changed violently and swiftly many times.

Hilina Pali is a steep cliff that offers a fine view of the Big Island's southeast seacoast. Late afternoon is a good time to visit the pali. On your way you will see fine examples of pahoehoe lava along this edge of the Kau Desert.

In Bird Park (Kipuka Puaulu), off of Mauna Loa Road, a nature trail leads through open meadows and forest—one of the richest concentrations of native plants in Hawaii. Kipukas are islands of old surface or soil surrounded by more recent lava flows, and on the slopes of Mauna Loa these kipukas support grassy meadows dotted with clumps of koa, ohia, soapberry, kolea, and mamani trees.

Chain of Craters Road passes along several huge pit craters formed in prehistoric time and several areas of recent volcanic activity which temporarily buried the road. The road now ends near Mauna Ulu, where lavas have permanently buried or blocked the pavement. Short trails cross these fresh landscapes to volcanic features and impressive views.

The coastal section of the park is accessible via Hawaii 130 from Keaau. The road leads past the reli-gious heiau (temple) of Wahaula, near the Wahaula Visitor Center, and skirts along the coastline past the historic Hawaiian villages of Kamoamoa and Lae

Apuki. It ends near Puu Loa, one of the great concentrations of petroglyphs in Hawaii.

Interpretive programs, including evening talks, nature walks, and other activities, are offered at Kilauea and the coastal section during the summer season. You can get a schedule from either visitor center or by writing to the park.

Volcano Art Center, housed in historic 1877 Volcano House, is just a few steps from Kilauea Visitor Center. Features include a gallery and seminars and workshops on painting, print making, pottery, music and dance, and other art forms.

LODGING: Volcano House, on the rim of Kilauea Crater, is a privately operated franchise, open all year. Reservations can be made through: Volcano House, Hawaii Volcanoes National Park, HI 96718. There are numerous accommodations in Hilo and all over the island.

Within the park, Namakani Paio camper cabins, operated by Volcano House, and Kipuka Nene provide shelters, fireplaces, wood, and water. Kamoamoa provides picnic shelters and fireplaces, but no water is available. Backcountry hikers can obtain permission from park headquarters for free use of the equipped overnight rest houses on Mauna Loa, accessible by an arduous climb requiring three or four days. Camper cabins at Namakani Paio provide bunks, outdoor grills, tables, and benches. Rest rooms, showers, and laundry facilities are nearby.

HOW TO GET THERE: Hilo, Hawaii, is served by major airlines with direct flights from mainland cities. There are several flights daily from Honolulu, Oahu, to

Hilo and Kailua-Kona. Unscheduled ships are also available. Taxis meet all planes and ships, and cars can be rented in Hilo and Kailua-Kona. Hawaii Road 11, south from Hilo or around southern Hawaii from Kailua, lead to the park.

HOT SPRINGS NATIONAL PARK

ARKANSAS

Hot Springs is a highly unusual national park in many respects, the most important being its dual function as a national health spa and recreation area. Because of its beneficial thermal waters, Hot Springs was also the first natural resource in the country to be put under federal protection. During the ensuing 150 years, the idea of preserving such natural wonders gradually evolved into the present system of federal parklands, which everyone can use and enjoy.

First-time visitors to this lovely park in the Zig Zag Mountains are usually surprised to find that it's small enough to be nearly surrounded by a bustling resort city, yet so perfectly maintained in its natural state that a stroll along its wooded trails is like taking a step backward in time.

Long before the first Europeans came to these shores, Indians already had discovered the wonders of the hot springs of Arkansas. Tradition says this was hallowed ground; here warriors laid aside their arms and, regardless of tribe or tongue, bathed in peace.

This area, as a part of the greater Louisiana Territory, had been alternately claimed by France and Spain since the mid-1600s. However, the area saw little development and settlement until after the United States purchased Louisiana in 1803. Crude canvas shacks and log cabins were the first bathing facilities.

Medicinal bathing, traditional since ancient times, was reaching peak popularity in Europe, where great spas developed. These traditions, transplanted to the United States, caused the hot springs of Arkansas to become Hot Springs Reservation, a federally protected area. Thus, in 1832, was born a great national idea—that this country's natural heritage be held in trust for all people, for all time.

Although the modern bathtub, whirlpool machines, and chlorinated swimming pools have replaced social bathing in the style of the ancients, the tradition endures. Hot Springs National Park keeps its restful yet holiday air not only in its water programs but also along its quiet streets, on the Promenade, and on its wooded hillsides. The Hot Springs tradition is ageless.

The underground pathway of the thermal water begins as rainwater and soaks through highly fractured rocks located northwest of the springs. The water penetrates deeply into the earth's crust, where it is heated by coming in contact with a mass of hot rock. Years later the thermal water emerges from the torrid depths through a fault, or ancient break, in the earth's crust. Geologists have determined, through hydrogen isotope (Tritium) analyses, that a small amount of the thermal water is less than twenty years old, while most of it is thousands of years older.

Each day about four million liters (one million gallons) of water at 61°C (142°F) flows from the park's forty-seven springs. Chemical analysis shows the waters from these forty-seven springs to be practically identical. Unlike other thermal waters, Hot Springs water is remarkably pure and free of offensive odor or taste.

Of the forty-seven springs, forty-five are sealed; water is collected, carefully cooled, and piped to a central reservoir for bathhouse and therapy use. Complicated collecting and cooling systems provide visitors with pure water in properly tempered baths that do not lose the natural gases.

Two springs are kept open so visitors may see water emerging naturally. These—the Display Springs—are accessible from either Bathhouse Row or the Promenade. An audio station provides a message about the human and natural history of the springs.

Several drinking fountains on Reserve Avenue, along the Promenade, and on Bathhouse Row provide hot thermal water. Jug fountains are located on Reserve Avenue for those who wish to take the water home. Water from natural cold water springs may be obtained from jug fountains located at Happy Hollow Spring (on Fountain Street) and Whittington Avenue Spring. Water from park sources must not be sold or used commercially in any way.

The seventeen bathing establishments—nine in the park and eight in the city—use thermal waters of the park. All are concessioners of the federal government, subject to regulation and inspection. The baths—full immersion type—may be taken by direct application to the bathhouses, although a physician's advice is recommended. All bathhouses have facilities for whirlpool baths, showers, massages, and alcohol rubs.

Libbey Memorial Physical Medicine Center uses the thermal waters in its hydrotherapy program. Patients who suffer from arthritis, general injuries, or nervous-system damage often find relief in this therapy. Patients must be recommended by a local federally registered physician. A list of these physicians is available at park headquarters.

Hot Springs enjoys a favorable climate all year. The winters are mild and, except for infrequent short intervals, are conducive to outdoor recreation. The mild weather and warm sunshine are often decided aids to the bath treatments.

Visitors may hike or ride horseback on the lovely eighteen-mile network of wooded trails, drive on the park's scenic roads, and fish in nearby Lakes Catherine, Hamilton, or Ouachita. Boating and sporting supplies are available at the lakes for canoeing, motor boating, sailing, and fishing.

The five mountains of the park are clothed in dense oak-hickory forests with abundant shortleaf pine. Flowering trees are common in the understory and every season has its rewards. Particularly noteworthy are redbud and dogwood in spring, southern magnolia in summer, and colorful foliage in autumn. Wild flowers bloom all year.

LODGING: In the adjacent city of Hot Springs, accommodations are plentiful, ranging from hotels, motels, and cottages to apartments. Several of the hotels have bathhouses on the premises. For information and reservations, write: Hot Springs Chamber of Commerce, Hot Springs, AR 71901.

Gulpha Gorge Campground, within the park, provides trailer space, but no electricity or water connections. The campground area has fireplaces and tables for picnic use. Camping is limited to thirty days, except April 1–October 31 when fourteen days is the maximum limit.

HOW TO GET THERE: The nearest principal city is Little Rock. Trans-Texas, Delta, and Central airlines make daily scheduled stops at Memorial Airport, adjacent to the city of Hot Springs, two miles from the park, where rental cars are available. By bus, Arkansas Motor Coaches, Continental Trailways, Wolf and Midwest bus lines, with their connections, all provide service to Hot Springs. By car, from Interstate 30, Hot Springs National Park and the city of Hot Springs are on U.S. Highways 70 and 270, and State Road 7, which are all good, hard-surfaced roads.

CARLSBAD CAVERNS NATIONAL PARK

NEW MEXICO

The arid landscape in this particular section of southeastern New Mexico looks harsh and forbidding, at first glance appearing to lack the overwhelming beauty which characterizes so many of the other parks in the national system. Carlsbad Caverns is located in a ridge of barren limestone hills that rise from the desert sand dunes along the northern slopes of the Guadalupe Mountains and are covered with cactus and other spiny plants that seem to discourage closer inspection.

But there is far more here than casual observation reveals. Above ground, and especially below, Carlsbad Caverns is a unique testimony to the awesome power of time and nature. As you descend into the very mantle of the earth, a whole new world of strange and fantastic sights unfolds before your eyes. And once inside this chain of underground chambers it's easy to understand why Carlsbad is known as the "king of its kind."

Some sixty-six caves are preserved in the 46,753-acre park. Carlsbad, the largest, has one room with a floor area equal to fourteen football fields and enough height for the U.S. Capitol in one corner. Visitors can tour vast underground chambers; explore deep, winding canyons; study a Permian period fossil reef; view unusual desert plants; and when the migratory bat colony is in residence, witness spectacular evening bat flights.

The limestone in which the caverns formed was deposited near the edge of an inland arm of the sea during Permian times, about 250 million years ago. Its core is a fossil barrier reef built by lime-secreting algae and other marine organisms. To the north are layered rocks which formed in a lagoon behind the reef, and to the south are exposures of talus, or rock fragments, broken from the reef's crest by storms on the ancient sea.

In time, growth of the massive reef was halted and it became buried under layers of sediment. A pattern of cracks then appeared in the rock, which set the stage for the formation of the caverns. Rainwater, converted to a weak carbonic acid by absorption of carbon dioxide in the soil and decaying matter above, seeped into the cracks and worked its way down to the permanently saturated zone or water table. It then slowly dissolved the rock to create immense underground galleries.

As mountain-building forces raised the caverns

above the water table, air filled its chambers and mineral-laden water filtering in from the surface began to decorate the rooms with stalactite and stalagmite formations. A few of these are still slowly growing, but no change is noticed in a human lifetime.

For thousands of years, bats that winter in Mexico have used one portion of the main cavern as a summer home. From late spring until the first major frost in October or early November, these tiny flying mammals spiral out of the cavern entrance in incredible numbers at sunset each evening. They fly southeastward over the escarpment rim to feed at night on flying insects along the Black and Pecos rivers. Before sunup the colony returns to the cavern, where the bats sleep during the day. Up to five thousand bats per minute may boil up through the cavern opening, depending on weather conditions and the insect food supply.

More than a thousand years ago, prehistoric Indians left paintings on the entrance wall of Carlsbad Caverns and cooked agave and other desert plants in a rock pit just outside. They were attracted to the cavern because of the shelter it could provide, as were the Apache Indians of more recent times.

More permanent settlers arriving after the Civil War were attracted to the cavern by what appeared to be smoke against the sky; they would ride to the cave and discover that the dark cloud consisted of literally millions of bats streaming out of the opening. Later, finding huge guano deposits beneath the bat roost valuable as natural fertilizer, the settlers' interest in the cave became commercial. Mining claims were filed on the "Bat Cave" and more than 100,000 tons of guano were removed in 20 years.

James Larkin White, a young cowboy who was fas-

cinated by the cavern and its bats, became a foreman
for the guano mining companies and spent more than
20 years exploring, building trails and escorting people
through portions of the cavern he had discovered. His
efforts, along with those of others, led to a visit by
Robert Holley of the General Land Office, to a six-
month National Geographic Society expedition under
Dr. Willis T. Lee, and finally to designation of the cave
as a national monument in 1923. Additional land and
caves were added in 1930, when it became a national
park.

The landscape of the park holds as much interest as
the awesome caverns beneath. Elevations range from
3,600 feet above sea level at the base of the escarpment on the east boundary to 6,350 feet atop
Guadalupe Ridge on the west boundary. Slicing
through the rugged backcountry are numerous canyons with intriguing names like Slaughter, Bear, Walnut, Rattlesnake, Lefthood, Midnight, Yucca, and
Double.

The shape of the land in the park has created wide
variations in temperature, soil, sunlight, and moisture,
and these in turn have resulted in a wide variety of life-
forms. On the flatlands near the base of the mountains
are creosote bush and other drought-resistant shrubs.
In the canyons, black walnut, hackberry, oak, desert
willow, and other trees are common. The canyon walls
and ridge tops are covered mostly with agave, yucca,
sotol, ocotillo, and desert grasses; and at the higher
elevations are juniper, pine, Texas madrone, and occasionally a Douglas fir. In all, more than six hundred
plant species have been identified. In wet years, a succession of colorful annuals covers the canyons and
ridges with a carpet of blooms from spring into fall.

Wildlife abounds, although the nocturnal habits and natural camouflaging of many species keep them from being seen readily. Most commonly encountered among the mammals are jackrabbits, ringtails, raccoons, skunks, foxes, gophers, wood rats, mice, squirrels, porcupines, and mule deer. Seen less often are coyotes, badgers, bobcats, mountain lions, and elk.

More than two hundred species of birds, ranging in size from tiny hummingbirds to the majestic golden eagle, have been identified. During the summer, turkey vultures glide on thermal currents above the canyons, and cave swallows rear young in mud nests plastered high up on the walls of several caves.

The harsh land is also the home of many lizards and snakes. None should be feared, but the rattlesnakes should be respected. It is unlikely that you will see any, but be watchful on warm summer evenings and when traveling cross-country.

A variety of activities can be enjoyed both above and below ground. The visitor center is near the cavern entrance, which is 7 miles west of U.S. Highway 62/180 at the end of State Route 7. The center is open daily throughout the year. Information and orientation services, exhibits, and interpretive publications are available.

Underground interpretive trips are offered continuously from 8 A.M. to 3:15 P.M. in the winter and for longer hours during the summer. Visitors have a choice of either walking in through the natural entrance on a complete 3-mile trip or entering by elevator for a 1¼-mile walk around the Big Room. On both trips you return to the surface by elevator. Although you may walk at your own pace, the complete trip is somewhat strenuous and is not recommended for persons with walking or breathing problems. The most scenic portions of the Big Room are reached by a relatively level trail that will accommodate wheelchairs. A light sweater or jacket and comfortable walking shoes with rubber soles or heels are recommended.

Bat-flight programs are scheduled nightly at the entrance amphitheater during the summer. The starting time is adjusted periodically to fit the colony's flight pattern, but it is usually just before sunset. The exact time is posted daily in the visitor center.

Primitive lantern trips into New Cave, which is near the entrance of Slaughter Canyon, are available seasonally on a limited basis. Inquire at the information desk upon arrival. The trail to this cave involves a strenuous climb (500 feet in elevation) and should be attempted only by those in good physical condition.

Nature trails near the cavern entrance and along the Walnut Canyon entrance road offer an opportunity to become acquainted with plants of this semiarid land. Guided walks into the desert are also scheduled periodically during the main travel season.

Sightseeing by car can be both enjoyable and educational when traveling the park entrance road as it winds through lower Walnut Canyon and then climbs to the top of the Capitan Reef Escarpment. Along the 7-mile route are opportunities to view exposures of the ancient reef and lagoon deposits, wildlife, and unusual desert plants. Roadside exhibits interpret natural features along the route. On clear days, a sweeping panorama of the entire reef escarpment and the Delaware Plain, extending more than 100 miles southward into Texas, awaits you on the reef crest.

Summers are usually warm and winters mild. However, extreme changes can come suddenly at any season of the year. In the caverns the temperature remains constant at 13°C (55°F) year round. Average annual precipitation is fourteen inches.

LODGING: Within the park there are no overnight accommodations, and camping is not permitted. However, numerous motels, hotels, campgrounds, and trailer parks are located nearby and around the city of Carlsbad. Picnic facilities are available within the park at Rattlesnake Springs. A restaurant, gift shop, nursery, and kennel are next to the visitor center. Lunches and refreshments are available underground.

HOW TO GET THERE: Carlsbad Caverns National Park is on U.S. Highway 62/180 20 miles southwest of Carlsbad, New Mexico, and 150 miles east of El Paso, Texas. Both cities are served by bus and air transportation, and both have rental cars and bus service to the park.

BIG
BEND
NATIONAL
PARK

TEXAS

If you've ever wondered what the Old West was really like before the advent of modern superhighways and fast-food restaurants, Big Bend National Park is the place to find out. Nestled in the curve of the mighty Rio Grande River in southern Texas, this huge park is a study in contrasts between seemingly limitless deserts and bizarre mountain ranges that rise unexpectedly from the arid flatlands. This is raw, untamed country where you can see the well-preserved remains of animals that lived many millions of years ago, smell the aroma of creosote bushes, and hear the calls of unusual birds.

The hazards posed by the plant and animal life, unpredictable flash floods, and potential rockslides only add to the sense of adventure and challenge which dominates this park. With proper precautions, danger can be easily avoided and the rugged terrain enjoyed to its fullest.

The park, open all year, offers the visitor a variety of exciting ways in which to experience this sense of adventure by automobile, on horseback, or by foot.

In summer, a trip to Santa Elena Canyon (forty-seven miles southwest of The Basin) should be made in early morning, for sunlight strikes the canyon walls for only one or two hours after sunrise, supplying just the right light for picture taking; soon thereafter, the walls are in shadow. The canyon is likely to be hot in summer at midday. In winter, sunshine enters the canyon only at sunset.

The high, sheer walls seem to overhang the winding river. To sense its awesome immensity and to feel its solitude you should walk into Santa Elena Canyon. A foot trail crosses Terlingua Creek to the base of the cliff on the United States side and leads upward to a panoramic overlook. From there the trail goes about three-quarters of a mile along the river. The picnic area at Santa Elena Canyon, providing shade and water, is a pleasant place to eat lunch.

On the way back to The Basin, you may want to visit historic Castolon or make a side trip to Terlingua, a ghost town whose period of quicksilver-mining prosperity lasted from 1900 to 1946. Today only a few families live in Terlingua, near the ruins of a store, a church, a school, and many adobe houses.

Boquillas Canyon, cut through the Sierra del Carmen by the Rio Grande, is the longest (twenty-five miles) of Big Bend's famous gorges. It is thirty-four miles by paved road from The Basin. In the evening the sun seems to set fire to the face of the Sierra del Carmen; across the river, the Mexican village of Boquillas glistens with golden light.

The path into the canyon is steeply uphill at first, and then it descends gently; part of the way it is shaded by the walls. This canyon, wider than Santa Elena, imparts a sense of grandeur. Near the mouth of the canyon is a large sand slide; you can reach its top in less than one-half hour. The view, from a little wind-hollowed cave, is worth the struggle.

Lost Mine Trail, a round trip of about four miles, begins in The Basin. Be sure to carry water. A self-guiding leaflet, available at the trailhead, names plants and identifies lookout points along the way. From the overlook at the head of the Juniper Canyon, you will be able to see many miles into Mexico. But the most breathtaking sight along the trail awaits you atop Lost Mine Ridge; from there you can see the park spread out all around you.

The fourteen-mile horseback trip to the South Rim is a real adventure. Sturdy mountain horses will carry you along forest trails, sometimes in and out of the rocky bed of a trickling stream, sometimes across a stretch of mountain meadow. Just as you think you are never going to get to the top, the sky suddenly appears all around you and you are looking at an incredible panorama. Spread out before you is a large part of Texas and an even larger slice of Mexico, with the Rio Grande marking the boundary. The trail to the South Rim can be hiked, too; but it is strenuous and not for novices.

After you have visited Big Bend's major attractions you may want to further explore this desert country. Motor tours over primitive roads offer a variety of scenery, history, and fascinating plants and animals. Plan your trip in advance, register at park headquarters, and obtain current road information from a park ranger. Since these roads are patrolled only at infrequent intervals, you will be on your own, and you must take necessary precautions.

If you leave the park by way of the road to Marathon, eighty miles north of The Basin, be sure to see the park's fossil exhibit (just north of the Tornillo Creek bridge) to learn more of Big Bend's ancient past. On your left as you drive north you will notice the Rosillos Mountains, which appear rosy or brown according to the angle of the sun. The drive into Dagger Flat (a side trip), interesting at any season, is particularly rewarding in spring, when yuccas and cactuses are in bloom. Some of the desert plants along the route are labeled. A few miles beyond the intersection with the road to Dagger Flat, you will leave the park at Persimmon Gap, having traveled a part of the Comanche Trail, which few men dared follow a hundred years ago.

Winter is nippy in the mountains and comfortably warm during the day in the lowlands. Once or twice a year snow falls in the mountains. Spring weather arrives early with a slow succession of blooms beginning in late February and reaching the mountain heights in May. Some desert plants bloom throughout the year.

Midsummer temperatures in the desert and river valley are likely to hover above 100° during the day. This is the best time of year to go to the mountains. In The Basin (5,400-foot elevation) daytime temperatures average a comfortable 85° and nights are cool. Autumn sunshine and air are usually gentle and warm.

LODGING: At Chisos Basin, the center of activity most of the year, the Chisos Mountain Lodge includes motel units, rustic cottages, dining facilities, a supply store, and campground. For reservations, write: National Park Concessions, Inc., Big Bend National Park, TX 79834. Lodging is also available in Alpine, seventy-seven miles away.

Both Chisos Basin and Rio Grande Village campgrounds include water and comfort stations. Trailer sites with utility connections are located at Rio Grande Village and Panther Junction. Pay showers are at the lodge. Chisos and Rio Grande camping is limited to fourteen days.

Park headquarters provides literature which outlines self-guided tours, trails, and points of interest. Naturalist programs and illustrated talks are given year round. Hiking trails offer impressive vistas of the desert, plains, and distant mountain ranges. Arrangements can be made for saddle horses, pack animals, and guides at the Chisos Remuda for full-day horseback trips to the South Rim, overlooking the Rio Grande. River float trips (November through February) provide rugged and enjoyable experiences. Equipment is not available within the park grounds, but information can be obtained from: Villa de la Mina, Inc., Resort and River Float Trips, Box 47, Terlingua, TX 79852, about ten miles west of the park.

HOW TO GET THERE: The nearest principal city is El Paso, Texas. There is no public transportation directly to the park, although bus and rail companies serve the nearby Texas towns of Alpine, seventy-seven miles away, and Marathon, thirty-nine miles away. Auto rentals are available at Alpine. By car, there are three paved approach roads to the park: U.S. Highway 385 from Marathon to the north entrance; State Road 118 from Alpine to the west entrance; and U.S. Highway 67 from Marfa to Presidio, then Route 170 from Presidio to the west entrance.

GUADALUPE MOUNTAINS NATIONAL PARK

TEXAS

The Guadalupe Mountains have often been likened to an island in the desert, or silent sentinels standing guard over the hostile beauty of the surrounding plains. If you could see them from the air, these rocky outcrops would look like a giant V with the point in Texas and the two arms extending into New Mexico.

At first glance there seems to be nothing particularly remarkable about these barren mountain peaks and the new 76,000-acre park which lies astride their most rugged portions. There is no hint, until you get quite close to them, that they contain the most extensive fossil reef complex known to man. And here, too, sheltered by the highest point in Texas, 8,751-foot-high

Guadalupe Peak, are the unique remnants of forest plants and animals which have struggled to survive since the end of the last ice age 10,000 years ago.

In the park you can explore desert lowlands, superb canyons, and forested mountains. You can study geology, visit historic sites, and see plants and animals uncommon to the surrounding semiarid lowlands. Those who climb into the high country can enjoy outstanding views across the Salt Basin to the west, the Delaware Basin to the south and east, and into the deeply cut canyons to the north.

The rocks which make up the Guadalupe Mountains were formed during the Permian period, 225 to 280 million years ago. An inland sea which covered more than 10,000 square miles of Texas and New Mexico controlled their formation. It was in the shallow water near the shore of this sea that the Capitan barrier reef was built by lime-secreting algae and other organisms. As the reef grew upward and seaward, upon talus broken loose by storms, sediments were deposited in a lagoon between reef and land.

In time, the arm of the sea filling the Delaware Basin was cut off from the rest of the ocean, and the basin became excessively salty. Deposits of mineral salts gradually filled the basin to the height of the long-dead reef and buried it. A series of earth movements eventually raised the region dramatically, tilting its western edge upward. Erosion cut away the softer sediments, and additional movements helped shape the mountain range.

Vegetation typical of the southwestern deserts, including creosote bush, lechuguilla, Parry agave, yucca, and sotol, is found at the lower elevations. The high country contains a forest of ponderosa pine,

Douglas fir, limber pine, and a few aspens left over from a forest that covered this area thousands of years ago, when the climate was cooler and the rainfall was greater than they are today.

In the sheltered canyons, where moisture is more abundant, ferns, bigtooth maple, chokecherry, walnut, hop hornbeam, Texas madrone, and other species occur with vegetation from higher and lower elevations. Protection of these rare associations of plants is of paramount importance.

Animals commonly seen include wapiti, mule deer, wild turkey, ringtail, raccoon, porcupine, kit and gray foxes, coyote, and bobcat. Black bears and cougars pay occasional visits. More than two hundred species of birds and seventy species of reptiles and amphibians have been identified.

For the past 12,000 years, the mountain caves, springs, plants, and wildlife provided shelter and sustenance to various groups of people. Spanish conquistadors passed the Guadalupes on their journeys north from Mexico in the late 1500s and found the Mescalero Apaches inhabiting this area. Military surveyors mapping a transcontinental route to the California goldfields in 1849 passed along the base of the Guadalupes just south of El Capitan.

A route was opened through Guadalupe Pass in 1858, and it was used for eleven months by the Butterfield Overland Mail Line to carry mail and passengers from St. Louis to San Francisco. The first eastbound and westbound stagecoaches to travel the new route met just west of Guadalupe Pass on September 28, 1858. Pine Springs ("The Pinery") Station was a regular stop for changing teams on the four-horse, Celerity stagecoaches.

Shortly after the Civil War, ranching activities began and the area was soon settled. At times the settlers had to contend with outlaws, cattle rustlers, and Apache raiders.

In this semiarid climate, the summers are generally warm and the winters mild. But severe and sudden changes in the weather often occur. You can expect strong winds in spring and autumn, and electrical storms—sometimes accompanied by heavy downpours and flash flooding—in summer. Considerable variation, especially in temperature, between higher and lower elevations and between the eastern and western sides of the range is also common.

Sightseeing by car is possible from U.S. 62/180 which passes through the park, offering spectacular views of El Capitan, Guadalupe Peak, and the eastern and western escarpments. Scenic, historic Guadalupe Pass has picnic areas provided by the State of Texas. The National Park Service Frijole Information Station, 1 mile east of Pine Springs, is open daily.

McKittrick Canyon, noted for both its scenery and scientific importance, is open for day-use foot travel. A stream surfaces and disappears at various places along the canyon bottom. Rare and interesting plant communities are on the floor and lower slopes of the canyon. In autumn, the colors of the foliage are outstanding. A striking cross section of the Capitan reef complex, which includes the massive reef-core, forereef, and back-reef deposits, can be seen in the 1,900-foot-high north wall of McKittrick Canyon.

Until development is completed, public facilities and staffing at this new national park are extremely limited. People visiting the backcountry should be prepared to "rough it."

The park offers some fine opportunities to backpack in deserts and forests. However, water is not available and trails are faint. Before venturing into the park's interior, backpackers must make thorough preparations and check in at the information station to obtain campsite locations and to register destination and time of departure. They also should check in upon their return.

The park contains 63 miles of rugged mountain trails. Most are in poor condition and some routes are ill-defined. For safety, hikers should check in at the information station and have a good topographic map of the high country. Maps may be purchased at the information station. Good boots and adequate water supplies are essential.

The low-desert areas of the park lend themselves to horseback travel, but the mountain trails are steep and rough. Horses are not permitted in McKittrick Canyon.

LODGING: Overnight accommodations and food service facilities are available at cities some distance from the park: Carlsbad, N.M. (55 miles); El Paso, Tex. (110 miles); White's City, N.M. (34 miles); Dell City, Tex. (44 miles); and Van Horn, Tex. (65 miles).

Camping is limited to the primitive drive-in campground in Pine Spring Canyon and designated backcountry sites. Wood fires are not allowed in the backcountry, but containerized fuel stoves are permitted. The small, primitive campground at Pine Spring Canyon has tables, trash cans, and pit toilets. Water can be carried from the information station. The campground turnoff is 1 mile southwest of Frijole Information Station.

HOW TO GET THERE: Guadalupe National Park is on U.S. Highway 62/180 between El Paso, Texas, and Carlsbad, New Mexico. Both cities have rental cars, and both have bus and air transportation to the park. Adjacent on the northeast side of the park is Carlsbad Caverns National Park, also on U.S. Highway 62/180.

BISCAYNE NATIONAL PARK

FLORIDA

Both above the water and beneath its sun-dappled surface, the delights of nature are boundless in Biscayne National Park. This is truly a park of rare aquatic beauty, composed of long narrow islands floating just offshore and multicolored coral reefs, where brilliantly hued fish dart in and out among the swaying sea plants.

Biscayne is one of the largest marine preserves administered by the National Park System. Within its 180,000 acres (including thirty-two keys—or small islands) you can observe the intermingling of plant and animal communities from both the Temperate and

Tropic zones or learn about the complex and fascinating building process of a coral reef.

The limestone reefs owe their existence to groups of animals and plants that deposit calcium around themselves as a protective shell. The park's reefs are made up predominantly of the marine animal "coral," both living and dead, but calcareous algae (plants) and bryozoans (animals) also contribute to the process.

Lime building of the corals progresses best at temperatures of 20°C (68°F) and warmer. Besides warm water, corals require moving salt water, a firm foundation to start on (succeeding generations build on top of the limestone "houses" of their ancestors), and water no deeper than two hundred feet. The Biscayne reefs, which continue southward into John Pennekamp State Park and the southern Florida Keys, lie in waters generally no deeper than forty feet.

Among the colorful fish to see here are grunt, porkfish, wrasse, queen angelfish, and neon gobies. Sponges, sea "grasses," hard corals—and their plant-like relatives, the sea feathers and sea whips—cover the bottom. Algae are common marine plants taking many different shapes and ranging from blue-green to dull reds and browns.

In the waters off the southern coast of Florida, low islands or reefs are called "keys." The park has about thirty-two keys forming an almost continuous north-south chain. Woody vegetation covers them almost completely. Mangroves invade the sea along much of the shoreline, and a surprising variety of tropical hardwoods dominates the higher interior. Rapidly returning second growth is recreating much of the hardwood forest that was disturbed or destroyed by early inhabitants. There are some remnant stands of larger trees, including mahoganies.

The keys are home to such land mammals as the raccoon, marsh rabbit, and the exotic Mexican red-bellied squirrel. Water birds are common to the area, and Arsenicker Keys are nesting sites for many of these birds.

A well-sheltered section of Florida's Biscayne Bay lies between the keys and the Florida coast. Its waters, averaging eight to ten feet, shoal to shallow banks on each side that average three to five feet. The Intracoastal Waterway crosses the bay north to south. East of the keys, the ocean floor slopes gently to depths of ten to fifteen feet in Hawk Channel—a natural safe passage for larger boats traveling up and down the keys. Seaward of Hawk Channel is a wide band of highly varied subaquatic terrain consisting primarily of coral patch reefs and turtle grass. The protective outlying barrier reefs are just inside the park's eastern boundary. Beyond these reefs, the ocean floor drops off rapidly into the depths of the Florida current (Gulf Stream).

The old shipping routes of European powers, especially Spain and England, passed close to the Florida Keys, and in later years schooners trading along the coast picked their way through these waters. Voyages of the early sailing ships were always fraught with danger. Strong currents and high winds, storms and violent hurricanes, and the ever-present reefs and shoals made passage through the Florida Straits a risky business.

But natural dangers weren't the only threat to coastal sailors. Pirates lurked among the keys, waiting to pounce upon ships crippled by the sea, turning those disasters to their own sinister advantage. Caesar Creek—named for that notorious pirate of the Florida Keys, Black Caesar—reminds us of those turbulent days.

Even more vivid reminders are the shipwrecks lying below the waters—some dating back to the relatively primitive sailing ships of the sixteenth century. Some shipwrecks, though, are much more recent, giving us fair warning that despite our modern equipment, we're still at the mercy of the sea's hidden reefs and sudden storms.

Boating and fishing are the most popular pastimes in Biscayne National Park. There's a boat launching ramp near park headquarters at Convoy Point and a small marina at Elliott Key Harbor. Fishing is permitted in accordance with Florida law; no fishing license is required for saltwater fishing.

Swimming, snorkeling, and scuba diving are also popular, and one of the most exciting things you can do here is investigate a typical patch reef. Four such reef areas, including one shipwreck, are marked by mooring buoys, where you can tie your boat and explore. These reefs are two to three miles east of Elliott Key and Old Rhodes Key; detailed information and maps are available at park headquarters and at the ranger station on Elliott Key.

Because most of the shoreline in the park is exposed, rough, coral rock, there are few sandy beaches from which to swim. Also, there are no guarded swimming areas.

Park headquarters, located on the mainland at Convoy Point, has a free public boat ramp which is accessible twenty-four hours a day. In addition, there is a locked, overnight parking area for vehicles and boat trailers.

Elliott Key Harbor is seven miles across Biscayne Bay from Convoy Point. Facilities in the harbor include seventy boat slips and a campground area, both free and both operated on a first-come, first-served basis. However, fresh water, electrical hookups, food service, and garbage collection are not available.

Elliott Key also has a visitor center which offers interpretive programs, books, and marine charts. Picnic grounds are located on this key, as well as a one-and-a-half-mile self-guided nature trail which takes you through a hardwood hammock and along the ocean side of the island.

LODGING: Motels, campgrounds, gasoline, and other supplies are available in the nearby town of Homestead. Many well-supplied marinas are located along the mainland coast and in the Florida Keys. Check your charts or ask a park ranger.

HOW TO GET THERE: Coming from all points north of Biscayne National Park: proceed to Florida Turnpike Extension leading south to Tallahassee Road exit. Signs prior to exit will indicate "Homestead Air Force Base—turn right next exit." Continue south on Tallahassee Road to North Canal Drive. Proceed east on N. Canal Drive until you reach the Homestead Bayfront Park and Biscayne National Park signs. Turn left and proceed to park headquarters. Coming from all points south of Biscayne National Park: drive on U.S. 1 until you reach the intersection of U.S. 1 and North Canal Drive. Turn right and proceed eight miles east until you reach the Homestead Bayfront Park and Biscayne National Park signs. Turn left and proceed to park headquarters.

Everglades National Park is about a half-hour drive south from Convoy Point Headquarters. John Pennekamp Coral Reef State Park can be reached by driving south on U.S. 1.

EVERGLADES NATIONAL PARK

FLORIDA

The Everglades is a vast, mysterious, fascinating expanse of mangroves and pines, cypress, and mahogany. But above all it is grass—more than one hundred species of grasses—gently rippling in the soft subtropical breeze.

From afar, the inland stretches of this rolling grassland look like dry, solid prairie extending to the horizon in every direction. That, however, is only nature's illusion. The name "Everglades" means "River of Grass," and that's literally what this area is: a river flowing through grass. This unusual freshwater river is six inches deep and fifty miles wide, meandering slowly toward the sea along a riverbed that drops a mere fifteen feet along its course to Florida Bay.

The park boundary only partly contains the watery expanse for which it is named. An area of this marshy land and open water larger than Delaware were set aside as a park in 1947. But its great size can neither protect the environment from the disruptive commercial agriculture and industry around it nor assure that endangered species finding havens here will survive. Human concern and prudent management must now play a strong environmental role.

Climate governs Everglades life. The nearly uniform climate makes the park a year-round attraction, but there are two distinct seasons: summer is wet and winter dry. Heavy rains fall during intense storms in late May through October. Warm, humid conditions bring abundant insects (carry repellent in summer months) important to food chains. Precipitation can exceed fifty inches a year.

The Everglades is best known for its abundance and variety of birdlife. At Flamingo you can watch roseate spoonbills, large pink birds often mistaken for flamingos. The flamingos no longer regularly visit southern Florida, if indeed they ever did. Reddish egrets and endangered great white herons live and breed in Florida Bay. Some fifty pairs of endangered southern bald eagles nest along the coast. Look for the eagles from the breezeway of the Flamingo Visitor Center.

Large populations of Cape Sable sparrows, once found at Cape Sable and Big Cypress, are almost gone. Only widely scattered individuals remain. Taylor Slough's muhly grass prairie supports an active population, but non-native, exotic plants threaten to close in the open prairie this sparrow depends on for its survival. Short-tailed hawks prey on the sparrow, and ants can kill its nestlings. When abundant habitat fostered an abundance of Cape Sable sparrows, this natural predation posed no great threat to the species.

Other rare and endangered wildlife species found here include the Florida panther, manatee, Everglades mink, green sea turtle, loggerhead turtle, brown pelican, Florida sandhill crane, Everglades kite, short-tailed hawk, peregrine falcon, and crocodile. Other species also require the special protection Everglades National Park provides for survival. These include the alligator, Florida mangrove cuckoo, osprey, and round-tailed muskrat.

The rare, shy, harmless manatee weighs close to a ton and measures more than fifteen feet in length. It is entirely herbivorous, a docile, plant-eating mammal. Man's motorboats and propellors pose the greatest threat to this easygoing sea cow. The Florida panther (cougar) is among North America's rarest mammals. The major threat to these big cats, rarely seen in the pinelands or along the park road, is loss of the extensive habitat over which they stalk their prey.

The alligator is the best-known Everglades citizen. Unfortunately, its hide has been greatly prized for high-fashion shoes and handbags. The alligator once waged a losing battle against poachers and habitat loss, but has now staged a comeback under nationwide protection. Recently seventy-five percent of the nation's alligators were reclassified as threatened rather than endangered. The alligator has earned the title "keeper of the Everglades." It cleans out the large holes dissolved in the Everglades' limestone bed which function as oases in the dry winter season. Fish, turtles, snails, and other freshwater animals seek refuge in these life-rich solution holes, which become feeding grounds for alligators, birds, and mammals until the rains return. Survivors, both predators and prey, then quit the holes to repopulate the Everglades.

Crocodiles, less common than alligators, are distinguished by their narrower snouts and greenish gray color. You would be lucky indeed to see one of these shy and secretive creatures, which are mostly found in the Florida Bay area. The crocodile's survival hinges on the preservation of its dwindling habitat, which somewhat overlaps the alligator's.

Human beings are as much a part of the Everglades as the alligator. But our conflicting actions as consumers and conservers have irrevocably changed southern Florida, altering the Everglades ecosystem. Concern for protecting rookeries of herons, ibis, and other wading birds from commercial plume hunting motivated creation of the park. Ironically, millions of people now seek sanctuary here from similar problems in our synthetic world. Ultimately, places like the Everglades may be the last refuge not just of eagles, crocodiles, and wood storks but of people, too.

Fishing is permitted in the park under Florida laws, but spearguns are prohibited. Freshwater rod-and-reel fishing requires a Florida license, but saltwater fishing does not. Inquire or watch for signs about the few no-fishing areas.

The four most sought-after fish in the Everglades are snapper, snook, trout, and redfish. These good eating fish are caught all year round. Purchase shrimp for bait at the Flamingo Marina. Baits you can catch yourself are finger mullet and pinfish.

Flamingo Marina accommodates boats up to 18.3 meters (sixty feet) long, with ample boat trailer parking and free launch ramp access. Slip fees are based on boat length. Rent small powered skiffs, houseboats, and canoes at the marina and ask about the many services offered. Purchase navigation charts in Homestead, Miami, Everglades City, or at the marinas and visitor center.

A marked ninety-nine-mile Wilderness Waterway offers inland boating from Everglades City to Flamingo. Whether by boat or by canoe, this waterway provides an ideal way to experience the Everglades for those who have the time. The Flamingo area offers four marked canoe trails: Bear Lake, West Lake, Hells Bay, and Noble Hammock. Ask a park ranger for specific information.

Coot Bay provides access for canoe travel into Whitewater Bay. Mrazek Pond features large numbers of migratory and resident birds during several midwinter weeks.

Flordia Bay lies largely within Everglades National Park. Most of its islands are closed to boat landings to protect nesting birds. Check at the Key Largo or Flamingo ranger stations or the visitor center to see which islands are open.

Birdwatching, perhaps some of America's finest, lures many people back to the Everglades time after time. This area is unique because some species that are rare or endangered throughout the United States or the world are relatively common in the park's protected habitat.

Hiking trails are provided in the Flamingo area. Round-trip distances range from four miles on the Bear Lake, Christian Point, and Snake Bight trails to fourteen miles on Alligator Creek Trail. Many also serve as bike trails. Inquire at the Flamingo Visitor Center for more details.

Long Pine Key Nature Trail offers hiking and biking

in the pines. It returns to the main road just east of the
Pahay-okee Trail. Its length is seven miles.

Shark Valley. A tram ride and other naturalist-
conducted activities are provided in this biologically
rich and diverse area. Abundant wildlife can be seen
most of the year, especially in winter.

The nonprofit Everglades Natural History Association makes books and pamphlets available at the
visitor center or by mail. Write the association before
you visit. Address: P.O. Box 279, Homestead, FL
33030.

For boat sightseeing and fishing trips from Flamingo, write to the Everglades Park Co. The ninety-
nine-mile Wilderness Waterway boat trail requires
from one day by powerboat to several days by canoe.
Arrangements can be made upon arrival at Flamingo
or Everglades. Airboats and glades buggies can be
rented just north of the park at several locations along
Tamiami Trail between Miami and Naples. Sightseeing
boats in the Ten Thousand Islands and mangrove
swamp are operated by Everglades National Park Boat
Tours, P.O. Box 119, Everglades City, FL 33929.
Trips originate at the Gulf Coast Ranger Station in
Everglades City on Fla. 29. Sandwiches and drinks
can be obtained here also.

LODGING: Accommodations within the park are concentrated at Flamingo, where the visitor center, a restaurant and motel, a boat marina, campground, picnic
area, and service station are located. For hotel reservations, write: Everglades Park Co., Inc., 18494
S. Federal Highway, Miami, FL 33157. Accommodations are also abundant in the nearby towns of Homestead, Flordia City, Everglades, and Miami.

Camping sites are available at Long Pine Key and
Flamingo campgrounds. Camping at Flamingo is limited to seven days from December 15 through April 15.
Drinking fountains, tables, charcoal burners, and rest
rooms are available at both campgrounds. House trailers are permitted, but there are no utility hookups.
There is no charge for camping on beaches or for backcountry camping, but a permit is required from park
headquarters. Camper rentals and supplies are available in Homestead, Flordia City, and other nearby
towns. ·

HOW TO GET THERE: The nearest major city is
Miami, 35 miles away, where rental cars and motor
coach tours to the Everglades are available. Rental
cars are also available in Coral Gables and Homestead, Florida. By car from Miami, take U.S. Highway
441 to Homestead and Florida City, then State Road
27 to the park entrance and Flamingo City, within the
park. The western entrance is accessible from U.S.
Highway 41 to State Road 29, south of Everglades
City. By boat, cruisers use inland waterways to Coot
Bay, Flamingo, and Everglades City.

MAMMOTH CAVE NATIONAL PARK

KENTUCKY

With over two thousand known caves and many more undiscovered ones, south central Kentucky is known as the cave capital of the United States. Of all these caves, however, the most famous and overwhelming is Mammoth Cave.

The Mammoth complex is so huge, so vast, that only 150 miles of its passageways have been explored and charted. Here you'll find breathtaking rock formations of cascading stone, domes, deep pits, historical and archeological remains, and even a subterranean crystal lake.

Geologists have dated the cave's formation back more than 300 million years to when shallow inland seas covered much of the region. Gradually, as the seas drained away, the underlying strata of porous limestone were exposed to weather and water seepage, with the resulting erosion creating the unusual formations we see today.

Although Mammoth Cave was officially discovered in 1799, there is evidence that man has walked its passageways and chambers for more than 4,500 years. Early Indians lighted their way through the darkness with blazing torches, and during the War of 1812 miners used oil lamps to search for the nitrates used in making gunpowder. Today's visitors, however, can see the cave's wonders courtesy of modern electricity.

When you arrive at Mammoth Cave National Park, your first stop ought to be the visitor center, where you can obtain current information on cave tour schedules and aboveground activities. An illustrated program is also presented throughout the day to give you additional background on the caves.

Cave trips are offered all year, varying in length (from one to six hours) and in times of departures. Except for the special wheelchair tours for the handicapped, many of these underground trips are quite strenuous and require a good deal of stooping and walking over uneven terrain. The temperature down in the cave remains a constant 54°F (12°C) and the humidity 87%, so it would be advisable to take along a sweater or light jacket in addition to a sturdy pair of walking shoes.

To see more of the 52,000 surface acres in Mammoth Cave National Park, hike the self-guiding nature trails and longer hiking trails that lead through hardwood forests to a variety of features, including springs that emerge from the cave system.

In summer, interpreters present programs nightly in

an outdoor amphitheater and lead a variety of nature walks over these woodland trails. Some activities are scheduled in the spring and fall. You can also get an appreciation of the Green River and its forest wildlife by taking a one-hour cruise on the boat *Miss Green River II*. Buy your tickets at the visitor center from the concessioner. Season: April through October.

LODGING: Mammoth Cave Hotel, a motel-type lodge, and electrically heated cottages are open all year. Unheated cabins are available from May to September. If you expect to stay in the park in summer, we suggest that you write (National Park Concessions, Inc., Mammoth Cave, KY 42259) for rates and that you make your reservations well in advance. Accommodations are also available in nearby communities. For information on areas outside the park, write to the Department of Public Information, Capitol Annex Building, Frankfort, KY 40601.

A 145-site campground and a picnic area are available near the visitor center. A free primitive campground with 12 sites is located at Houchins Ferry. Free backcountry campsites are also available but require a permit, which may be obtained at park headquarters.

HOW TO GET THERE: Mammoth Cave National Park is about halfway between Nashville, Tennessee, and Louisville, Kentucky, just off Interstate 65. State Road 70 runs through the park, connecting I-65 on the southeast and the Western Kentucky Parkway to the northwest. Air, train, bus connections, and taxis are available in Nashville, and in Louisville and Cave City, Kentucky.

GREAT SMOKY MOUNTAINS NATIONAL PARK

NORTH CAROLINA— TENNESSEE

Perhaps more than any other mountains in the United States, the Great Smokies evoke images of America at its pioneer best. Although the pioneers are gone now, their legacy lives on in the rustic settlements they built in the isolated valleys of these magnificent mountains. Many of those settlements have been preserved as reminders of the rugged but colorful lives of those hardy mountain people.

The Great Smokies, named for the smokelike haze that hangs over the densely foliated ridges, are the majestic climax of the Appalachian Highlands. Despite the presence of man since the earliest days of this country, the Great Smoky Mountains National Park remains virtually unspoiled, containing the finest examples of temperate deciduous forests in the world.

Fertile soils and heavy rains, over a long period, have caused a world-renowned variety of flora to develop. Some 1,400 kinds of flowering plants grow in the park. Within the coves, broadleaf trees predominate; while along the crest, which rises to more than six thousand feet, conifer forests like those of Central Canada find suitable climate.

The park is maintained in its natural and wild condition. Motorists must drive defensively and be alert for hazards caused by changing natural conditions. Hikers must be prepared to meet nature on its own terms. The main roads offer only an introduction to the Smokies. At Cades Cove an eleven-mile loop road leads past open fields, pioneer homesteads, and little frame churches where mountain people lived and worshiped almost unnoticed for a century. At the Oconaluftee Pioneer Museum in North Carolina, exhibits, live demonstrations, and an early-twentieth-century farmstead tell the story of the mountain people more fully. A scenic high mountain road winds its way through Newfound Gap to Clingmans Dome; there, a half-mile walk to an observation tower provides an excellent panorama of the countryside on clear days. In summer you can expect extremely heavy traffic on this route.

From mid-June to Labor Day you may enjoy evening programs and nature walks at most developed campgrounds. During the spring and fall these activities are scheduled on a limited basis. For further information about interpretive events, inquire at any park visitor center or ranger station.

The eight hundred miles of horse and foot trails offer the most rewarding experiences; trails wind along streams and through forests into the high country. Forget life's routines. Pick a trail and hike into the forest stillness of the Smokies. For the "do-it-yourself" naturalist, there are several short, self-guiding nature trails. Pick up the explanatory leaflet at the beginning of each trail. As you walk, read about the relationship of plants to their woodland habitat.

A free backcountry camping permit is required for all overnight hiking parties and can be obtained at any ranger station or visitor center. Because of overcrowding, it is necessary to ration overnight use of the sixty-eight miles of Appalachian Trail within the park. Five other popular areas, Mt. Le Conte, Laurel Gap, Kephart Prong, Scott Gap, and Rich Mountain, are also rationed. Arrangements for a permit must be made after you arrive in the park. There are many uncrowded trails in the park, however. A listing of trailside campsites, for use in planning alternate hiking routes, is available upon request. Pets are permitted in the park if on a leash or under other physical control at all times. They may not be taken on trails or cross-country hikes.

There are seven developed campgrounds and three primitive camping areas in the park.

Many of the park's streams provide fishing for rainbow trout and brown trout. In certain streams, managed on a fishing-for-fun plan, you may fish the year round, but you must carefully release all fish under twelve inches. The regular season is from April

15 through October 15; Tennessee or North Carolina fishing licenses are required, but not trout stamps. Local regulations are posted on streams and can be obtained at any park ranger station or visitor center. The possession of any brook trout is prohibited, except for those caught in designated children's streams, April 15 to October 15 inclusive.

Wild flowers and migrating birds attract many visitors in late April and early May. If you intend to hike or camp in the spring, bring warm clothing and be prepared for a variety of weather conditions, including frequent rainstorms. Summer days are warm, and nights are usually cool. At higher elevations, temperatures may range from fifteen to twenty degrees lower than those in the valleys. During June and July, the blooming of rhododendron is the outstanding natural event. July and August usually bring the heaviest rainfall, and thunderstorms sometimes come without warning. For greatest comfort on summer hikes, carry a raincoat and insect repellent.

Autumn's pageantry of color usually reaches its peak during the middle of October. To many visitors, this is the finest time of the year. Autumn days are cool and clear, ideal for hiking. Winter is the most unpredictable season, yet you shouldn't discount it as a time to visit the Smokies. A quiet peace pervades the park. At times the fog, moving over the mountaintops, blankets the conifers in frost. However, be prepared for icy road conditions and sudden snowstorms. From November through March, winter gear and clothing suitable for survival in deep snow and −20°F temperatures are necessary. This includes a sleeping bag adequate to −20°, waterproof matches or fire starter,

food, and other items available at ranger stations and
visitor centers.

LODGING: Most neighboring towns have gas, food,
lodging, and camping supplies. Many private
campgrounds operate outside the park. For information, write to the chambers of commerce of nearby
towns in North Carolina and Tennessee. Accessible
only by trail, Le Conte Lodge offers accommodations
within the park from mid-April to late October. Allow
a half-day hike up a mountain trail to reach this se-
cluded retreat. Reservations are necessary; call or
write: Le Conte Lodge, Gatlinburg, TN 37738.

Overnight hotel accommodations and food service
are provided at Wonderland Hotel, at Elkmont, June 1
to October 31.

Saddle horses are available at Cades Cove,
Smokemont, Dudley Creek, Cosby, and Two-Mile
Branch near Gatlinburg, from approximately April 1 to
October 31.

A word about bears. Bears may appear tame, but
they are dangerous wild animals and should not be
approached closely, teased, or frightened—especially
when cubs are present. Feeding bears is dangerous
and is a violation of park regulations. Dependence on
unnatural foods may make bears easy prey for
poachers. If a bear approaches your car, stay inside
with the windows closed.

HOW TO GET THERE: Located on the border of Ten-
nessee and North Carolina; the nearest principal city is
Knoxville, Tennessee, fifty miles from where U.S.
Highway 441 leads to the north park entrance at Gat-

linburg. Asheville, North Carolina, thirty miles away, is served by Delta, United, and Piedmont airlines. Rental cars and bus connections are available at both cities. From Asheville, take Interstate 40 west to U.S. Highway 276, which runs south to U.S. Highway 19, leading to the south entrance at Cherokee.

VIRGIN ISLANDS NATIONAL PARK

ST. JOHN, U.S. VIRGIN ISLANDS

For lavish, untrammeled tropical beauty, there is no place quite like St. John in the U.S. Virgin Islands. Stately coconut palms sway in the gentle trade winds, while the warm, azure waters of the Caribbean wash over white sand beaches and fanciful coral reefs.

The U.S. Virgin Islands may not be a state, but they're definitely a state of mind—a tropical state where relaxation and enjoyment are the norm instead of the exception. And nowhere is this more evident than in the Virgin Islands National Park, located on the smallest of three major American-owned islands.

Growing from the rock outcrops bordering numerous bays and from small rocky cays (islands) are the coral reefs. These fringing reefs are a complex community of interacting marine plants and animals. The basic building blocks of reefs are hard corals—including brain, elkhorn, star, finger, and staghorn—and soft corals (gorgonians), especially sea fans and sea whips. Within the corals are a variety of fish, including parrot, sturgeon, angelfish, grunt, and snapper.

Closely dependent upon the reefs are the sand beaches for which these islands are so well known. Without the growth of the living corals that comprise the reefs, the beaches could not exist.

Man has been an inhabitant of these islands for centuries. Long before the birth of Christ, seafaring men using stone tools and bone implements hacked logs into canoes, swam and fished in the clear waters of the Virgin Islands. Later, tribes of tall black-haired people from South America—farmers, pottery makers, warriors, and rock carvers—drifted with the winds and current through the curving necklace of islands now called the Lesser Antilles.

On November 4, 1493, Christopher Columbus, with a fleet of seventeen ships, discovered the Lesser Antilles. By mid-November he had found an island he named Santa Cruz, or St. Croix. A few leagues northward, the Italian explorer then charted a chain of green, mountainous islands he christened Las Once Mille Virgines—the Virgin Islands. The Spanish claims resulting from Columbus' voyages began two centuries of international wars for supremacy of the West Indies.

Against this background, the island of St. John slowly awakened to the visits of occasional freebooters, runaway slaves, castaways, and Dutch timber cutters. In 1717, Denmark took control, initiating a period of prosperity during which slave labor built many sugar and cotton plantations. With the abolition of slavery in 1848, St. John gradually reverted to its former quiet existence.

On March 31, 1917, the United States purchased the Virgin Islands from Denmark. The U.S. Navy managed the islands until 1931, when the Territory of the Virgin Islands was created. The Territory is administered by the U.S. Department of the Interior. As a result of congressional legislation and the donation of lands to the government by Laurance S. Rockefeller and the Jackson Hole Preserve Corporation, Virgin Islands National Park was established on December 1, 1956.

Opportunities abound in the park for a wide range of activities—from quiet, contemplative afternoons on the beach to rugged 6-mile hikes across the interior of the island.

Swimming and snorkeling are excellent at St. John's many fine beaches. Snorkel equipment can be rented at Trunk and Cinnamon bays, and scuba gear can be rented and serviced on both St. John and St. Thomas.

Saltwater fishing is good all year, and no license is required. Off-the-shore rod and reel fishing is permitted, but not in the vicinity of public swimming or snorkeling beaches. Boats for deep-sea fishing, drift fishing, or shoreline trolling may be chartered on St.

John and St. Thomas. Charter sail- and powerboats with operators are available on St. John, St. Thomas, and nearby British Tortola.

The Red Hook Contact Station on St. Thomas and the Cruz Bay Visitor Center on St. John provide orientation talks, exhibits, maps, and literature about park features. Guided snorkel trips, hikes, cultural demonstrations, and evening programs are offered throughout the year. A schedule of interpretive activities is posted on the park's bulletin boards and may be obtained at the visitor center in Cruz Bay. Self-guiding walking trails are marked at Annaberg, Cinnamon Bay, Reef Bay, and Salt Pond Bay.

Hiking trails on St. John range from easy walks to difficult climbs, from well maintained to brushy, and from short to long. Bring hiking shoes and light clothing. Small knapsacks and belt canteens are also advisable since water is not available along hiking trails.

There are many points of interest to see in the park, and the easiest way in which to see them is by taking the 15-mile tour by auto or taxi over Centerline Road and back via the North Shore Road. This route includes some of the island's most spectacular scenery, including the ruins of the Annaberg sugar plantation and several of the island's most popular beaches. For those who are nervous about driving on the left-hand side of the road, native guided taxi tours are available. These are operated from Cruz Bay, and a typical tour can take up to two and a half hours. If you plan to rent a car, however, be certain to make reservations well in advance.

Island highlights you won't want to miss include:

1. Cruz Bay, the administrative seat of St. John, has a few food stores and gift shops. Stop at the park head-

quarters and visitor center there for park orientation and publications.

2. Trunk Bay has one of the best beaches in the world and offers a sign-posted underwater nature trail for snorkelers. Lifeguards are on duty daily from 9 A.M. to 4 P.M. Facilities include changing rooms, toilets, pay telephones, a picnic area, and snack bar.

3. Cinnamon Bay, the location of Cinnamon Bay Camp, has a camp store and cafeteria. Lifeguard services are provided from 9 A.M. to 4 P.M. daily. A 1-mile self-guiding nature trail is located across from the camp entrance.

4. The Leinster Bay area contains a mangrove swamp, reef flat, and the partially restored ruins of the Annaberg sugar mill factory complex. From seaward, this complex, located above Leinster Bay on St. John's rugged north shore, is reminiscent of an ancient European castle. The beautiful, thick-walled old buildings, constructed of cleverly fitted stone, native coral, and yellow and red Danish ballast brick, were familiar to the eighteenth- and early nineteenth-century Danes, Dutchmen, and slaves who toiled here. Under the hot Caribbean sun they worked endlessly to produce crude brown sugar, rich dark molasses, and strong rum for export to North America and Europe.

5. Coral Bay, the site of the first established sugar plantation on St. John, was first settled in 1717. The site was selected because of its well-protected harbor.

6. Salt Pond Bay and nearby Lameshur Bay are generally calm during the winter, when stormy seas make snorkeling and swimming hazardous on the north shore beaches. A side trail leads to a salt pond, then to the rugged, windswept, coral rubble beach at Drunk Bay. Another trail winds through a growth of

barrel cactus, called Turk's head, to Ram Head, with its magnificent views of St. John's south shore and the British Virgin Islands.

7. Four-wheel-drive vehicles are required for the drive to Lameshur Bay. A picnic area, toilets, ranger station, and research station are located in this area, once known for its bay oil, lime juice, and cattle production. Several interesting hiking trails connect Lameshur Bay with Reef Bay, Europa Bay, Yawzi Point, and Bordeaux Mountain Road.

8. Reef Bay Valley contains mysterious petroglyphs (rock carvings), some of which are attributed to West African origin and others to Taino Indians. Also within the valley are ruins of the Reef Bay Estate house and steam-powered sugar mill ruins, the last to operate on the island. Reef Bay is accessible from Centerline Road by a shady, 2.6-mile downhill hiking trail that traverses a unique subtropical, moist forest.

The climate here in the Virgin Islands is ideal. The yearly temperature averages 26°C (79°F) and varies little between winter and summer. Temperatures rarely exceed 37°C (99°F) or fall below 18°C (64°F). Rainfall averages approximately forty inches per year, coming mostly in brief night showers.

LODGING: Caneel Bay Plantation provides lodging and complete dining facilities. Meals are also served to non-guests, but by reservation only. A wide variety of facilities and accommodations are also available on the nearby island of St. Thomas. See your travel agent for reservations.

Within the park, Cinnamon Bay Campground provides campsites and cottage units, and a lovely beach with picnic tables and charcoal grills. Complete camping equipment, cooking utensils, food, and supplies can be rented or purchased there. For reservations for sites, cottages, and equipment, write: Cinnamon Bay Campground, P.O. Box 4930, St. John, U.S. Virgin Islands 00801.

HOW TO GET THERE: Both Charlotte Amalie, St. Thomas, and San Juan, Puerto Rico, have scheduled airline service from major cities in the United States. Taxi or bus transportation is available from Charlotte Amalie to the Red Hook public dock, where a ferry operates daily to and from Cruz Bay, St. John. Once on St. John, taxi service is available for a very minimal charge, or you-drive-it jeeps are available for rent by the week. St. John is also served by amphibious aircraft from St. Thomas and St. Croix. Private or charter boats are welcome.

SHENANDOAH NATIONAL PARK

VIRGINIA

At peace with the ages and at peace with nature. That, in a few words, sums up the serene beauty of Shenandoah National Park, located deep in the Blue Ridge Mountains of Virginia. These softly rounded mountain crests are among the oldest in the world and wear their age with a grace and dignity that belies the scenic wilderness of their hills, valleys, and hollows.

The park itself stretches out like a long, slender ribbon over the ridgetops of these ancient Appalachians, with 105-mile-long Skyline Drive its most famous feature. Just a short hike away from many of the Drive's seventy-five overlooks are trout-filled mountain pools and wild gardens of vines, shrubs, and brilliant wild flowers.

Shenandoah National Park lies astride a spectacularly beautiful part of the Blue Ridge, which forms the eastern rampart of the Appalachian Range from Pennsylvania to Georgia. The Shenandoah River, from which the park's name is derived, lies to the west, flowing northeastward beneath the Blue Ridge and the Allegheny mountains. Massanutten, the 40-mile-long straight-profiled mountain you see from many Skyline Drive overlooks, lies between the North and South forks of the Shenandoah. To the east of the Blue Ridge is rolling Piedmont country.

From the mid-eighteenth century on into the 1900s the hollows, ridges, and slopes that now constitute the national park were the home of mountain people. These hardy folk eked out a marginal existence by growing corn, beans, cabbages, and apples; by raising chickens, hogs, and cows; and by producing from the bounty of the forest and the harvest of their stony fields such market commodities as tanbark, honey, moonshine, and furs. Theirs was a highly self-sufficient culture. They developed their own techniques for smoking meats, rendering hogs, preserving vegetables and fruits for winter use, and making household furnishings and farm implements. They devised their own recreational pursuits, created their own music, and passed on their traditions from generation to generation.

During the first decades of this century, many of the mountain people left this land, which had become steadily less productive, in search of an easier life in the lowlands. The lumber companies had depleted the forests; most of the game was gone; the soil was worn out from misuse and much of it washed down the slopes; and cash was always scarce. When the plans for a new 300-square-mile national park to be carved out of the Blue Ridge were taking shape, it was necessary to make provisions for the future of the remaining mountaineers. New communities were established in the valleys below the Blue Ridge, and the families moved down into government-financed homes that were closer to schools, jobs, and the amenities of civilization. With improvement in the economic lot of the mountain folk, the crafts they had developed over generations to enable them to exist in the isolated and harsh environment came into disuse. Today, only a few old-timers retain the skills that enabled them to fashion finished products from the raw materials of the mountains, using only their hands and their homemade tools.

Following establishment of the park, cessation of timber-cutting operations, and relocation of the mountain people, nature rapidly began to heal the scars of man's long exploitation of the land. Vegetation soon masked the stone walls, rail fences, and rusting barbwire; and pines, locusts, and other pioneer forest trees reclaimed the cut-over forests and worn-out fields. Today, few signs remain as evidence of the mountain culture. Here and there old apple trees bear blemished fruit, but the crop is harvested by black bears and white-tailed deer. Raccoons, opossums, skunks, squirrels, turkeys, and woodland songbirds again abound, and beavers have returned to the fringes of the park. On the other hand, animals that adapted to grassy or bushy environs, such as the cottontail, quail, and red fox, declined in numbers as the pastures, cornfields, and farmyards were gradually taken over by the new forest. The landscape, even without the late, lamented American chestnut, is regaining the aspect of the pristine scene that greeted the settlers who moved west from the coastal plain or east from the Shenandoah Valley a century ago.

There are 390 miles of trails. A 94-mile section is the Appalachian Trail, following the crest of the Blue Ridge Mountains. Saddle horses can be rented at Skyland and Big Meadows. Orientation programs, literature, and exhibits are available at Dickey Ridge, Matthews Arm, Skyland, Big Meadows, Lewis Mountain, and Loft Mountain. There are also nightly campfire programs at Matthews Arm, Big Meadows, Lewis Mountain, and Loft Mountain. The park is open all year, but most activities and facilities are closed in the winter.

LODGING: Accomodations are available in the park's central district at Skyland, Big Meadows, and Lewis Mountain. For reservations, write: ARA–Virginia Sky-Line Company, Inc., Box 727, Luray, VA 22835. Six trail cabins for hikers are available with advance reservations through the Potomac Appalachian Trail Club, 1718 N Street, N.W., Washington, D.C. 20036.

Within the park, Matthews Arm, Lewis Mountain, Loft Mountain, and Big Meadows Campground provide tent and trailer sites with outdoor fireplaces, fountains, tables, benches, and comfort stations, but no utility connections. Showers and laundry facilities are available at Big Meadows and Loft Mountain. Picnic areas and trailside shelters are also available. The park requires backcountry camping permits and accepts reservations.

HOW TO GET THERE: Major highways connect with the park's Skyline Drive. The Drive extends 105 miles from Front Royal to Rockfish Gap, where it connects with the Blue Ridge Parkway. Entrance roads on the west connect the park with Interstate 81 at Harrissonburg and Luray; to the east, Sperryville (on U.S. 211) and Ruckersville (on U.S. 33) connect with U.S. Highway 29. The nearest principal cities served by scheduled airlines are Washington, D.C., about 100 miles away; Richmond, 100 miles; and Charlottesville, Virginia, 25 miles. All have bus lines and rental car companies which can provide transportation to the park.

ACADIA NATIONAL PARK

MAINE

For four hundred years the rocky coast of Maine has been an irresistible lure for those who love the sea, and nowhere is this lure more compelling than the wildly beautiful archipelago comprising Acadia National Park.

Although Acadia is spread out over numerous small islands and the Schoodic Peninsula on the mainland, the major portion of this park is located on Mount Desert Island. As its name implies, this island is a series of rounded granite mountains boasting the highest elevation on the East Coast. The highest dome, Cadillac Mountain, rises 1,530 feet above the blue Atlantic, offering breathtaking panoramas across the island and the sea to the rockbound mainland coast.

The sea is all pervading; it encircles, it thrusts inland, it fogs. In the midday sun, its bright-blue surface is studded with lobster buoys. White boats of lobstermen, trailing plumes of shrieking gulls, toss on shoreward swells in fearless disregard of rocky cliff and ledge. In fog, all is gray and muted. Engines mutter out to sea. The lobster boat is a blurred shape in a formless world. The water's leaden surface heaves, and kelp strands stir uneasily in the sucking tide. At sundown, the ocean glows in pastel shades of pink, mauve, and gold; gulls wing silently home to distant islands; and like fireflies, first here then there, the navigational aids on reef, island, and headland flash their silent warnings.

The tidal zone, twice daily exposed to air and drowned by water, is an exciting place to visit. As the water drops away, tide pools brimming with life are exposed, and you can watch marine animals going about the business of living. Blue mussels and barnacles strain microscopic bits of life from cool salt water. Legions of periwinkles feed by scraping algae from rocks and ledges, while other snails fasten death grips on shellfish, drilling holes in their shells and drawing out the flesh. In shadowed crevices flowerlike anemones extend their fleshy tentacles. Under camouflage of shell and weed fragments, spiny sea urchins huddle together, awaiting the next tide and safety from the gull's cold eye.

Behind the sea are the forests and mountains of Acadia, made easy for exploring by the forty-mile system of carriage paths. These broad, smooth, graveled byways encircle Jordan Pond and Eagle Lake and wind around the flanks of Sargent and Penobscot mountains. They offer stunning views of Somes Sound and Frenchman Bay, and they lead you along beaver-dammed brooks. Grades are gentle and vistas long. Here small children run and jump while parents or grandparents stroll. If you prefer, you can ride in the style of earlier days, by horse-drawn carriage. The loop around Eagle Lake is a bicycle path.

Who built these carriage paths? Who had the vision of a national park here? This park was neither carved from public lands nor bought with public funds. Many people loved Mount Desert Island, Schoodic Peninsula, and the nearby islands. Residents of Maine and summer visitors alike donated time and resources to preserve Acadia's beauty. Men such as George B. Dorr and Charles W. Eliot, a former president of Harvard, saw the dangers of development and acted to avoid them. John D. Rockefeller, Jr., played a critical role. He built the many miles of carriage paths and gave more than eleven thousand acres (about one-third of the park's area) to Acadia National Park.

An Acadia experience involves more than forest and sea. There were people living on this island when Champlain named it l'Isle des Mont-deserts in 1604. The story of those people is told in the Abbe Museum at Sieur de Monts Spring through exhibits and Indian artifacts. Visit Islesford Museum on Little Cranberry Island; ride over and back on the ferry and see the museum's ship models, tools, and pictures, which speak of island life in the nineteenth and early twentieth centuries.

Nearby villages testify to the variety of life-styles on the island today. Northeast Harbor is a major summer colony whose harbor shelters a host of sailboats, large and small. Bar Harbor caters to tourists; it offers a wide variety of accommodations and amusements.

Bass Harbor and Southwest Harbor on the west side of the island and Winter Harbor at Schoodic retain more of the true flavor of Maine coastal villages. The men who earn their living from the sea—lobstermen, fishermen, boat builders, and coastguardsmen—tie up here; canneries, lobster pounds, and boatyards have not yet been replaced by summer homes and motels.

Don't neglect the opportunities for exploring marine environments. On conducted tide-pool walks you'll learn about the plants and animals inhabiting microhabitats between land and sea. On a naturalist-led cruise you may see porpoises, seals, eagles, and nesting colonies of seabirds, or watch an osprey catch a fish and carry it to a nest of hungry youngsters. You can explore an offshore island and reflect upon the lonely life of a lighthouse keeper's family.

Make sure to drive Park Loop Road. From this twenty-mile scenic drive connecting lakes, mountains, and seashore, you can branch off onto Cadillac Mountain Summit Road, which leads to the highest point on the Atlantic coast. At various points along the loop road you can stop to view glacier-carved valleys and lakes, high surf-pounded cliffs, and magnificent remnants of the northern coniferous forest that once extended unbroken over the region.

Boat trips are available at nearly all the island villages. You have a choice of scheduled sightseeing voyages or your own cruise by charter boat. Fishing is permitted in accordance with state laws; no license is required for saltwater angling. Lifeguards are on duty in summer at Echo Lake for freshwater swimming and at Sand Beach for bathing in the icy surf.

Auto-touring, hiking, snowmobiles, cross-country skiing, and snowshoeing in the winter; hikes, walks, swimming, horseback riding, bicycling, boating, and carriage rides in the summer are popular activities. Equipment can be rented in towns on the island.

Campfire programs are conducted in July and August. Boat cruises operate in late June through August for a modest fee. Scenic boat trips, park bus tours and taxi tours can be arranged in any town on the island. Restaurants and souvenirs within the park are located at Jordan Pond, Cadillac Mountain, and Thunderhole.

LODGING: There are no motels or hotels in the park, but lodging is available in all towns on Mount Desert Island. For rates and reservations, write to the chambers of commerce in Bar Harbor, Northeast Harbor, Southwest Harbor, and Winter Harbor, Maine.

There are two national park campgrounds: Blackwoods, at Otter Creek (open all year); and Seawall, at Manset (closed from October 15 to May 15). Facilities include water, rest rooms, and a camping station for trailers. Park campgrounds are filled to capacity by noon during July and August. The park accepts reservations for backcountry camping.

HOW TO GET THERE: The nearest international airport is forty miles from the park at Bangor, Maine. Air service is available during summer from Bangor to Bar Harbor Airport in Trenton, which is eight miles from the park. Greyhound schedules year-round daily bus service from Bangor and Trenton to the park. Taxi service and rental cars are available in all major towns. Take Maine 3 to the island; Maine 186 to the peninsula.

ISLE ROYALE NATIONAL PARK

MICHIGAN

In the northwest corner of Lake Superior lies a lovely wilderness archipelago unspoiled by roads, cars, telephones, or other modern intrusions. Here it's truly possible to "get away from it all" and return to a closeness with nature.

Isle Royale, and the more than two hundred small islands that surround it, is a region of undisturbed woodlands, refreshing lakes, and rugged, scenic shores accessible only by boat or floatplane. Travel on or around the island is accomplished by boat, or by foot on the 160 miles of hiking trails that crisscross this enchanting land.

Isle Royale is the creation of volcanoes, ice, and water. Its billion-year-old rocks are basalt lava flows layered with river-deposited sandstone and conglomerate. Originally horizontal, these rock beds were bent downward long ago to form the great basin now occupied by Lake Superior. Isle Royale is on the northwest rim of this basin.

Within the last 3 million years, numerous glaciers have covered Isle Royale, ground smooth the surfaces of its rocks, gouged out basins that are now lakes, and exposed layers of the softer sandstone and conglomerate. Water has eroded these soft rock strata into valleys that now extend the full length of the island. Between these valleys, the rock beds of hard basalt form long ridges, such as massive Greenstone Ridge, backbone of the island.

Long before Europeans saw Isle Royale, Indians mined copper here. Using hand-held beach cobbles, they hammered out chunks of pure copper from the hard bedrock. Archeologists have excavated their shallow mining pits, some of which date as far back as 4,500 years. When the French took possession of the island in 1669, they found Indians living here who did not remember the copper miners of old. It was the French, lured to the island by the fur trade, who named it Isle Royale.

In 1783, Isle Royale became part of the United States, though it was recognized as Chippewa territory until 1843, when the tribe ceded it to the United States. Prospectors swarmed over the island and burned large acreages of forest to expose copper outcroppings and to clear space for mining settlements. Lumbering for local needs also flourished. Mining continued until 1899, and the ruins of many of these activities are still evident. The amount of copper on the island had been adequate for the crude tools of ancient Indians but was insufficient for commercial mining.

In the early 1900s when Isle Royale became popular for summer homes and excursion boat tours, many visitors realized the island's value as a wilderness retreat. The movement to preserve it, spearheaded by Albert Stoll, Jr., a Detroit newspaperman, resulted in the establishment of the national park on April 3, 1940.

Forests dominate the scenery and the ecology of the park. Evergreens and hardwoods meet on Isle Royale and form an outstanding example of forest transition. The interior and upland regions of the park have pure hardwood stands, whereas the cool, moist shores and lake borders tend to have mixed evergreen forests. Despite the short summer growing season, Isle Royale has several hundred species of wild flowers.

Isle Royale is 15 miles from the nearest mainland shore, and the only animals that live here today are those that could fly, swim, or drift across the water barrier, or cross the ice that occasionally forms a bridge to Canada. More than two hundred kinds of birds have been listed here, and the red squirrel is the most frequently observed small mammal. Other common mammals include the beaver, red fox, snowshoe hare, and moose.

Moose are found throughout the park and are often seen wading in the shallow inland lakes. They were not on the island before 1900, but soon thereafter a number of them either swam or ventured over the ice from Canada and have since flourished. Wolves, rarely observed by people, prey upon the moose, culling the herds and keeping the population down to levels the island can support.

To help you enjoy this natural area, park rangers conduct nature walks and evening slide programs. The schedule is posted at campgrounds and ranger stations. Self-guiding nature trails with interpretive signs and exhibits are further aids to your understanding of this park.

Swimming is not recommended at Isle Royale because of the extremely cold water of Lake Superior and the leeches in the warmer inland lakes. Diving activities must be registered at a ranger station on a daily basis.

Michigan fishing regulations apply and a state license is required in all Lake Superior waters, but no license is required for Isle Royale's inland lakes or streams. Ranger stations have information on fishing and regulations. Equipment can be obtained at the Rock Harbor store or at Windigo. Guided fishing trips are offered at Rock Harbor. A free folder on fishing is available at all information and ranger stations.

The marina at Rock Harbor Lodge is open from late June to Labor Day. Most docks at the park will accommodate cruisers of moderate draft. Holding-tank pump-out stations are located at Mott Island and at Windigo. Boating regulations and marine weather forecasts can be obtained at headquarters and ranger stations. Lake Survey Chart #14976, "Isle Royale," is recommended for anyone navigating the park's waters. This chart can be purchased from the park or the U.S. Lake Survey, 630 Federal Bldg., 231 Lafayette Blvd., Detroit, MI 48226. A topographic map of Isle Royale also can be purchased at the park or from the Geological Survey, U.S. Department of the Interior, Washington, D.C. 20240.

Transportation from the mainland to Isle Royale is

by boat or floatplane. Reservations are recommended. Because the waters of Lake Superior are often rough, it is not safe to use boats of twenty feet or less to go to the island. However, such boats can be transported to Isle Royale on the *Ranger III*. Private boat operators will transport small runabouts and canoes. Gasoline for your boat cannot be carried on commercial boats or planes but may be purchased at Rock Harbor and Windigo. Departure points are as follows:

Houghton to Rock Harbor (May to October): For schedules, rates, and reservations for the NPS boat *Ranger III,* write to the Superintendent, Isle Royale National Park, Houghton, MI 49931.

Copper Harbor to Rock Harbor (late June to Labor Day): also pre- and post-season charter trips. Write to Isle Royale Queen II, Copper Harbor, MI 49918.

Grand Portage to Windigo (late June to Labor Day) and Grand Portage to Rock Harbor via Windigo (May to October): Write to Silvertson Brothers, 366 Lake Avenue South, Duluth, MN 55802. One boat circumnavigates Isle Royale and will discharge and pick up passengers at various points.

Houghton to Windigo via Rock Harbor (late June to Labor Day): Write to Isle Royale Seaplane Service, Box 371, Houghton MI 49931.

All camping parties and those traveling in their own boats are required, upon arrival, to register at an information or ranger station.

Isle Royale National Park is open to visitors from about May 15 to October 20. Midsummer temperatures rarely exceed 80°; evenings are usually cool. Rain, frequent throughout the season, provides moisture for the lush north woods and the lakes and streams that make Isle Royale the kind of park it is.

LODGING: Within the park, Rock Harbor Lodge is open from late June through early September and has complete services, including regular rooms, housekeeping units, dining facilities, gift shops, food stores, a marina with electricity and water hookups, boat rentals, and guided fishing and sightseeing tours. Lodging is also available at Windigo Inn at Washington Harbor on the southwest end of the island. For reservations, write: National Park Concessions, Inc., Rock Harbor Lodge, Houghton, MI 49931 (summer) or Mammoth Cave, KY 42259 (winter).

Isle Royale has thirty-one lakeside and trailside campgrounds, most having fireplaces, tables, and tent sites. Campsites cannot be reserved. Basic food staples, specialized camping foods, and white gas may be purchased at the Rock Harbor store or at Windigo. All campers must obtain a camping permit.

HOW TO GET THERE: Isle Royale National Park is in Lake Superior, just south of Ontario. Scheduled air transportation is available to Houghton, Michigan, as well as bus service to Houghton and Grand Portage, Minnesota. The island is accessible only by boat or seaplane, and both require reservations. Boats are available from Houghton and Copper Harbor, Michigan, and Grand Portage, Minnesota, to Windigo Inn on Isle Royale. Crossing time is four hours from Copper Harbor and six hours from Houghton. Arrival and return passages are scheduled on alternating days. Daily air service is available from Houghton to Rock Harbor Lodge and Windigo Inn on Isle Royale.

VOYAGEURS NATIONAL PARK

MINNESOTA

The romantic epoch of the French-Canadian fur trader has left an indelible imprint on the lake country of northern Minnesota. For 150 years these colorful voyageurs in their fragile bark canoes provided the only consistent means of transportation for goods and furs in this region.

Voyageurs National Park, named in memory of these courageous men, lies along the U.S.-Canadian border east of International Falls, Minnesota. This is, however, a park still in the making; the park service is continuing to acquire land within the designated boundaries, and visitor facilities are still under development.

Most of the parkland is on the heavily forested and

relatively undeveloped Kabetogama Peninsula. Stands of fir, spruce, pine, aspen, and birch reach down to the water's edge, broken here and there by bogs, sand beaches, and cliffs. The peninsula is accessible principally by water, and its interior holds a number of lakes that can be reached only on foot.

The north shore of the peninsula has a sharply broken front, with many small bays and hidden coves. Numerous small islands lie off the south shore, and along both shores are many places with smooth, glaciated rock well suited for camping and picnicking.

The waters surrounding the peninsula range from narrows of less than one hundred feet in width to lakes several kilometers across, irregular in shape, dotted with islands, and accented with rocky points and promontories. Four lakes dominate the park area: Namakan, Kabetogama, Rainy, and Sand Point.

The trading posts and forts of the old French-Canadian fur companies were located west of the park, near International Falls. These posts served as the link between Grand Portage, a trading terminal on Lake Superior that is now preserved as a National Park System area, and the remote Northwest.

The voyageur's "canoe has long since vanished from the northern waters," Grace Lee Nute wrote. "His red cap is seen no more, a bright spot against the blue of Lake Superior; his sprightly French conversation, punctuated with inimitable gestures, his exaggerated courtesy, his incurable romanticism, his songs, and his superstitions are gone."

Though the colorful voyageur is gone, his land is not. Since 1971, when Congress authorized establishment of Voyageurs National Park, a sizable portion of it has been preserved to look much as it did during the voyageur days of the late eighteenth and early nineteenth centuries. The park, which encompasses 219,400 acres, much of it water, has all the wildness and immense scale associated with the northern lakes region: a land surface shaped by continental glaciation into an endless system of internal waterways, and a sense of vastness reinforced by the uniformity of the forest mantle.

A land and water environment, the park offers considerable recreational potential. Some of the nearby resorts provide bathing beaches, fishing launches, plus motorboat and water skiing rentals. Fishing is one of the outstanding recreational resources of the park, and outfitters in nearby communities can provide full equipment, furnish guides, and arrange flights to remote fishing lakes.

Crane Lake Gorge is one of the scenic wonders of Crane Lake, where the Vermilion River tumbles through a narrow chasm between vertical rock walls before it flows into the lake. There are trails on both sides of the canyon and many plants and mosses on the moist forest floor.

Historically, the park is a treasure trove. Underwater archeologists have recovered parts of voyageur canoes, muzzle-loading rifles, beads intended for Indian trade, and other artifacts.

LODGING: Privately owned resorts, summer homes, and marinas lie at the south end of Crane Lake and numerous nearby communities, such as International Falls, Kabetogama, Orr, and Crane Lake. Their facilities cover the whole spectrum of outdoor recreation. Houseboat rentals are available at Ash River, Crane Lake, and east of International Falls.

Within the boundaries of the park, open to the public, there are two primitive campground areas accessible by water. Both are open all year for fourteen-day stays. Private campgrounds are located near International Falls and Lake Kabetogama. The State of Minnesota and the U.S. Forest Service provide additional campsites in or near the park area. Camping supplies are available at Ash River, Crane Lake, and International Falls. Federal campsites are located in the Namakan–Sand Point area, north of Crane Lake.

HOW TO GET THERE: U.S. 53 from Duluth connects with the park by surfaced roads in four places. Access to the interior is by boat. North Central Airlines links Duluth to International Falls, where rental cars and buses are available.

MESA VERDE NATIONAL PARK

COLORADO

For over six hundred years a group of agricultural Indians occupied the area we know today as Mesa Verde in the southwestern corner of Colorado. They farmed the rich soil of the mesa top and built elaborate stone apartment dwellings in the caves of the cliffs below. Then, two centuries before Christopher Columbus arrived in the New World, these "cliff dwellers" abandoned their homes and disappeared, never to return again. To this day we don't know why they left.

When these people departed, they left their villages and many of their personal possessions behind. Today these relics are preserved in Mesa Verde National

Park, which occupies part of a large plateau rising high above Montezuma and Mancos valleys.

Archeologists who studied the relics have named the earliest inhabitants "Basket Makers" in recognition of their impressive skill in that craft. They also made pottery, but at this stage in their history the pottery lacked the quality of their baskets. At first these people lived in pithouses, dwellings dug into the ground so that the walls of the pit were the walls of the house. They clustered their pithouses to form small villages, usually on the mesa top, but occasionally in the caves of the cliffs. Crops of beans, corn, and squash were grown in the rich, red, windblown soil of the mesa top. Dogs and turkeys were their only domestic animals. The turkeys seem to have been raised primarily for their feathers, which were woven into blankets for the cold winter months.

For many years the Basket Makers prospered on the mesa. By the middle of the eighth century their descendants, whom we know as Pueblo Indians, had begun building houses above ground. They set poles upright in the ground to form the outline of a house, then wove sticks among the poles. They made the roof the same way and added a thick coating of mud to weatherproof both roof and walls. The houses were built one against another in a long, curving row. Frequently, they built one or two deep pithouses in front of the crescent-shaped row houses. Perhaps these were the beginnings of the underground religious rooms—kivas—of later times.

Before the year 1000, stone masonry began to replace the pole-and-mud construction. Sturdy, compact apartmentlike buildings were built, and by the twelfth century, they were exceptionally well made. Some stood as high as three stories and contained more than fifty rooms. Often the rooms were built around courtyards that contained several kivas.

Near the end of the twelfth century something caused the Mesa Verde people to make another great change in their lives, for they began to abandon their houses on the mesa top and move down into the caves in the cliffs. There they built the cliff dwellings we find today. Why did they make this drastic move? The caves may have been uncomfortable places to live—hot in summer, cold in winter. Living in the caves required a difficult climb up and down the cliffs to reach the cornfields, and it must also have been hazardous for the children and old people. One guess is that this was a time of warfare—either with local Indians fighting among themselves or with a foreign enemy tribe—and the caves were sought out for defensive purposes.

At any rate this period of living in cliff dwellings lasted less than a hundred years, and before the close of the thirteenth century the cliff dwellers left Mesa Verde forever. What caused the abandonment remains a mystery. Perhaps the people tired of strife. Perhaps they left because of drought. We know that the thirteenth century, particularly the last half, was a time of repeated drought and successive crop failures.

We think that when the cliff dwellers left here they traveled to the south and southeast—down to the valley of the Rio Grande and its tributaries. They may have joined existing villages of Pueblo Indians, or they may have established villages of their own. Perhaps both. Whatever happened, it seems likely that some of the Pueblo Indians in central New Mexico are at least partly descended from the cliff dwellers.

After the Indians left, the cliff dwellings lay silent for centuries. The Spaniards came into the area in the mid-eighteenth century, but did not find the ruins. The name Mesa Verde, which means "green table," surely dates from the time of their explorations. Not until 1874 was the two-story Cliff Palace discovered. But it was still fourteen years before the many canyons of the mesa began to be explored. In 1906, the area became a national park, and the period of scientific excavation began.

Tours to the cliff dwellings are conducted year round when weather and trail conditions permit. The museum of the Mesa Verde Indian artifacts is also open year round. Reservations for wrangler-guided horseback rides of one, two, and four hours, starting at Morfield Village, from Memorial Day to Labor Day can be made through: MV Pack and Saddle Horse Co., Mesa Verde National Park, CO 81330. The Ruins Road, along which the sequence of pre-Columbian architectural development is completely displayed, is open all year. During winter, only one loop is accessible.

Visits to the cliffside ruins tend to be quite strenuous and elevations rather high (altitudes in the park range from 7,000 to 8,500 feet above sea level), so visitors with heart and respiratory ailments should take special precautions not to overexert themselves. Daytime temperatures in the summer are usually quite comfortable, although the temperature can go as high as 100°F (38°C). Winter temperatures range from a high of 40°F (4°C) to a low of 15°F (−9°C), and snow-covered ground is predominant.

LODGING: Within the park, Far View Lodge at
Navajo Hill is open from May through October 15.
From June to early September reservations should be
made through: Mesa Verde Co., P.O. Box 277, Man-
cos, CO 81328. Meals and snacks are served at Far
View Terrace Restaurant and at park headquarters.
Accommodations are also available in nearby
Durango, Cortez, and Mancos.

Morfield Campground, for both tent and trailer
camping, is open all year and is the only area where
camping is permitted. The limit is fourteen days.
Facilities include rest rooms, tables, benches, and
fireplaces. Fuel and carry-out food is available at
Morfield Village. There are no utility hookups, but the
campground has a holding tank disposal station. Picnicking is permitted at the park headquarters area, in
Chapin Mesa, near the comfort stations on Ruins
Road.

HOW TO GET THERE: Mesa Verde National Park is
on the southwestern border of Colorado, on U.S.
Highway 160, between Cortez and Mancos, Colorado.
Cortez and Durango are served daily by Frontier Airlines. The nearest railroads are at Grand Junction, Colorado, and Gallup, New Mexico. Rental cars are
available at airline and rail points. Bus service from
Durango to the park center is scheduled twice daily by
Continental Trailways during the summer.

ROCKY MOUNTAIN NATIONAL PARK

COLORADO

The cloud-capped summits of the Rocky Mountains have proved irresistible to adventurers since the first Spanish explorers discovered this incredible range two centuries ago, and for good reason. Their sheer beauty is exquisite and unparalleled, brought about by a combination of towering peaks and forested dells, rushing streams and still, deep lakes, all laced together by a carpet of brilliant mountain wild flowers.

Although young in geological terms, the Rockies appear to us as ageless and unchanging, impervious to the ravages of time and weather. That's because these mountains are so young and not yet ground down and worn away by the forces of erosion. Thus they include

145

some of the highest elevations in the National Park System, creating a veritable hikers' and climbers' paradise.

The Rockies had their beginning about 300 million years ago when this area was uplifted from shallow inland seas. Cycles of invasion by the seas and renewed uplift of the land followed until the last sea withdrew, about 70 million years ago, never to return. Alternating periods of uplift, volcanic activity, and erosion came next. About 5 to 7 million years ago, forces within the earth initiated a final broad uplift of the Rocky Mountain region. In the park, the overall effect was to raise the mountains to their present altitudes of more than 12,000 feet. Deep erosion followed. Shallow valleys eventually became winding V-shaped canyons 600 to 1,500 feet deep.

Signs of several periods of glacial activity are evident throughout the park. The quarrying action of glaciers has left sheer rock faces like those on Longs Peak. Broad, U-shaped valleys denote the passing of giant glaciers through the V-shaped stream-cut valleys. The glacier-deposited ridges, heaps, and scattered masses of unsorted rock debris known as moraines can be clearly seen in Moraine Park. Chains of lakes linked by streams, such as the Gorge Lakes (visible from Trail Ridge Road), now fill depressions that were scoured out by glaciers.

As you travel from the valleys to the high peaks, you will notice changes in plant life due largely to increasing wetness, exposure, and coolness. At lower elevations, where the climate is relatively warm and dry, open stands of ponderosa pine and juniper grow on the slopes facing the sun; on cooler north slopes Douglas fir is mixed with them. The lovely blue spruce graces streamsides, and dense stands of lodgepole pine grow in some places. Here and there appear groves of aspen, which turn a golden yellow in autumn. Delighting the eye at ground level such wild flowers as American pasqueflower, Rocky Mountain iris, plains erysimum (known locally as "western wallflower"), and penstemon dot meadows and glades.

Above 9,000 feet or so, forests of Engelmann spruce, subalpine fir, and limber pine take over. Openings in these cool, dark forests produce wild flower gardens of rare beauty and luxuriance. Here the blue Rocky Mountain columbine—the State flower—seems to reach its best development. At the upper edges of this zone, where cold winds constantly blow, the trees are twisted and grotesque, often squat and ground-hugging. Then the trees disappear and you are in alpine tundra—open expanses of dwarf vegetation like that in arctic regions. Here plants hug the ground closely, an adaptation against the desiccating winds, and produce seeds quickly, an adaptation to the brief summers. Grasses, mosses, lichens, and many bright-blossoming plants create patterns of endless variety and surprise. Trail Ridge Road snakes for eleven miles through this Lilliputian plant world above tree line. Respect the fragile life here. Even a footprint can cause great damage.

As you explore this magnificent setting of valleys and high mountain peaks, forests, and tundra, occasional glimpses of wildlife will add moments of excitement.

Many small mammals seem always to be around, but larger animals such as wapiti (American elk) and deer are generally seen only just after dawn or in late evening. If you startle a mule deer as you hike the trails, it will bound off characteristically touching all four feet at once.

Bighorn—the living symbol of Rocky Mountain National Park—venture out into Horseshoe Park near Sheep Lake where there is a mineral lick. Observe them from the parking lot. Specimen Mountain, a prime lambing ground and grazing area for the bighorn, has been closed to entry above the crater to protect the sheep from harassment.

Above tree line in the tundra area, the yellow-bellied marmot, similar to the woodchuck in appearance, suns itself on the rocks. Another common but inconspicuous animal of the tundra is the tiny pika. The wild, eerie, yipping song of the coyote is familiar on autumn and winter evenings at Moraine Park and Horseshoe Park. Beaver, which are abundant in almost every stream, are easy to observe. All you need do is spend a little time in the evening around their ponds and lodges. They begin working around sunset and continue long after darkness. As they go about their business, they probably won't pay attention to you.

For numbers of species and individuals seen, bird-watching is the most rewarding of wildlife-observation activities in the park. Of the more than 150 kinds regularly encountered, the most common are the familiar robin, bluebird, chickadee, and junco. A good field guide, some understanding of the distribution and habits of birds, and good habits of observation on your part should lead to such exciting finds as the golden or bald eagles, white-tailed ptarmigan, Steller's jay, and dipper.

In the mountain streams and lakes are four species

of trout: German brown, brook, rainbow, and cutthroat. These cold waters may not produce large fish,
but the superb mountain scenery will enhance your
experience. Trout populations are maintained by natural reproduction. Fishing (with license) is permitted all
year in low-altitude waters and from June through October in high-altitude waters.

For those visitors who do not have the time or
stamina to explore the mountains on foot, the park's
road system provides an enjoyable way to see the
Rockies' splendor by car. Please bear in mind, though,
that some of these roads reach extremely high altitudes, so visitors with heart conditions or other
physical impairments should be careful not to overexert themselves.

From the east, Trail Ride Road (closed in winter)
takes a winding course upward, reaches 12,183 feet,
and then descends to Grand Lake. Take three or four
hours for this fifty-mile scenic drive, stopping at the
overlooks to absorb far-spreading views of Rocky
Mountain's peaks and valleys. As you travel along Tail
Ridge itself, above tree line, you are on the "roof of the
world," with superlative vistas of glacier-carved peaks
on every side. For a closer look at the alpine world,
walk to Forest Canyon Overlook or take the half-hour
round trip Tundra Trail. Remember the alpine tundra
ecosystem is extremely fragile; use it lightly by staying
on the paths where they are provided. Stop at Fall
River Pass (11,796 feet) to visit the Alpine Visitor Center. The exhibits will help you understand some of the
things you have seen and felt along Trail Ridge Road.

Fall River Road (closed in winter), the original road
crossing the mountains, is open from Horseshoe Park
Junction to Fall River Pass. West of Endovalley Picnic

Area, the road is one-way uphill. The gravel road switchbacks up a narrow mountain valley, offering an early-day motoring experience.

Take Bear Lake Road if you have the time—an extra hour or so will do it. This is one of the few paved roads in the Rockies that leads to the heart of a high mountain basin. The area is heavily used and often congested. Parking here and at Glacier Gorge Junction may not be available. For these reasons, a free shuttle bus system has been initiated between the shuttle parking area near Glacier Basin Campground and Bear Lake. The system operates from late June through Labor Day.

There are over three hundred miles of walking trails and climbs of varying difficulty. Most trails can be traveled on horseback, and horses can be rented at Glacier Basin and Moraine, or from nearby ranches and hotels. Guided walks, campfire programs, and visitor center exhibits are provided during summer; orientation films at headquarters are provided all year. Winter activities, centered at Hidden Valley, include skiing, ice skating, platter sliding, and snowshoeing— Fridays through Sundays.

A backcountry-use permit is required for all trips in the backcountry, summer or winter, and for all mountain climbing involving the use of technical climbing equipment.

LODGING: The few overnight accommodations within the park boundaries are privately owned. Estes Park and Grand Lake are the principal tourist centers and are adjacent to the park. For information regarding their accommodations and facilities, write: Chamber of Commerce, Estes Park, CO 80517; and the Chamber of Commerce, Grand Lake, CO 80447.

Within the park, each campground has comfort stations, piped water, and trash receptacles. Each campsite has parking space, table, fireplace, and tent space. Trailers are permitted (except at Endovalley), but there are no utility hookups available. Sewage dump stations are at Moraine Park, Glacier Basin, and Timber Creek. Most campgrounds operate in summer only. At Longs Peak, the camping limit is three days; seven days throughout the remainder of the park. Backcountry camping permit required.

HOW TO GET THERE: The nearest principal rail, air, and bus terminals are at Denver, Colorado, sixty-five miles from Estes Park; and at Cheyenne, Wyoming, ninety-one miles away. In summer, Gray Line Tours makes connections with transcontinental airlines, railroads, and bus lines at Denver. Ft. Collins is also served by bus lines. Rental cars are available in all connecting points above, and in Estes Park. U.S. Highway 34 (Trail Ridge Road) connects with U.S. Highway 40 and Interstate 70 (via U.S. 40) on the southwest (closes in mid-October); U.S. 36 and Interstate 25, leading to Denver, on the east.

GLACIER NATIONAL PARK

MONTANA

Ruggedly beautiful scenery, exceptional wildlife and solitude are the magnets that draw adventuresome visitors to Glacier National Park all year round. This park, famous for its thousand waterfalls tumbling into sparkling lakes and streams, its sharply etched peaks and knife-edged ridges girdled with evergreen forests, is also one of the last strongholds of the proud grizzly bear and the glorious setting for a multitude of different trees and plants.

Glacier National Park is often called "The Crown of the Continent" because it lies astride the Continental Divide, spilling over the Montana border into Canada's Waterton Lakes National Park. Waters from

153

its icy peaks flow northeast to Hudson Bay, southeast to the Gulf of Mexico, and westward to the Pacific.

To understand the "personality" of Glacier you must look to the geological past. The rocks that now loom so loftily in Glacier were deposited as sediments more than a billion years ago. For millions of years thick beds of ooze solidified into limestone; later sediments covered the limestone and became mudstone, and these in turn were overlaid with sediments that compacted into additional limestone. These strata show as streaks on the sides of Glacier's thousand-foot precipices.

About seventy million years ago, stresses in the earth's crust acted on the deeply buried mudstones, sandstones, and limestones of the old sea bottom. As the tensions and strains became acute, the rock was warped and finally broken; the western part, a thousand meters thick, slid over the eastern. The pressures continued for millions of years until a gigantic three-hundred-mile section of the earth's crust had been moved more than thirty-seven miles to the east, capping young rock with strata more than one billion years old. This same process created other mountain systems throughout the world; few overthrusts, however, have been as great as this—the Lewis Overthrust of Glacier.

The carving of the park's rugged landscape was principally the work of glaciers during the last three million years. The moving ice deepened the main valleys and cut back the base of the cliffs to form U-shaped valley profiles. Tributary valleys were not worn as deep and thus have become hanging valleys over which streams plunge, sometimes a hundred meters, to the floor of the main valley below. Glacial ice, by plucking away the mountainside, has formed hudge ampitheaters, called cirques, at high elevations. In many of these cirques, recent glaciers can be seen still performing the same kind of work, on a smaller scale, as their predecessors. The valleys, in turn, were partially filled with glacier melt water, forming the lakes for which Glacier National Park is so well known.

Because of Glacier's size and range in elevation, a wide variety of plant and animal life finds suitable habitats within its boundaries. Only the hardiest plants and animals are able to survive the alpine environment on the windblown mountain summits; lower, in the western valleys, luxuriant Pacific-type forests support a large and diverse plant-and-animal community. Plains on the Atlantic drainage side of the Continental Divide provide an expansive view of grassy, flower-covered meadows that are a soft contrast to the rugged defiles seen in the distance.

The eastern slopes, more exposed to cold winds and receiving less moisture, have open forests of Engelmann spruce, subalpine fir, lodgepole pine, Douglas fir, and limber pine. The western slopes, benefiting from warmer, moister Pacific winds, have denser forests of larch, fir, spruce, and lodgepole, and in the Lake McDonald Valley, red cedar and hemlock.

The park's brilliant floral displays begin in early spring and progress up the mountainside as the snow recedes, culminating in the unrivaled alpine summer show. They are most accessible near Logan Pass, along Going-to-the-Sun Road. These high-altitude wild flowers must survive in a severe climate with only a few summer months in which to grow. Some plants to look for in the alpine gardens are heather, gentian, bear grass, glacier lily, and stunted subalpine fir.

Glacier's wildlife includes the bighorn, mountain goat, moose, wapiti (American elk), grizzly and black bears, and white-tailed and mule deer, all living in a natural environment relatively untouched by man. The beaver, hoary marmot, river otter, marten, pika, and other smaller mammals are important members of Glacier's fauna. Among the more noticeable birds are the osprey, water ouzel, ptarmigan, Clark's nut-cracker, thrushes, and sparrows.

Legends of the Blackfoot and Kutenai Indian tribes indicate that they long held this area in awe and knew of Lake McDonald and St. Mary Lake. Over present park trails came western Indians to hunt bison on the plains, and in the cool mountain uplands they fished, hunted, and found relief from the summer heat. Today the Kutenai live on a reservation southwest of the park, the Blackfeet on a reservation just to the east of the park. The Kutenai once controlled a vast area immediately east of the Rockies but were driven west and over the mountains by the Blackfeet.

Unlike many western and Plains tribes, the Black-feet have no clear-cut record of migration or origin. This Indian nation now resides on four reservations in southern Alberta and northern Montana, gradually losing the ways of their forefathers and taking on modern dress and the English language. At Browning, thirteen miles east of East Glacier, a museum is maintained by the Bureau of Indian Affairs, U.S. Department of the Interior, to interpret the customs and ways of life of the Plains Indian.

The area of the park was probably seen by members

of the Lewis and Clark Expedition in 1806, but it was not explored by frontiersmen until 1846 when Hugh Monroe, a Canadian trapper, visited St. Mary Lake. In the 1850s railroad surveyors made tentative explorations into the mountains.

To enjoy the park to its fullest, see the orientation film and exhibits at the St. Mary Visitor Center (late May to mid-October) and exhibits at Apgar Information Center (late May through mid-September) and Logan Pass Visitor Center (mid-June to mid-September). Guided walks, campfire programs, and other activities begin in mid-June and extend through August; some weekend activities are usually conducted in late May and in September and October. Schedules are at all ranger stations and visitor centers.

The naturalist program is one of the most extensive in the park system, and all program services are free except for the costs of lodging and boat rides. More than seven hundred miles of backcountry trails invite hikers and horseback riders to explore the alpine scenery, and hiking and saddle-horse trips, from two hours to one week, can be arranged through: Rocky Mountain Outfitters, Inc., Box 776, Columbia Falls, MT 59912. Launch trips from Many Glacier Hotel afford excellent views of mountain peaks from picturesque lakes, or small boats and fishing tackle can be rented from June 20 to October 15. For information on all-expense tours ranging from one to ten days, write: Glacier Park, Inc., East Glacier Park, MT 59434. Inquire at the visitor center about mountain climbing and off-trail hiking, which are permitted.

All backcountry hikers who intend to camp overnight on their own must obtain a backcountry camping permit. These permits, issued free, are available from

any ranger or information center during the summer.
In winter, permits may be obtained from park headquarters or the St. Mary Ranger Station.

Winter use is encouraged for those who enjoy the
out-of-doors in snow. Park roads remain unplowed in
winter, except for the Going-to-the-Sun Road between
park headquarters and Lake McDonald Lodge. Over-
the-snow vehicles are not permitted to operate in
Glacier. Ski touring and snowshoeing are becoming
more popular every year. For those interested in winter activities, write to the park for detailed information. There are no accommodations within the park
during the winter.

Glacier has many good fishing lakes and many miles
of swift-flowing streams. Rainbow, brook, and cutthroat trout occur in Swiftcurrent, Josephine, and
Grinnell lakes, as well as in the lakes of Upper Swiftcurrent Valley in the Many Glacier area and the Middle and North forks of the Flathead River on the park's
south and west boundaries.

If you desire more solitude, consider a campground
along a gravel road where only fireplaces, tables, and
pit toilets are provided—River, Bowman Creek, Bowman Lake, Cut Bank, Kintla Lake, Logging Creek,
and Quartz Creek. Because the roads are narrow and
rough, campers should inquire at a ranger station before attempting to pull a trailer or camper into those
areas. Paved roads provide access to eight of Glacier's
campgrounds—Apgar, Avalanche Creek, Fish Creek,
Many Glacier, Rising Sun, St. Mary, Two Medicine,
and Sprague Creek. Trailer space is provided in all
except Sprague Creek. All have fireplaces, tables,
sanitary facilities, and cold running water; there are no
utility connections.

LODGING: Accommodations range from large hotels, motor inns, and rustic cabins to backcountry villages and chalets. For reservations, write: Glacier Park, Inc., 1735 East Fort Lowell Rd., Tucson, AZ 85719. The use of backcountry chalets requires reservations through: Belton Chalets, West Glacier, MT 59936. Year-round motel and dining facilities are available in the nearby communities of Hungry Horse, Coram, Columbia Falls, Kalispell, Browning, East Glacier, St. Mary, and Babb.

HOW TO GET THERE: Air West, Frontier, and Northwestern airlines serve Great Falls, Montana, and Air West serves Kalispell, Montana, where rental cars are available. The park is on U.S. Highways 2 and 89. From Kalispell, U.S. Highway 2 leads to the southwest entrance; from Great Falls, go north on Interstate 15 to Shelby or U.S. 89 to Blackfoot, then U.S. Highway 2 to the east entrance. From Alberta, Canada, choose Routes 2 or 6. Bus lines connecting with Greyhound at Great Falls and Missoula stop twice daily at East Glacier and West Glacier Park. Amtrak's streamlined Empire Builder between Chicago and Seattle also stops daily at East and West Glacier.

THEODORE ROOSEVELT NATIONAL PARK

NORTH DAKOTA

In spite of the connotations of its name, the badlands of North Dakota is an area of much scenic interest and historic appeal. Here were the wide-open ranges of cowboy legend where the great cattle drives of a century ago took place; and here, too, were the massive herds of buffalo which came close to extinction at the hands of man.

It was the buffalo, in fact, which first brought Theodore Roosevelt out west to the badlands in 1883. He came to hunt these magnificent beasts but soon turned his attention to cattle ranching instead. Over the ensuing fifteen years he returned often to visit his two ranches, and no doubt while there began to formulate his philosophy of practical conservation.

The park, which was dedicated in his memory, actually consists of three parts, although only two, the North Unit and the South Unit, are easily accessible to visitors. The two units are approximately thirty-eight miles apart. In between is the Elkhorn Ranch Site, Roosevelt's second ranch, but it can only be reached from the South Unit by a rough dirt road of about twenty miles.

The badlands landscape of Theodore Roosevelt National Park straddles the final two hundred miles of the Little Missouri River and spans its valley for a distance of five to thirty miles. Moving waters carved this valley, one of many that have cut into the ancient, preglacial plains. Starting some sixty million years ago, the waters carried eroded materials eastward from the Rocky Mountains and deposited them as sediments on a vast lowland. Then followed a warm, rainy period of many centuries when a jungle covered a large area of the flat lowlands and swamps. Some of the swamp vegetation was buried by new layers of sediment and eventually became lignite, a type of soft coal.

During the final development of the plains, clouds of ash, from the mountain-building volcanoes to the west, drifted eastward and settled on this land. In time, the ash decomposed and today is exposed in layers of blue bentonite clay. After the plains had been thus developed, many streams that drained this land started to cut down through the soft strata and to sculpture the badlands in an infinite variety of buttes, tablelands, valleys, and gorges.

Starting some six thousand to three thousand years ago and continuing into the present, grass fires and lightning occasionally set fire to exposed veins of lignite. The heat from these fires bakes the surrounding sand and clay to a natural red-brick material, locally called "scoria." This red scoria, very resistant to erosion, is a late addition to the colorful rocks of the badlands.

The interdependent web of life of the badlands depends upon the grasses and upon available water. Without the grasses and other plants, the animals have no food. Without water, the plants have no life. Available water dictates location, kinds, quantity, and the success of plant growth. Rainfall is mostly from May through July and averages only fifteen inches a year.

Grasses can thrive on this amount of water. Therefore, they are the dominant vegetation and represent the oldest and most enduring ground cover. Bushes require more moisture than grasses, but some can grow here. The sagebrush, for instance, grows everywhere because its long roots can reach down in the soil to moisture. Trees are found only in locations most favorable to them because they require much water over a longer period.

There is enough moisture on riverbanks and in ravines to sustain groves of cottonwoods, which offer food and shelter for white-tailed and mule deer. The north-facing slopes get less sun and therefore have less evaporation. This permits the growth of green ash and juniper trees, whereas the warmer and drier south-facing drainages develop semiarid habitat plants such as yucca, cactus, greasewood, and a few specialized grasses.

Rabbits, beavers, raccoons, porcupines, and prairie dogs eat plants and, in turn, become food for coyotes, foxes, bobcats, golden eagles, and other predatory birds. Reptiles and smaller birds and mammals help to maintain control of the insect population.

Humans have caused many changes in the web of life here. In this area they hunted to extinction the wapiti (American elk), wolf, bighorn, bison ("buffalo"), and antelope. But the National Park Service and the state have restored the bighorn, bison, and antelope.

The park is open all year, but the best time to visit is from May through October. During the winter months, portions of the park road may be closed, depending on snow conditions.

In the South Unit of the park, a stop at the museum in the visitor center will enrich your visit. The restored Maltese Cross Cabin, used by Roosevelt on his visits, has been relocated behind this building.

Painted Canyon Overlook is about seven miles east of Medora along I-94, at Exit 8. Here on the upper margin of the badlands is a magnificent view of its topography and colors. Rest rooms, picnic shelters, tables, and water are available.

A small herd of feral horses may occasionally be seen in the area east of Painted Canyon. These are descendants of domestic horses that escaped from local ranches during the ranching heyday.

Saddle horses are for rent at Peaceful Valley in summer only. Guides are provided with all rides.

The Scenic Loop Road is a drive of about thirty-six miles along a good paved road. There are a number of interpretive turnouts for views of significant park features.

In the North Unit, a stop at the ranger station will help you plan and enjoy your visit. A scenic drive starts at the entrance station and ends at Oxbow Overlook. Along this thirteen-mile drive are several turnouts and interpretive signs.

A small herd of longhorn steers may be seen between the entrance station and Squaw Creek Campground. Some longhorns were trail-driven north from Texas along the Long-X Trail, which crosses the park.

When visiting the South Unit, be sure to stop in at Château de Mores State Historic Site. This twenty-seven room château across the river from Medora was built in 1884 by the Marquis de Mores for his wife. He was a wealthy French nobleman who built a slaughterhouse to process beef from his large herds for shipping to the eastern markets in the new refrigerated railroad cars. He also built the village, named for his wife, Medora, and persuaded the Northern Pacific Railroad to build a station there. He was an acquaintance of Theodore Roosevelt. The château is open to visitors all year, depending on the weather.

LODGING: There are no overnight facilities within the park grounds. Near the South Unit—Medora has stores for supplies, service stations, restaurants, motels, and souvenir shops. Near the North Unit—Watford City, fifteen miles north of the park entrance, has food stores, service stations, motels, camping, restaurants, and souvenir and other shops.

HOW TO GET THERE: The South Unit of the park is bounded on the south by I-94 and is adjacent to the town of Medora. The North Unit is thirty-eight miles north of the South Unit, adjacent to and west of U.S. 85. The town of Watford City is fifteen miles north of the North Unit. Both units of the park are bisected by the Little Missouri River.

BADLANDS NATIONAL PARK

SOUTH DAKOTA

There is a unique and fearsome beauty in the badlands of South Dakota, where bizarre spires and pinnacles rise above massive buttes, and steep-walled gorges edge vast seas of grass.

Although this seemingly desolate land is far from being devoid of life, the animals that live here now pale in comparison to the vast numbers and variety of wildlife which flourished in this region millions of years ago. These long-dead species, however, left behind a legacy in the form of the world's greatest fossil beds from the Oligocene epoch of the "age of mammals." Among the fossilized skeletons to be found in Badlands National Park are those of small camels and three-toed horses, saber-toothed cats and gigantic rhinoceros-like beasts.

These animals lived twenty-five to thirty-five million years ago, when the land of the White River was a broad, marshy plain crossed by sluggish streams from the highlands. As time passed, streams laden with silt from the highlands deposited layer upon layer of sediment over the remains of animals that had died.

Volcanic activity to the west, perhaps in the Yellowstone region, hurled great quantities of finely fragmented material into the air. The prevailing westerly winds bore the dust eastward and deposited at as an ashen blanket, to be washed by streams and spread as the whitish layers of today's badlands. Over succeeding millions of years the climate also changed. With new, dry winds from the north and diminishing rain, today's grasslands gradually replaced the swamps and silted marshes.

Today the annual precipitation is about sixteen inches, and the prairies persist. Water still drains from the highlands, but now it cuts into the land. Tributaries of the White River carve away the soft, sedimentary layers into fins and expose them to the action of rain and water, creating spires, pinnacles, and saw-toothed ridges. Beneath a capping layer of sandstone, a deposit of clay may suddenly fall away, leaving a shallow cave. Or a section of several acres may slump into a gully below. Few landmarks remain for many generations.

This raw, arid landscape supports little life. The water it receives sometimes comes in torrential storms that do little but tear away at its soft surface and at whatever small plants may be fastened there. Temperatures on sunny days frequently soar into the 90s F (30s C) or higher; chilly winter days may quickly become bitterly cold.

Yet for some animals and plants there are certain advantages here. Swifts and cliff swallows find the cliff faces fine for nesting, and rock wrens build in the crevasses. Golden eagles occasionally nest on the high buttes. Junipers patch the canyons and passes with green; they seem to prefer the protected corners of the badlands. Yuccas thrive on the disturbed and broken slopes and valleys. Clusters of life have become established where water is adequate. Green islands of cottonwoods and wild rose are filled with birds and other small animals.

Here and there is a prairie dog town. And close by are badgers and coyotes that prey on the prairie dogs. Porcupines, chipmunks, and mice may also be seen. Jackrabbits and cottontails live here too, as do snakes—bull snakes, racers, and prairie rattlesnakes.

Westward settlement in the nineteenth century doomed many large mammals of the plains, but some have returned. Deer and pronghorn are here again, and the National Park Service has reintroduced bison and bighorn in an effort to restore the scene of the 1800s.

French-Canadian trappers in search of beaver to the west were the first men to record their impressions of the badlands. They described the region appropriately as *les mauvaises terres à traverser* (bad lands to travel across). Indians in the area called it *mako sica* (bad land).

The Arikara was the first tribe of Indians to be noted on the western Dakota plains. By the mid-nineteenth century, however, the Sioux ruled this area, and during the next century their culture, based on the hunting of the abundant bison, flourished. The westward movement of the growing United States brought in the army, the miner, the homesteader, and the face of the plains and the life of the native people changed. Forty years of intermittent warfare brought to an end the Sioux way of life and the beginning of the reservation system.

Travelers to the Dakotas in the early 1800s were astounded to find huge herds of bison darkening large sections of the prairie. Herds were measured not in number of animals, but by the area they covered. One herd in 1862 measured five by twelve miles and another in 1839 covered an area thirty by forty-five miles. That is an area of bison a little larger than the state of Rhode Island.

Fewer than one thousand bison, however, survived out of a population once estimated at sixty million. Today, under the protection of state and national parks, bison are making a comeback. Badlands National Park has a herd of three hundred bison in the Sage Creek Wilderness Area that can sometimes be seen from Sage Creek Road. For your protection enjoy them from a distance, for a large bull can weigh as much as a small car and run faster than a horse. Respect the bison in their natural environment.

In 1976, two years before the Badlands were raised in status from a national monument to a national park, the protected area was expanded to include a new South Unit. This addition more than doubled the total park area to 244,000 acres. At the same time, Congress set aside approximately 60,000 acres in the Sage Creek Basin of the North Unit as a designated Wilderness Area. This roadless wilderness will be protected from all future development while leaving it available for hiking and backpacking.

There are only a handful of backcountry trails in the park because they are so difficult to maintain in an area where erosion constantly changes the topography. In the Wilderness Area, however, you may wish to hike the eight-mile-long Prairie Breaks Trail, which begins and ends at the Sage Creek Primitive Campground.

The Prairie Breaks Trail is a foot- and horse-path consisting of two loops laid out across rolling grasslands in the Sage Creek Basin and identified by conspicuous color-tipped metal stakes. The trail passes through mixed prairie grasslands made up of approximately fifty kinds of grasses, with blue grama, needle and thread, western wheatgrass, buffalo grass, and side oats grama being the most common.

Snowberry and the conspicuous tall silver sagebrush are the predominant shrubs. Scattered juniper groves with a few cottonwoods will also be encountered. Chances are good that you will see wildlife, including bison, mule deer, and pronghorn, particularly in the vicinity of wooded areas. The secretive coyote, as well as the badger, may be seen around any of the four active prairie dog towns along the route. You also may be fortunate enough to see white-tailed deer, bobcats, and sharp-tailed grouse. Chances of seeing prairie rattlesnakes, the only poisonous reptile in this area, are remote; however, high-topped hiking boots are recommended and care should be taken to watch where you step or reach.

The route is across ancient deposits of black mud (now shale) laid down more than sixty-eight million years ago on the bottom of a shallow inland sea. Later, between thirty-five and sixty-eight million years ago, an ancient land surface existed here which resulted in the weathering of this shale just under the old surface to the bright yellow hues you see today.

During the summer, hiking is advised only during the early morning or evening hours in order that you may increase your chances of seeing wildlife, and to escape the high midday temperatures which, at times, can climb to more than 100°F in the shade. Since there is no water along either loop, each hiker is strongly advised to take sufficient water and a snack or lunch. During wet weather you may have to make some detours, particularly along the three-mile loop where the normally dry creek beds may carry some runoff water.

The park is open all year, but the most popular seasons are summer, spring, and autumn. A visit in winter, when sharp peaks may be mantled in snow, can also be rewarding; although blizzards, characteristic of the northern Great Plains, may temporarily block roads.

Displays, exhibits, and recorded slide programs in the visitor center near Cedar Pass will help you become acquainted with the area. There are wayside exhibits along the park road and along the self-guiding trails. Evening campfire programs are given at the Sholly Memorial Amphitheater in summer.

LODGING: The Cedar Pass Lodge is operated by the Oglala Sioux Pass Concession Enterprises. It is open from May 1 to October 15. Reservations should be made during summer months either by phone or writing. The lodge provides cabins and a café. You can write to P.O. Box 71, Interior, SD 57750 for current reservation information. There are accommodations available year round in Wall and Kadoka (thirty miles north and twenty-seven miles east respectively). Both cities are on Interstate 90.

There are three campgrounds in the park and others located in nearby towns. No permit is required for backcountry camping.

HOW TO GET THERE: The Cedar Pass entrance to the park is 75 miles east of Rapid City, via Interstate 90. Take the Badlands National Park exit going south for eight miles to the northeast entrance on Highway 240. Also from Rapid City, you can enter the park at the Pinnacles entrance from the west via Interstate 90, turning south on Alt. 16 at the town of Wall. The main visitor center is at the Cedar Pass entrance.

WIND CAVE NATIONAL PARK

SOUTH DAKOTA

The dense forests and rippling grass prairies of the Black Hills were once the stamping grounds of gold prospectors and hardy pioneers. Today, a century later, the gold and pioneers are gone, but the Black Hills still contain a treasure of natural beauty and phenomena that continue to attract Americans from all over the country.

The forty-four-square-mile Wind Cave National Park, located in the rolling grasslands along the southeastern flank of these hills, is particularly special. Not only does it preserve a part of the original prairie ecosystem, it also preserves a distinctly different type of underground limestone cavern.

Unlike most limestone caverns, the subterranean

passageways and rooms of Wind Cave do not contain stalactites and stalagmites, but instead are lined with colorful calcite crystals which are called boxwork or honeycomb formations. Unusual displays of "frost-work" and "popcorn" formations also can be seen, while deeper recesses of the cave feature huge helictite "bushes."

The cave derives its name from the gushes of wind that blow in or out of its mouth, apparently in response to the atmospheric pressure of the surrounding air. When the outside pressure drops, the wind blows outward from the cave; but when the atmospheric pressure rises, the wind rushes back in.

The limestone bed from which Wind Cave was formed is from 300 to 630 feet thick in the Black Hills region. It is known as the Pahasapa limestone, a rock formation deposited in a great inland sea during the Mississippian period, about 300 million years ago. After deposition of this limestone, several periods of elevation and subsidence occurred. During periods of submergence, the Pahasapa limestone was covered by several hundred feet of sediments. The last uplift of the land from beneath the sea began at the end of the Cretaceous period, some 60 million years ago. Geologists believe the formation of Wind Cave began during this uplift.

Tom Bingham, a Black Hills pioneer, is credited with the discovery of the cave in 1881 while deer hunting. He was attracted by a strange whistling and, after searching about in the undergrowth, discovered that it was caused by wind escaping through a small hole in some rocks. For several years after its discovery, the area including the cave entrance lay open to claims. The South Dakota Mining Company filed location certificates on the cave in 1890. That same year, Jesse D. McDonald, accompanied by his sons, Elmer and Alvin, came to manage the property for the company. They made the first serious exploration of the cave and conducted the first guided tours.

Alvin McDonald discovered many of the passageways and rooms and kept an extensive diary in which he estimated distances; kept a record of explorations; and named rooms, interesting formations, and chief routes. A plaque now marks his grave near the cave entrance.

In 1892, the elder McDonald and several other people, including John and Charles Stabler, formed the "Wonderful Wind Cave Improvement Company" and took over the property. This company, after opening passages and building stairways, operated the cave and guided visitors. On January 9, 1903, President Theodore Roosevelt signed a bill establishing Wind Cave National Park.

The park above ground is a sanctuary for many species of animals native to the Great Plains and the Rocky Mountains before the arrival of American pioneers. One of the park's main attractions is its bison herd. It is a rare day that you won't see at least a few of these huge, shaggy beasts. As you drive through the park, you will notice several towns of black-tailed prairie dogs, a remnant of those that once covered many square miles of the Great Plains. Stop and watch the antics of these quick-moving little rodents and visit the roadside exhibit near one of the towns to learn about their habits.

Here, too, is the graceful pronghorn, swiftest of North American mammals, and the only horned species in the world that sheds its horn sheath annually. True antelopes never shed horns or sheaths. Its tan-and-white coat and conspicuous white rump patch help to identify the pronghorn. Among the other mammals of the park are elk, deer, coyote, badger, and raccoon.

The long list of park birds includes meadowlarks, woodpeckers, warblers, chickadees, sharp-tailed grouse, kingbirds, bluebirds, and magpies.

Summer is the most popular time to visit the park. Cave tours are conducted from April through October, although many Black Hills attractions are open only from June through early September. A wide variety of activities are available both above and below ground. Subterranean activities include ranger-guided regular tours, special candlelight tours, and half-day spelunking tours. Guided surface tours include a half-day nature hike and a wildlife caravan via auto from the visitor center. Evening campfire programs and visitor center exhibits on the area's human and natural history are free. Fees are charged for the cave tours, but surface tours are free, as is entrance to the park.

Mount Rushmore National Memorial is located twenty-five miles north of Wind Cave National Park. This spectacular granite sculpture memorializes four American Presidents: George Washington, Thomas Jefferson, Theodore Roosevelt, and Abraham Lincoln.

The faces were carved to a scale of men 465 feet tall. On an average, the heads measure 60 feet from chin to top, with each nose 20 feet long, each mouth 18 feet wide, and the eyes 11 feet across.

The sculpture is best viewed under morning light. Each night from June 1 to Labor Day, floodlights illuminate the faces.

LODGING: Although there are no facilities within Wind Cave Park, information on nearby motels, hotels, trailer courts, supplies, and garages can be obtained by writing: Chamber of Commerce, 630 N. River, Hot Springs, SD 57747; or Chamber of Comerce, 402 Mt. Rushmore Road, Custer, SD 57730.

Elk Mountain, the only park campground, is open May 15 to September 15. Wood, water, picnic tables, comfort stations, and fireplaces are provided, but electrical, water, and sewer hookups are not available. Sandwiches and light lunches are sold in the visitor center during summer. There are numerous private and public campgrounds in the southern Black Hills.

HOW TO GET THERE: Rapid City has the nearest principal airport, bus and train stations, and rental cars. Rapid City is connected with Hot Springs, South Dakota, by State Road 79. U.S. Highway 385 leads to the park entrance from Hot Springs on the south or from Pringle on the west. Mount Rushmore is twenty-five miles southwest of Rapid City (via U.S. 16) and three miles from Keystone, South Dakota.

ARCHES NATIONAL PARK

UTAH

Deep in the heart of the famed red-rock region of southeastern Utah are found the country's most superb natural stone arches, windows, spires, and pinnacles. These weird stone shapes, some of them resembling figures of men and animals, balanced rocks and narrow mazelike canyons, are the creations of water, wind, rain, frost, and sun working together as powerful forces of erosion.

Although Arches National Park, situated across the Colorado River from the historic Mormon settlement of Moab, is a relatively small preserve, it contains some of the most majestic examples of nature at work.

The rock in which the arches have formed was deposited as sand about 150 million years ago, during the

Jurassic period. This 300-foot layer, called the Entrada Sandstone, is believed to have been laid down mainly by wind. Its characteristics suggest that it accumulated in a vast coastal desert. In time, it was buried by new layers and hardened into rock.

The rock was then uplifted, twisted, and severely cracked several times. Later, after erosion had stripped away the overlying layers, the Entrada Sandstone was exposed to weathering, and the formation of arches began. Water entering cracks in the sandstone dissolved some of the cementing material, and running water and wind removed the loose sand. Cracks were widened into narrow canyons separated by fins. More rapid weathering of softer areas in some of these vertical walls resulted in undercutting. The quarrying by water and frost persisted, perforating the fins, enlarging the perforations, or windows, and smoothing their contours until large, graceful arches were the final creation.

Some arches, such as Delicate Arch, have been left isolated by erosion of surrounding fins. Of course, the continued thinning of arches by weathering will eventually result in their collapse. You can see all stages of their development and decay in the park.

Local wildlife is characteristic of the sparse pinyon-and-juniper forest communities of Great Basin Desert. Larger mammals, such as deer, coyotes, and foxes, are present but are most active at night. You may, however, see birds, ground squirrels, kangaroo rats and other rodents, rabbits, and small reptiles. From May to August, except in abnormally dry years, colorful displays of wild flowers carpet moist places, particularly in Salt Valley.

You can reach most of the scenic features of the park from the road, but the trails will yield much that is missed by motorists. A paved entrance road leaves U.S. 163 at the park visitor center five miles north of Moab, climbs the sandstone cliffs behind the visitor center, and passes first through the Courthouse Towers section. Here you may want to take the easy one-mile hike through Park Avenue, a narrow corridor through towering red-rock walls topped by an orderly array of towers and spires, which resembles the sky-scrapers of a great city. As there are parking areas at each end of the trail, one member of your party can drive around to pick up the hikers. There are exciting views of the La Sal Mountains, Courthouse Canyon, and The Windows section from the parking areas and roadside turnouts.

In the east central part of the park, which is the most readily accessible, a great mass of the Entrada Sand-stone towers over the surrounding plain. In these walls the forces of nature have carved eight immense arches and many smaller windows, passageways, coves, pin-nacles, spires, and balanced rocks. Here are Double Arch, Parade of the Elephants, Cove of the Caves, North and South Windows, Balanced Rock, and other erosional features. This section is twelve miles from the visitor center, but a paved road enables you to drive within easy walking distances of most of these features.

On the way, stop and view the grandeur of Delicate Arch, with its unsurpassed setting of cliffs and massive "slickrock" domes, the gorge of the Colorado River beyond, and the snow-capped peaks of the La Sal Mountains in the distance. A graded road leads to within one and a half miles of Delicate Arch; there is a foot trail the rest of the way. This is also the site of the Wolfe Ranch Environmental Study Area.

Fiery Furnace, an intricate maze of narrow passageways and high sandstone walls, gets its name from its glow in the light of the setting sun. The guided hike here in summer gives an "inside" view of the red-rock country.

The road ends in the Devils Garden section, nine miles north of Balanced Rock. From the end of this road near Skyline Arch, trails lead to Fin Canyon, Tunnel Arch, and Landscape Arch (one mile), Double-O Arch (two miles), and many other arches found in this part of the park. Landscape Arch, 291 feet long, is believed to be the longest natural-stone span in the world. Prehistoric Indians used part of the Landscape Arch area, perhaps as a winter campground. They made arrowpoints and other stone implements from the chalcedony that litters the ground.

Another area which has not been adequately investigated because of the difficult terrain is Klondike Bluffs. The Klondike Bluffs parking area is eight miles by dirt road from Skyline Arch. A one-mile marked route leads from the parking area to Tower Arch. Inquire about road conditions before attempting this trip.

During the summer, campfire talks are given nightly at the campground amphitheater. Although park roads provide many scenic features, the self-guiding park trails lead to some of the park's most impressive features, which are missed by motorists. Guided hikes are conducted through the maze of narrow passageways of Fiery Furnace. Information regarding hikes and activities is available from the visitor center. The park is open all year and a small entrance fee is charged.

LODGING: Although there is no food or lodging within the park, both are available in Moab, Utah. For information and reservations, write to the Chamber of Commerce in Moab, Utah.

Devil's Garden Campground, eighteen miles north of the visitor center, is open with water April through November and open the rest of the year without water. Stays are limited to fourteen days. A free backcountry permit is required.

HOW TO GET THERE: Located in east-central Utah, the closest principal city is Salt Lake City, Utah, which lies to the northwest. However, nearby Moab is served by Frontier Airlines. Rental cars are available from both cities. From Moab, take U.S. 163/191 northwest to State Road 279 at the southwest park entrance.

BRYCE CANYON NATIONAL PARK

UTAH

From ancient Indians to modern-day travelers, the reaction to Bryce Canyon remains much the same: surprise and wonderment tinged with the sensation that there's something almost supernatural about the fantastic and alien rock formations which prompt the human imagination to run wild.

More than a hundred years ago, T. C. Baily, U.S. Deputy Surveyor, penned these words in an effort to describe the indescribable:

> . . . the surface breaks off almost perpendicularly to a depth of several hundred feet—seems indeed

as though the bottom had dropped out and left rocks standing in all shapes and forms as lone sentinels over the grotesque and picturesque scenes. There are thousands of red, white, purple, and vermillion colored rocks, of all sizes, resembling sentinels on the walls of castles, monks, and priests in their robes, cathedrals and congregations . . . presenting the wildest and most wonderful scene that the eye of man ever beheld . . .

Written at Sunset Point, these words were among the first to describe an impression of the Bryce Canyon Amphitheater, whose moods vary with weather, season, and sunlight. The Bryce Amphitheater is only one of numerous alcoves cut into the Pink Cliffs, a twenty-mile escarpment exposed on the eastern edge of the Paunsaugunt Plateau. Bordering this winding cliff line is the badland topography, famous for its vivid colors and fragile forms.

In this high section of the Colorado Plateau are rock strata from the most recent chapter of geological history. Formed from compacted sediments, these Tertiary strata cap a grand sequence of rock layers, the most ancient of which are seen in the depths of the Grand Canyon. At nearby Zion Canyon, the massive amber-colored sandstones represent the earth's middle history; at Bryce Canyon, these Zion rock layers are buried. Thus, the Pink Cliffs of Bryce are a colorful frosting on a geological layer cake, though these cliffs represent sixteen thousand feet of rock and a billion years of geological history.

The Pink Cliffs, known collectively as the Wasatch Formation, are an accumulation of sand, silt, and lime washed into inland lakes from surrounding highlands and later compacted into layers of rock. These sediments began to accumulate about sixty million years ago. After the deposition stopped, about thirteen millions years ago, the then-existing sediments were consolidated and uplifted by powerful pressures from within the earth. Slowly the lands of southern Utah rose from what was then sea level to mountainous heights. During these continuing and unequal upheavals, huge blocks of the earth's crust fractured and separated. The slow and persistent forces of erosion widened the gaps between massive blocks of rock, and in time, these became separate tablelands or plateaus that differed in elevation by thousands of feet.

The freestanding forms were and are fractured rocks sculptured by several physical forces. Erosional processes are one force. Those act somewhat uniformly at a given location, but hardness of rock types determines whether a particular block of rock will endure as a freestanding form or will erode down to a pile of rock fragments. Limestone and siltstone are hard and durable rocks in arid climates. Where they form the bulk of a wall or act as a protective helmet for spires, the destructive processes of erosion are diverted, and in places, postponed. Rocks that are less hard, such as shales, poorly cemented sandstones, and conglomerates, are weaker and therefore erode more rapidly. The forces of uplift and faulting create a pattern of cracks into which water intrudes and freezes. Cracks widen and channels deepen from the freezing and thawing action, from chemical changes in the rocks caused by water and air, from plant root penetration, and raindrop erosion.

After immense periods of time, this jointing system creates a rough topography. In the flash-flood season of late summer, streams pour through established channels, scour them and wash fallen debris down toward the Paria River. Parts of walls are split off, and isolated columns are undermined and collapse. The same processes that were so active in the past are still active today. The beatings of these erosive forces are also the creative agents forming new landscapes as the canyon rim retreats westward. What you see tomorrow will be different from what you saw yesterday.

Rocks, plants, wildlife, and even climate are interlocking agents. Where it is not too steep, the surface of the landscape is a living carpet upon which plants and animals continue their life cycles in nature's harmony. Bryce Canyon's summer wild-flower displays include sego lilies, yellow evening primrose, wild iris, Indian paintbrush, and blue flax. In autumn, rabbit brush, goldenrod, gumweed, and Senecio splash yellows and golds along the roadsides.

The most common wildlife the visitor may see are the chipmunks and golden-mantled ground squirrels. The yellow-bellied marmot, badger, bobcat, porcupine, gray fox, and pine squirrel are also present. The mule deer, the park's largest mammal, may generally be seen browsing the meadows in early morning or evening. The cougar and coyote are considered rare.

Possibly the first white explorers to view the Pink Cliffs from a distance were Fathers Escalante and Dominguez in 1776, when these Spanish missionaries searched for a connecting route between the prospering missions of New Mexico and the new missions of central California. The federal survey parties which explored the interior West a century ago barely touched the Bryce Canyon area.

As part of the Mormon Church's plan to colonize

southern Utah, some Mormons settled in the valley east of the Paunsaugunt Plateau in 1874. One settler built his cabin on a tributary that drained a large amphitheater. His name was Ebenezer Bryce. Though he grazed cattle here for only a few years, he left a name for the park and a vivid description of the place: "A hellava place to lose a cow!"

It was not until the second decade of the 1900s that articles about the magnificent scenery began to appear in the public press. Bryce Canyon gained sufficient national attention to become a national monument on June 8, 1923. In 1928, Congress doubled the area and made it a national park, one of the world's most intricately eroded and strikingly beautiful sections of badland topography.

From late April through October, days are pleasant and nights cool. In late July and throughout August, thundershowers are fairly common. Winter lasts on the plateau from November through March, with days that can be delightfully bright and crisp. Four major vantage points on the short tour from Sunset Point to Paria View are maintained during winter, when deep snow transforms Bryce Canyon into another land of enchantment.

The park's visitor center should be the first stop. Here, information and orientation are provided. See the short slide program and exhibits depicting the forces that shape the landscape. Ask about the various interpretive programs being offered. Each of the numerous vantage points has its own display of curious and beautiful formations. From the park's southern end, at Rainbow Point, you can look back along the colorful escarpment.

A short tour is recommended for those with limited

time. Four spectacular views may be seen within two hours. Sunset Point, Inspiration Point, Bryce Point, and Paria View comprise the most scenic concentration of sculptured red rocks. You may also wish to stop at Fairyland View if you did not see it on the way into the park. Except for Fairyland View and Sunset Point, the vantage points are not designed for trailers. Trailers should be unhooked and parked at the visitor center parking lot or at Sunset Point prior to your tour.

On hiking trails in Bryce Canyon, the walking is hardest on your return trip—it's all uphill! Wear stout walking shoes. You may wish to carry water. At Sunset Point, the Navajo Loop Trail is a good place to start. A self-guiding booklet about the Queen's Garden Trail from Sunrise Point may be purchased at the visitor center or trail box. A backcountry permit is required for overnight trips, which are allowed only on the Under-the-Rim Trail south of Bryce Point.

Less oxygen is available to breathe at Bryce because of its altitude (eight thousand to nine thousand feet above sea level). Therefore, heart patients and visitors with high blood pressure should not subject themselves to strenuous climbs.

Guided walks and campfire talks by park rangers are given daily from mid-May through October 1. These include a "special" walk leaving the visitor center, the Bristlecone Walk from Rainbow Point, and the Rim Loop Walk from Sunset Point. Evening programs are given in both campgrounds. Check at the visitor center for departure times.

For children, ages six to twelve, the Environmental Day Center offers morning and afternoon learning sessions.

Riding horseback is another way to see the colorful amphitheaters and inner canyons. Morning and afternoon trips, conducted by a concession wrangler, begin at the corral just below the lodge. Where horses and hikers use the same trail, be prepared for an inevitable meeting. Hikers are required to stand aside quietly and allow the horses to pass.

Winter activities include cross-country skiing, snowshoeing, overnight camping, and snowmobiling. Registration is required.

LODGING: Bryce Canyon Lodge, open from mid-May to October 1, consists of cottages with and without baths, dining rooms, a recreation hall, gift shop, and coffee shop. For reservations, write: TWA Services, P.O. Box 400, Cedar City, UT 84720. Other motels and services are located in Panguitch, twenty-six miles away, and at Ruby's Inn, outside the park.

North Campground, east of the visitor center, is open May 1 to November 1. Sunset, a mile south, is open June 1 to Labor Day. Campsites have tables and fireplaces and are near water and rest rooms. Camping is limited to fourteen days. A free backcountry permit is required.

HOW TO GET THERE: The nearest principal cities with frequent air service and rental cars are Salt Lake City, Phoenix, and Las Vegas. Nearby Cedar City, Utah, also has rental cars and is served by Hughes Airwest. Main bus lines operate from Salt Lake City and Los Angeles to Cedar City, where park passengers can transfer to Utah Parks Company buses. By car from Cedar City, on Interstate 15, take State Road 14 east, then U.S. Highway 89 north to State Road 12, which leads to the west park entrance. State Road 12 from Boulder and Canonville leads to the east park entrance. From Zion National Park, take State Road 15 east to Mt. Carmel Junction, then U.S. 89 north to State Road 12, which leads to the park.

CANYONLANDS NATIONAL PARK

UTAH

Towering spires, broad mesas, stately arches, roaring rapids, and more than one hundred miles of canyons—these are the hallmarks of Canyonlands National Park, truly a masterpiece of varied color and form.

Ruined villages and ancient drawings (petroglyphs) indicate that man has inhabited this exciting region since prehistoric times, although the landscape has undoubtedly changed a good deal since the first campfire was lighted in the shelter of an overhanging cliff. The landscape is always changing, even today, as it's rearranged and resculptured by the forces of erosion.

Most of the resculpturing that has occurred was done by the Colorado River and its tributaries as they gouged through layers of salt, sandstone and limestone laid down by an inland sea some 300 million years ago. As the salt washed away, the more resistant rock layers settled down into the cavities to create the canyons and strange new rock formations.

But Canyonlands is more than just a piece of scenic real estate; it's also a piece of American history. The roads and trails which wind through this park were once ridden by cowboys and sheepherders as they tended their livestock, and the convenient campsite where hikers rest tonight may well have been an Indian camp 900 years ago.

The desert lands look desolate and empty but are very much occupied by plant and animal life. Bighorn sheep, mule deer, cougars, bobcats, coyotes, foxes, and pronghorn are present, as well as rodents in great variety and numbers, various kinds of other small mammals, and some reptiles. Along the rivers are beaver, shorebirds, ducks, and other wetland animals.

Birdlife in Canyonlands is especially diverse because of the wide range of habitats. Totally different conditions may occur within very short distances, and bird watchers find a rich variety of species throughout the year.

Like everything else at Canyonlands, travel conditions vary greatly. Depending upon which parts of the park you visit and upon the type of motor vehicle you are driving, you may be traveling on paved roads; dirt roads suitable to any type of vehicle; easy four-wheel-drive routes; or steep, rocky, and hazardous four-wheel-drive trails.

Island in the Sky's dirt roads—dusty and a little rough but suited to any vehicle—end at overlooks of a vast expanse of canyons, gorges, spires, towers, and buttes. From these vantage points, you look down at the White Rim, more than a thousand feet below, and catch glimpses of the rivers a thousand feet below the White Rim. The road to Upheaval Dome provides easy access to a remarkable craterlike feature caused by movement of salt far below the surface.

The White Rim Trail offers backcountry enthusiasts more than a hundred miles of easy four-wheel-drive travel. Shafer Trail, for which a four-wheel-drive vehicle is advised, is a thrilling route, but it involves some hazardous driving.

You travel about thirty miles through magnificent canyon country to reach The Needles district. All passenger cars must stop at Elephant Hill, a forty-degree grade traversable only by four-wheel-drive vehicles. You can hike miles of trails, take concession-operated jeep tours from nearby towns, or rent four-wheel-drive vehicles at a resort immediately outside the park. Visitors to Chesler Park, Salt Creek, and other areas in The Needles district travel into the canyons amid the remarkable erosional features that give the area its name.

You can see much of The Maze district by four-wheel-drive vehicle but can get into The Maze itself only on foot. Travel to the Maze Overlook, Horseshoe Canyon, and the Land of Standing Rocks can provide a severe test for even the best four-wheel-drive vehicle. Because it is remote and lightly traveled, parties visiting The Maze district should include at least two vehicles.

Each year, thousands of people travel through the park by boat or raft. For many, the ultimate recreational experience at Canyonlands is a float trip down either the Green River or the Colorado River and then through Cataract Canyon. It is a never-to-be-forgotten journey. Commercially operated float trips, led by licensed guides, are the most popular. Private groups with proper equipment and experience may attempt the trip after obtaining a permit from the superintendent.

This is desert country, so annual precipitation averages only five to nine inches, much of which falls as late-summer thundershowers and winter snow. Annual temperatures vary from 20° below zero to 110° above, but the normal temperature range in any one area is generally much less. Since clear desert skies and lack of dense vegetation tend to encourage very rapid cooling at nightfall and rapid warming in the morning, a daily range of 25° to 30° is not unusual.

Nights are fairly cold from December through February, but daytime temperatures are generally pleasant even in midwinter. The winter season is usually short, with very little snow. Spring and autumn tend to be long and very pleasant, except that high winds accompanied by sand- or dust-storms are common in spring. Spring and autumn are best for hiking and exploring.

LODGING: Facilities are not available within the park, but nearby Moab, Monticello, and Hauksville provide a full range of services. Write: Chamber of Commerce Information Center, Moab, UT 84532 for information. Canyonlands Resort (near The Needles entrance) offers fuel, snacks, limited supplies, and scenic flights over the park.

Year-round camping is provided at Squaw Flat, thirty-eight miles west of U.S. 160, and Green River Overlook, thirty-two miles southwest of U.S. 160. Campsites include tables, fireplaces, and pit toilets,

but no utility hook-ups or water. Camping is limited to
fourteen days. A free backcountry permit is required.

HOW TO GET THERE: The nearest principal city is
Salt Lake City, Utah. However, nearby Moab is
served by Frontier Airlines and bus lines. Rental cars
are available from both cities. By car from Moab, go
north on U.S. Highway 163/191 to State Road 279
south, which leads to the east park entrance.

CAPITOL REEF NATIONAL PARK

UTAH

T he little known desert land of south central Utah is the site of one of the most spectacular tilted cliffs (monocline) in the United States. Extending for nearly a hundred miles from Thousand Lake Mountain to the Colorado River, Capitol Reef is composed of deeply colored and luminous bands of sandstone and shale.

Although most people usually don't associate the term "reef" with the desert, in this case it's used to mean a ridge of rock which forms a barrier. The reef derives its name from one of its high points, Capitol Dome, which rises a thousand feet above the Fremont River and stretches for twenty miles. This particular formation earned that name because of its resemblance to the dome of the U.S. Capitol Building.

The rock you see today in the park was laid down, layer upon layer, in past ages. At times this area was a tidal flat whose ripple marks are now hardened into stone. At other times sand dunes drifted across the land, and they eventually were consolidated into crisscrossing beds of sandstone.

Capitol Reef is located on the Colorado Plateau. The reef and the Rocky Mountains began rising to their present heights toward the end of the "age of dinosaurs." Pressures on the rock increased as the plateau rose and resulted in the folding of the rock into a hundred-mile-long formation called the Waterpocket Fold, considered unique by geologists because of its great size and a primary reason for the establishment of the park. As the rock was folding, it was also eroding, creating cliff faces, arches, monoliths, and canyons.

Your first impression of the park may be of the contrast between the lush growth along the Fremont River and the barrenness of the cliffs and terraces. The year-round water of the Fremont River, which allows cottonwood and the willow to grow, creates this contrast.

Though the Fremont River is an oasis, there is abundant life in other, drier parts of the park. On the more gentle slopes and terraces you'll find pinyon jay, pinyon pine, and Utah juniper, all adapted for living in a dry climate. A twisted juniper growing from a crack in sandstone is a testimony not only to how hard life is in this desert but also to how hardy life is.

In the narrow canyons and washes, water appears in a flash and mostly disappears in a few hours. Plants grow wherever they can gain a foothold. While risking being swept away in a flash flood, the living things in the sheltered canyons enjoy milder conditions than their counterparts on exposed slopes and cliff faces.

The sandy floor, piles of rock debris, and water-worn holes in the canyon walls make ideal homes for such animals as the side-blotched lizard, antelope squirrel, and canyon wren. Toward dusk, the first bats appear, hunting insects that may be attracted to moisture. Pockets of water often remain after a rain; that's how Waterpocket Fold got its name. These pockets, or tanks, hold surprising kinds of wildlife, including shrimp and spadefoot toad tadpoles. Tadpoles go through their life cycles so rapidly that when the pocket of water dries, they have become toads and can survive until the next rain, buried in the sand in a protective mucus coat.

To the daytime visitor it may seem that few animals live in the park except for lizards, chipmunks, and squirrels. But most, like the ring-tailed cat, fox, and deer, simply come out at night. Wildlife viewing is best at dawn, dusk, and after dark. Remember though, to the animals this place is home; we are merely visitors. Please do not feed, chase, or capture any animal in the park.

Human beings inhabited the Capitol Reef area as long ago as A.D. 800—and perhaps much earlier. The Fremont Indians lived along the Fremont River and other permanent watercourses for about four hundred years. They left petroglyphs—carvings on rocks—that still elude translation. The petroglyphs may have had to do with hunting, for they show desert bighorn sheep and figures of people. They may have had religious significance, or perhaps they were doodles. Study the petroglyphs and come up with your own interpretations.

Around A.D. 1200 the Fremont people left, possibly because of prolonged drought. Later, Paiute Indians lived in the area, passing through Capitol Reef while hunting game and gathering food plants. But humans did not again live in the park the year round until 1880, when Mormon settlers established a community, later called Fruita, where the visitor center and campground are today. These people earned their living from the crops and orchards they planted. Like the Fremont Indians before them, the Mormon settlers irrigated their crops from the Fremont River and Sulphur Creek. Small lime kilns were operated, making use of Capitol Reef's limestone deposits. In the early 1900s and the late 1940s several small uranium mines were worked. Cattle have grazed Capitol Reef since the early days of Fruita, and some of the park's roads and trails originally served as cattle drive routes. Today, grazing is being phased out.

With the establishment of Capitol Reef National Monument in 1937, land use began to change. The last residents of Fruita left in the late 1960s, and in 1971 a greatly expanded Capitol Reef was designated a national park.

Capitol Reef has a desert environment, so be sure to carry water with you, even on short hikes. You'll find your trip more pleasant and certainly safer. Most water in Capitol Reef is contaminated with minerals or by animals. Potable water comes out of labeled taps at the visitor center and at the nearby picnic area and campground. Water from any other source is not recommended for human consumption. Backcountry users should carry their own water.

Evening programs, conducted by park naturalists, and displays of early Indian artifacts and relics are at the visitor center. Park roads pass overlooks into the deep zigzag canyon and the spectacular monoliths. Self-guiding hiking trails range from the easy to the strenuous. One-day trips in four-wheel-drive station wagons are conducted by Sleeping Rainbow Guest Ranch, P.O. Box 93, Torrey, UT 84775. For seven-day trips combining jeeping and backpacking, write: Peace and Quiet, Inc., P.O. Box 163, Salt Lake City, UT 84110. Nearby are Arches, Canyonlands, Bryce, and Zion national parks. Capitol Reef is open all year.

LODGING: There are no overnight facilities within the park. Food and lodging are available in nearby Torrey, Bicknell, Loa, Fish Lake, and Hanksville. All facilities are privately owned, and many are closed during winter. Information may be obtained by writing to the respective chambers of commerce.

The only park campground is on the Scenic Drive near the Fremont River. Facilities include tables, fireplaces, and modern rest rooms. Firewood, trailer hookups, and holding tank dumps are not available. Camping is limited to fourteen days. A permit is required for backcountry camping.

HOW TO GET THERE: The nearest principal city is Salt Lake City, Utah. Cedar City, west of the park, is served by Hughes Airwest; Moab, east of the park, is served by Frontier Airlines. The nearest other airport is in Richfield, Utah, seventy-two miles northwest of

the park. Salt Lake City, Cedar City, Moab, and
Richfield are all served by bus lines and rental car
companies. The main access to the park is via State
Road 24, an all-weather road passing through the park
and connecting with new Interstate 70 to the northeast
(near Green River) and with U.S. Highway 89 to the
northwest (near Salina).

ZION NATIONAL PARK

UTAH

Exotic temples of stone, networks of deeply etched finger canyons, prehistoric Indian ruins, hanging gardens—these are just a few of the many fabulous sights to be found in the unique plateau and canyon country of Zion National Park.

This park is named for its principal gorge, Zion Canyon, which was carved out of the southern Utah desert plateau by the Virgin River. The walls of the canyon and the eroded slopes reveal an infinite variety of colors—from vivid splashes to gentle pastels—which constantly change during the course of the day to create different atmospheres, different moods.

As geologist Clarence E. Dutton wrote in 1882:

Nothing can exceed the wonderful beauty of
Zion . . . In the nobility and beauty of the sculp-
tures there is no comparison . . . There is an elo-
quence to their forms which stirs the imagination
with a singular power, and kindles in the mind a
glowing response.

When people of European origin first discovered
this area, native Americans of the Paiute tribe were
claiming the region. The Escalante-Dominguez party
of Spanish padres was the first group of Europeans to
explore this part of southern Utah. Skirting the great
canyons, they crossed the Virgin River near Hurricane, Utah, in 1776, and beheld the glories of this
area.

Fifty years passed before trappers and fur traders
reached the Zion region. Jedediah Smith, one of the
most daring, led a party of sixteen men from Great Salt
Lake south through the valleys to the Virgin River in
search of pelts. Through this and a later expedition
down the Virgin River, Smith provided information to
guide other exploring parties to the area over the next
few years. But it was Capt. John C. Fremont who,
from his 1843–44 explorations, supplied the detailed
information which led the Mormon pioneers to a mass
migration into the Great Salt Lake valley in 1847.
Within little more than a decade, the Mormons had
established small settlements as far south as the Virgin
River and had discovered Zion Canyon.

From that time to the present, the story parallels the
settling and development of Utah by the Mormons and
others. The colorful canyons, first thought of as obsta-

cles to be avoided, soon became choice places for retreat and relaxation.

Like so many pages of a book, rock layers of the towering cliffs and slopes in the Zion region tell a fascinating geological story of natural processes operating through more than 200 million years. These layers reveal that successive occurrences of vast inland seas, ponds and lakes, raging rivers, tropical lowlands, tremendous earth upheavals, and the constant forces of erosion have all played a part in forming this region.

About 60 million years ago, when the Zion country was near sea level, a very gradual uplift of the entire region began. Over a period of many millions of years, the land was lifted thousands of feet and, because of the tremendous stresses, was broken into great blocks. The cleavage lines which separate these blocks are known as faults, and lesser fractures within the blocks are called joints. Along these planes of weakness, many canyons have been formed by the process of erosion. In the Finger Canyons area, in the northwest corner of the Park, the forces of deformation have folded the strata, and great blocks of bedrock have been thrust up and over themselves. There the towering "fingers" of Navajo Sandstone resemble the bows of ships riding up on a beach.

Later tilting of the Markagunt Plateau, of which the Kolob Terrace of Zion National Park is a part, permitted development of fast-moving streams along the south and west margins of the plateau. These rushing waters rapidly carved their way into the terrace's rock layers, continually deepening their crooked channels. Billions of tons of rock were ground up and carried away, finally exposing the remains of that great ancient desert, now called Navajo Sandstone.

The varieties of plants and animals in the park provide a pleasing change from the impact of great stone masses that form the walls of the canyon. It is these very walls, though, that create diverse environments for the plants and animals.

The Virgin River, running along the floor of Zion Canyon, supports a narrow corridor of riparian woodland where broadleaf trees, birds, and small mammals abound. On narrow ledges above the river are drier benches and open areas of pinyon-juniper woodland. Thickets of short evergreens and oaks are interrupted by open flats covered with low shrubs. These areas are preferred by birds for nesting and by deer for browsing.

The high country vegetation is predominantly ponderosa pine, quaking aspen, white fir, Douglas fir, and many kinds of shrubs. Many of the resident birds in the park migrate from the canyons to the high country in the summer, then back when the snow falls.

Many side canyons have been cut back into the walls of the main canyon. These offer shade and moisture from springs, providing an ideal environment for many of the high country birds and other animals to live at much lower elevations. Pines and firs also grow in these side canyons, providing food and protection for the small animals associated with them. If there is enough moisture, cottonwoods and box elders will also be present. Around the mouths of these canyons is more pinyon-juniper woodland. This association of environments allows you to enjoy all three in a small area without climbing from the floor of Zion Canyon to the plateau top.

From December to March, snow may fall intermittently but usually lasts only a day or two on the canyon floor. Maximum winter temperatures average 12°C (54°F); the average minimum is −1°C (30°F). May to October daytime temperatures may range from 22°C (72°F) to 39°C (102°F); nighttime, from 7°C (45°F) to 23°C (73°F).

The park is open all year, although summer is the principal visiting season, with maximum park services and programs. Illustrated talks and guided trips are scheduled daily during summer and several times a week in spring and autumn. Scenic drives and self-guided walking and hiking trails offer vantage points for striking views and include most points of interest. Technical rock climbing is permitted after registering at park headquarters. Arrangements for guided horseback trips may be made at Zion Lodge. Fishing is allowed (with license) all year.

LODGING: Within the park, TWA Services, Inc., Box 400, Cedar City, UT 84720, operates Zion Lodge, open from mid-May through October 6. The lodge has cabin accommodations and requires advance reservations. A dining room, cafeteria, grocery store, medical assistance, and automotive service are also available within the park. Nearby Cedar City provides year-round accommodations and facilities.

Within the park are South and Watchman campgrounds. The camping limit is fourteen days. Both campgrounds have fire grates, tables, tap water, ice machines, picnic sites, rest rooms, and a sanitary disposal station for trailers, but no utility hookups. Numerous other camping facilities are available in Cedar City. A permit is required for backcountry camping.

HOW TO GET THERE: The nearest principal cities include Salt Lake City, Las Vegas, and Phoenix. Cedar City, sixty miles from the park, is served by Hughes Airwest. In summer, the Utah Parks Company furnishes bus service from Cedar City, but there is no common carrier service to the park the rest of the year, so a rental car is a must. Bus connections and rental cars are available at all cities listed above. Zion National Park borders Interstate 15 on the west and State Road 15 on the south.

GRAND TETON NATIONAL PARK

WYOMING

Towering starkly blue-gray above the sagebrush flats, the massive silhouette of the Grand Tetons creates a ruggedly magnificent skyline 40 miles long. These jagged peaks, carved out of solid rock by mammoth glaciers, soar more than a mile above the morainal lakes of Jackson Hole. Glacial remnants of the Ice Age still cling to the steep slopes, feeding the frigidly cold streams that tumble down to the rivers and lakes below.

In geological terms, the Grand Tetons are not only a young mountain range but also an unusually striking example of a fault-block mountain range. The steep eastern front is the result of a recent uplift of the range along a great fracture line, or fault, in the earth's crust. The Teton fault shows signs of movement within the last few thousand years, indicating that the process is still going on.

In striking contrast to the youth of the mountain range is the great age of the rocks themselves. Recent datings by geophysicists reveal that some of the crystalline rocks are about two and a half billion years old! Yet these once-molten veins penetrate rocks that were already ancient and metamorphosed into gneiss when these intrusions came up from below. Here, then, some of the oldest rocks in the world have been brought to light by one of the most recent mountain uplifts.

Erosion has completely cut away great segments of the mountain mass—erosion that probably began with the very first uplift of the mountain block. As uplift proceeded, erosion continued more intensely with increases in the gradients of the mountain streams. These rushing torrents tore away rocks, creating gorges. Then came the profound sculpturing of the Ice Age. During the past million years several periods of intense mountain glaciation have occurred. At the head of each gorge more snow piled up in winter than would melt the following summer. Great masses of snow slowly changed to glacial ice. In response to the inexorable pull of gravity, these masses became streams of creeping ice which plucked off bits of the canyon wall here and ground away rock obstructions there.

Fluctuations in the climate melted away this ice sheet, only to bring back glaciers of smaller size during more recent cold periods. As recently as nine thousand years ago, valley glaciers flowed from the crest of the Teton Range down to Jackson Hole. Crescent mounds (terminal moraines) left at the snouts of these most recent glaciers are now the natural dams for the lakes at the foot of mountain slopes. Again the climate moderated and became about what it is today. The ice melted away and, retreating gradually, once again exposed the canyon bottoms. The forces of rain, wind, landslides, and other agents of erosion resumed their attack on the uplifted range. Ice sculpturing is evident in all the major canyons of the park. Although the present glaciers are a mere vestige of the king-size masses of the Ice Age, they are still quarrying away into the face of the mountains. No one can confidently predict whether glaciers will once again extend and fill these valleys or when another mountain uplift might occur. There is no reason to think, however, that either process has come to an end. Thousands of years from now the scene may be quite different from that which delights the visitor today.

Because most of the ice has vanished, you can see the effect these glaciers had on the landscape. At the head of each canyon is a rounded natural amphitheater, called a cirque. These were the gathering places for mountain glaciers from which great ice tongues extended downward. The U-shaped valleys were carved out by the now-vanished ice. Smaller tributary glaciers plucked away at each of the higher peaks of the range. This detailed sculpturing resulted in the noble spires that extend along the range and culminate in the majestic cathedral-like pinnacle of Grand Teton. Much of the rock waste carried down from the eroding mountain range was strewn in the valley, making up a great deal of the present flat floor of Jackson Hole.

Until 1800, Indians held undisputed sway over the country dominated by the Three Tetons, frequently coming across the passes into the basins on warring or hunting expeditions. The Tetons probably first became known to white men in 1807, when the intrepid John Colter crossed the range on the journey that also made him the discoverer of the Yellowstone country. In 1811, the Astorians, under Wilson Price Hunt, entered Jackson Hole and crossed the range on their expedition to the mouth of the Columbia. In the late 1880s came the first settlers. They entered by the Gros Ventre River and Teton Pass and settled first in the southern end of the valley.

In 1929 the Teton Range and the lovely lakes at the mouths of its deep canyons were assured protection by the establishment of Grand Teton National Park. But it was obvious that part of the valley, with its own charms, was also in need of protection. Thus, the Jackson Hole area was made a National Monument in 1943; in 1950, Congress set aside the upper valley in a greater Grand Teton National Park. The gross area of the park is now 485 square miles, of which about ninety-eight percent is in federal ownership.

All of Grand Teton National Park is a wildlife sanctuary. Look in the valley for elk, mule deer, and bison. Mule deer and elk range from the lowest parts of the valley to the tree line. A pond-side vigil may reward you with the sight of moose feeding on aquatic vegetation. Wildlife viewing is best in the early morning and late afternoon hours. All native animals are wild; some may attack unpredictably, so do not feed or approach them. Photograph them from a safe distance, using telephoto lenses for closeups. Attendants at the visitor centers can help you identify and locate such species as moose, elk, bighorn, pronghorn, beaver, trumpeter swans, and eagles. Bird and mammal checklists are available at visitor centers.

A summer visitor to Jackson Hole can expect to see only a fraction of the floral displays of wild geranium, scarlet gilia, balsamroot, blue lupine, larkspur, fleabanes, penstemons, and cream-colored clusters of wild buckwheat. A traveler can scarcely pass through the valley, however, without encountering the Indian paintbrush, Wyoming's State flower. The bracts and upper leaves (not the flowers) give the plant the appearance of a brush dipped in red paint. In the high country are small clumps of tiny, brilliant, blue-flowered alpine forget-me-nots. On mountain slopes can be seen blue columbine and glacier lily.

It is doubtful if anyone views the rugged Teton Range without at least wondering what it must be like to stand on the summits of the peaks. Thus, mountain climbing has become a major outdoor activity in the park. Climbing instruction and guide service are available in the park area in summer. Low-cost bunk space and a cookout shelter are available for registered climbers at the Grand Teton Climber's Ranch.

The visitor centers provide fur trade and Indian craft exhibits, movies, literature, and auto tape tours. Major park roads are open all year, affording vistas of the majestic Tetons against a clear blue sky. The lakes accommodate a variety of water sports. During summer, fishing and boating equipment can be rented at Moran. Swimming is permitted in certain areas. Snake River float trips can be arranged from Jackson, Moran, and Moose. Mountain-climbing equipment can be rented in Moose or at Teton Villas. Corrals at Colter Bay, Jenny Lake, Jackson Lake Lodge, and on Rockefeller Parkway can make arrangements for one-hour or overnight horse trips. In winter, horse-drawn sleds schedule feeding trips into the midst of elk herds just south of the park. An aerial tramway above Teton Village is available for winter skiers. From February through April, snowshoe hikes, ski trips, snowmobile tours, and various equipment are available at the visitor center.

LODGING: For reservations to Jackson Lake Lodge, Jenny Lake Lodge, and Colter Bay Cabins, open during summer, write: Grand Teton Lodge Co., Moran, WY 83013. Reservations to Leeks Lodge can be made through: Leeks Lodge, Inc., Moran, WY 83013 (summer); or 2547 East 3d Street, Casper, WY 82601 (winter). The address of The American Alpine Club is Box 157, Moose, WY 83012. For year-round accommodations, write: Triangle-X Ranch, Moose, WY 83012.

The park contains five campgrounds and a trailer village, open from about the middle of May to mid-October, and two June–September campgrounds. Stays are limited to fourteen days, except at Jenny Lake, a ten-day site. The adjoining John D. Rockefeller, Jr., Memorial Parkway has two trailer villages and a campground on a June–September schedule. A free backcountry permit is required. Reservations for Colter Bay camping, including off-season stays, may be made by writing: Grand Teton Lodge Co., Moran, WY 83013. Reservations available for backcountry camping.

HOW TO GET THERE: Grand Teton National Park is on U.S. Highways 26/287 and 89/287. The latter joins with U.S. 26/86 to form the Rockefeller Parkway, which links Grand Teton and Yellowstone Parks. From the south, at Rock Springs, U.S. Highway 187 leads to the park at Jackson. From the west, State Road 33/22 leads from Victor, Idaho, to Jackson. Jackson is served by Frontier Airlines. Rental cars and bus connections are available at Jackson and Rock Springs.

YELLOWSTONE NATIONAL PARK

WYOMING— MONTANA— IDAHO

Yellowstone is a glorious and mysterious region which has intrigued and inspired the human mind since the dawn of man. The sheer splendor of this high mountain plateau, with its streaming geysers and glacier-carved canyons, its icy cold streams and rainbow-hued pools, exerts such a powerful influence on the human spirit that it's small wonder it became the country's first national park in 1872.

This gigantic park covers 3,400 square miles, spilling over the borders of northwest Wyoming into Montana and Idaho. It's one of the largest parks in the nation and, understandably, one of the most popular. Since Yellowstone is the size of a small country, a visit here requires some forethought and planning in order to gain a true appreciation for this amazing land.

To many, Yellowstone is a fleeting glimpse of a geyser, a bear, or a canyon through the window of a passing car. But certainly Yellowstone is more than this. It is more than a collection of scenic features and natural curiosities.

Yellowstone is an idea, a philosophy, and a monument to farsighted conservationists who more than a hundred years ago foresaw the need to preserve a bit of primitive America; it is a symbol of America's reverence for the foundations of her greatness, the great untouched North American wilderness.

Walk out into the cool, crisp air of an early fall morning. Hear the frosty meadows crackle as dim shapes invade their stillness and the mountains ring with the age-old, wild notes of bull elk issuing their thrilling challenges. This is Yellowstone, a tremendous block of wild mountain country in which thousands of furred and feathered creatures are living and mating and dying in harmony with the natural rhythms that have ruled the land for millions of years.

In this natural scene, man is but a visitor who is privileged to share glimpses into the intimacies of nature—if he only has the time and patience. Here roads, campsites, and hotels are enclaves of civilization in a wilderness world in which nature remains sovereign.

In Yellowstone the two contrasting elements, fire and water, have combined to produce a land of natural wonders. It is a land born in the fires of thundering volcanoes and sculptured by glacial ice and running water into a fascinating landscape.

Although thousands of years have passed since Yellowstone's violent birth, the thermal features in the park bear testimony that at a comparatively shallow depth beneath us the fiery heart of the volcanoes still beats. Literally thousands of hot springs dot the thermal basins; gigantic columns of boiling water are hurled hundreds of feet into the air, causing the ground to shake; hissing steam vents punctuate the valley floors; and stumps of redwood forests, buried by volcanic ash and petrified in an upright position, stand out starkly on eroded mountainsides.

More recently, glaciers have reworked the land's surface by smoothing canyons and leaving a myriad of sparkling blue ponds and lakes scattered across the landscape. And now, mountain streams carve beautiful canyons and leap over resistant rock ledges in breathtaking cascades and waterfalls.

Geologically, Yellowstone is a young land, with the last of the lava flows burning their way across the surface less than 100,000 years ago. Soil development is shallow and pioneer plants are common. Even today, fire and water—in the form of thermal heat, snow, and rain—dominate the landscape and determine which plants and animals will make up Yellowstone's natural communities.

Visitors to Yellowstone are privileged to see in this vast array of natural features the culmination of several million years of exacting natural processes.

Old Faithful is the park's favorite attraction. But sharing the Upper Geyser Basin are numerous other geysers, including Riverside, Grand, Castle, and Beehive. Eruption times for the most predictable geysers are posted in the Old Faithful Visitor Center.

Downstream along the Firehole River, where it parallels Grand Loop Road, are the Midway and Lower Geyser basins. Boardwalk trails and side roads lead to points of interest in those areas. The Fountain Paint Pots Trail, in the Lower Basin, presents more varied hot-water phenomena in a concentrated area than any other trail in the park.

Norris Geyser Basin is Yellowstone's most active thermal area. Eruption times for the more predictable geysers are posted at the museum in summer. Besides the numerous geysers, a variety of fumaroles (steam vents) and hot springs makes Norris an interesting place to visit.

The thermal pools of Mammoth Hot Springs are quite different from other springs and geysers. Here the hot waters cascade over a series of delicately colored rimstone pools. Limestone dissolved in the waters deep beneath the surface is deposited rapidly to form terraces and pools that literally change from day to day.

Backcountry basins such as the Shoshone and Heart Lake basins deserve special consideration. If you have a day, hike to one of them; perhaps you will sense the awe felt by mountaineer Jim Bridger as he wandered amid the boiling cauldrons and hissing steam vents long ago.

Just as the west side of the Grand Loop draws those fascinated by the geysers, so the east side attracts those who love canyons and waterfalls, placid and violent waters, and the soaring heights of mountain wilderness.

The Grand Canyon of the Yellowstone leaves many

people breathless. Go to Artist Point, Inspiration Point, or Lookout Point. Look down at the deceptively tiny river below, at the wisps of steam and the pastel canyon walls. Here you can see ospreys far below as they wheel and soar over the canyon bottom. Or stand on the lip of the Lower Falls; watch the bottle-green Yellowstone River break into frothy white jets as it drops away into the canyon below; listen to its constant wild roar; feel the spray on your face.

Yellowstone Lake is a mixture of charm on summer days, anger in sudden storms, and beauty in the quiet of evening sunset. Sit on the shore with your back against a log, watch a sunset reflected on the Absaroka Mountains to the east, and let your mind drift. Unexpectedly, you hear the muted sounds of nature, the lapping of wavelets on the shore, and the murmur of birds in the spruce nearby. You feel a part of nature rather than apart from it.

Hike to the summit of windswept Mt. Washburn. The panorama below encompasses the whole park, and may include distant mountain ranges on clear days. Visible are the deep gash of the Grand Canyon of the Yellowstone, frigid Yellowstone Lake, and the expansive lodgepole pine forests of this high plateau.

Summer is an especially good time to observe the park's wildlife. Hayden Valley, between Fishing Bridge and Canyon, and Pelican Creek, east of Fishing Bridge, are prime moose territory. Hayden Valley is also an area to watch for bison and grizzly. Waterfowl and gulls frequent the Yellowstone River in this valley.

Lamar Valley, in the northeast section of the park, is good territory for seeing elk, bison, moose, pronghorn, coyote, bighorn, and grizzly, especially during the winter months. Look for bighorn sheep on the cliffs between Mammoth and Gardiner, Montana. Pronghorn may be sighted in the sagebrush flats surrounding the North Entrance, and elk are frequently seen in the meadows and forests along the road from Mammoth to Madison.

The Midway and Upper Geyser basins are also good areas to find elk and occasionally see bison. Near the South Entrance elk and moose frequent the forests and wetlands along the Lewis River. Old Faithful, Lake, Canyon, and the areas between the North Entrance and Tower are good areas for sighting mule deer.

Bears—all bears—head the list of dangerous animals in Yellowstone National Park. Despite their sleepy, friendly looks, bears claw and bite visitors each year and destroy thousands of dollars worth of equipment.

If you are caught in a "bear jam," stay in your car with the windows rolled up. When camping, don't store food in your tent! Food can be detected by bears even when it is tightly wrapped. Bears may come right in with you during the night. To discourage these uninvited guests, keep your food locked in the trunk of your car.

Never feed wild animals; most people who have been bitten were feeding animals, in violation of park regulations. Bison, moose, and elk, as well as some of the smaller animals, can be extremely dangerous, especially when approached too closely. Again, keep your distance or remain in your car.

The park includes 500 miles of public roads. Most major features are adjacent to Grand Loop Road. More than 1,000 miles of hiking trails lead to remote parts of the park. Some offer easy, part-day trips, while others require skill and endurance. Interpretive programs, visitor centers, conducted walks and hikes, self-guiding trails, and campfire programs are all geared to deeper appreciation and understanding of the park.

Trout fishing is excellent and requires a free permit. Boat ramps are available at Bridge Bay and Lewis Lake and include rowboats, outboard skiffs, and cabin cruisers. Scenicruiser bus excursions are available from Bridge Bay. In summer, horses can be rented for short trips from Canyon, Roosevelt, and Mammoth, or arrangements can be made for extended trips into the backcountry areas of the park. Winter activities include a wildlife show, cross-country skiing, snowshoeing, and snow-coach trails.

LODGING: Complete accommodations, from hotels to cabins, are available from mid-June to early September, when most facilities are filled to capacity. Limited accommodations are available within the park early and late in the season, when the park is less crowded. Advance reservations are required through: Yellowstone Park Co., Yellowstone National Park, WY 82190. Meals, light lunches, souvenirs, medical and hospital services, and transportation are also available within the park. Additional facilities are available in the nearby communities of Silver Gate, Moran, Cody, Cooke City, Livingston, Gardiner, Jackson, and West Yellowstone.

The majority of campgrounds are open from June through August or September. Limited camping is available all year. Camping is limited to thirty days, except from July 1 to early September when the limit is fourteen days. Most campsites have piped water and flush toilets, and some have sewage dump stations within the grounds. A trailer park at Fishing Bridge operates from June 1 to September 14, providing water, sewer, and electrical hookups. For reservations, write to the Yellowstone Park Co. Less-crowded campgrounds convenient to major park features are at Gallatin, Targhee, Teton, and Shoshone National Forest. A backcountry camping permit is required.

HOW TO GET THERE: In the northwest corner of Wyoming, Yellowstone National Park is accessible by five entrances: U.S. Highway 89 on the north at Gardiner; U.S. Highway 212 on the northeast at Silver Gate; U.S. Highways 16 and 14/20 at East Entrance; U.S. Highway 20/191 at West Yellowstone; U.S. Highway 89/287 at South Entrance. Within the park, West Yellowstone is served by Frontier and Western airlines, and bus lines. Nearby Billings, Butte, Bozeman, Cody, and Jackson also schedule frequent air service. Rental cars are available at all points served by air.

CRATER LAKE NATIONAL PARK

OREGON

Approximately 6,600 years ago Mount Mazama was an active volcano soaring 12,000 feet into the air; today it is a water-filled crater half that high.

Crater Lake, lying in the center of the now-dead volcano, is one of the deepest and most strikingly blue lakes in the world. Visitors marvel at the clarity of its waters and at the steep, stark gray walls which surround it—all the result of a tremendous volcanic explosion that shook the Cascade Range sixty-six centuries ago.

Lava, in the form of frothy, superheated pumice, was blown out in great quantities, and fine dust was carried hundreds of miles to the north and east by the prevailing winds. Other, but smaller, eruptions spewed out lava in a series of glowing avalanches, cracks opened beneath the volcano, and several cubic miles of molten rock drained away. These ejections and drainings left a vast cavity beneath the cone which now could not support its own weight and collapsed into the void.

After this destruction, additional volcanic activity within the caldera produced the cinder cone known as Wizard Island. Over the centuries the great caldera has accumulated water from rain and snow; today evaporation and seepage are balanced with precipitation, and the water level remains fairly constant.

The lake was discovered on June 12, 1853, by John Wesley Hillman, a young prospector and member of a party in search of a rumored Lost Cabin Mine. He named it Deep Blue Lake. Sixteen years later, visitors from Jacksonville gave the lake its present name.

Only six lakes in the world are deeper than Crater Lake. In the Western Hemisphere, only Great Slave Lake in Canada is deeper—by 83 feet. A sonic depth finder has measured the greatest depth of Crater Lake at 1,932 feet.

Many animals can be seen in the 250-square-mile park. Birds along the rim include Clark's nutcrackers, gray jays, and the blue Steller's jay. Eagles and hawks are often seen. Chipmunks and golden-mantled ground squirrels are common. Remember, these animals are wild; wild animals are dangerous. They may bite—and a small nip can be serious. At a distance or from the safety of your car, be on the lookout for deer and bears. Seldom seen are the Cascade red fox, coyote, pine marten, porcupine, bobcat, elk, and very rarely, the cougar.

Early visitors reported that Crater Lake originally contained no fish, but several species have been introduced. Recently, the practice of stocking has been discontinued, but rainbow trout, brown trout in small numbers, and kokanee salmon are known to be reproducing. The limited fish population is due to the lack of adequate food and suitable spawning grounds. The amazingly pure lake water supports comparatively little life, but an aquatic moss has been found at a record depth of 425 feet.

Wild flowers and evergreen forests of the park are typical of the Cascades. Principal trees surrounding the lake include mountain hemlock, Shasta and subalpine firs, lodgepole and whitebark pines, and in lower elevations beautiful stands of Douglas fir and ponderosa pine. Wild flowers of the high mountains appear late and disappear early, but displays of phlox, knotweed, and monkey flowers are brilliant.

The entire lake, cradled in the extinct volcano, can be viewed from the towering rim of lava cliffs. The deep, brilliant blue of the lake contrasts sharply with the evergreens, pines, firs, and hemlocks surrounding the lake.

The most popular overlook is the Rim Village area. A park naturalist is on duty in the Exhibit Building, located on the rim wall, where you can buy literature concerning the park. In front of and below the Exhibit Building, on the caldera wall, is Sinnott Memorial Overlook, with a broad terrace presenting a magnificent panorama. Here, talks explaining the origin of Crater Lake are presented throughout the day in summer.

Two nearby trails afford breathtaking vistas from precipitous vantage points: 1.7-mile Garfield Peak

Trail runs east along the rim wall, beginning behind the lodge and ending at the peak 1,900 feet above the lake; 1.5-mile Discovery Point Trail begins at the opposite end of Rim Village and leads to Discovery Point, where prospector John Wesley Hillman discovered the lake in 1853. This is an easy walk to the Discovery Point turnout on Rim Drive.

Rim Drive, a 33-mile route circling the caldera's edge, offers unexcelled observation points. Picnic areas along the way are available for short stops.

The Watchman, the first prominent peak along Rim Drive beyond Discovery Point, looms 1,800 feet above the lake. A .8-mile trail from the parking area leads to the summit and a fire lookout station. Exhibits in the public-use area locate notable park features, and a museum room vividly depicts park forests. There are exceptional views in all directions, including 14,000-foot Mount Shasta, about 100 miles away.

At 8,156 feet, neighboring Hillman Peak, named for the discoverer of the lake, is the highest point along the rim.

At North Junction the north entrance road joins Rim Drive. This area was devastated by glowing avalanches of frothy pumice that spewed from the volcano and only now is gradually being reclaimed by lodgepole pines. Prominent along the rim at this point is Llao Rock, a massive flow of obsidian-like dacite that fills an earlier glacial valley.

Cleetwood Trail descends the northern rim wall to Cleetwood Cove, the only access to the water. The 1.1-mile trail requires about one-half hour to go down and about three-quarters of an hour to return. Launch trips around the lake and to Wizard Island, which rises to 760 feet above the water, begin here. A trail to the top enables you to see the island's crater. Rowboats can be rented, but private boats are not permitted on the lake.

Cloudcap, reached by a short spur road from Rim Drive, offers an exhilarating panorama of the Crater Lake scene. To the east is two-peaked Mount Scott, which rises to 8,926 feet above sea level, the highest point in the park.

The famous Pinnacles are easily accessible at the end of a 6-mile branch road. They are striking spires of pumice and welded tuff rising 200 feet out of the Wheeler Creek canyon. Halfway to the Pinnacles is Lost Creek Campground.

A short trail at Sun Notch provides the best view of the unique dike remnant called Phantom Ship, which seemingly sails Crater Lake's blue waters.

At the Rim Drive and south entrance road junction, near park headquarters, is Castle Crest Wildflower Garden and nature trail. Three trails are easily accessible along the south entrance road: Godfrey Glen Trail, midway betwen Mazama Campground and park headquarters, skirts the edge of Munson Creek Canyon; Annie Crook Canyon Trail loops .7-miles into Annie Creek Canyon near Mazama Campground; and Oregon Skyline Trail, a part of the Pacific Crest Trail System, runs the entire north-south length of the park.

LODGING: Crater Lake Lodge, at Rim Village, is open from mid-June to mid-September and provides hotel rooms, sleeping cabins, cottages, a lounge, cocktail bar, dining room, and cafeteria. For reservations, write: Crater Lake Lodge, Inc., Crater Lake, OR

96704. Year-round acommodations are available near the park at Diamond Lake, Union Creek, Fort Klamath, Medford, and Klamath Falls.

Crater Lake National Park averages 50 feet of snowfall annually. Only the south and west entrance roads to Rim Village are open all year. On weekends and holidays, from mid-September to mid-June, light refreshments and souvenirs are available at the coffee shop in Rim Village. Carry towrope, shovel, and tire chains, which may be necessary at any time.

In summer, there is a branch post office in the administration building at park headquarters. Visitors not staying at the lodge or in cabins in Rim Village should have their mail addressed to General Delivery, Crater Lake, OR 97604.

Park campgrounds are open from about mid-June to the end of September, also depending on snow conditions. Check the map for locations. Trailers up to 18 feet can be accommodated, but there are no utility connections. Campsites cannot be reserved. They are assigned on a first-come, first-served basis. Once the campsites have been filled, campers should contact privately operated campgrounds in the area. A permit is necessary for overnight backcountry trail trips.

Fishing is permitted in park streams and in Crater Lake, and no fishing license is required. Regulations are available at park headquarters or from a park ranger.

HOW TO GET THERE: Nearby Medford and Klamath Falls are both served by Hughes Airwest and both cities have rental cars. By car from Klamath Falls, take U.S. Highway 97 north to State Road 62, which leads to the south entrance. From Medford and Interstate 5, take State Road 62 to the west entrance. From northern points, State Road 138 leads to the north entrance. Crater Lake Lodge buses operate from mid-June to mid-September from Klamath Falls to Crater Lake. Klamath Falls is served by railroad, and both Klamath and Medford are served by airlines and transcontinental buses.

MOUNT RAINIER NATIONAL PARK

WASHINGTON

Mount Rainier is a towering, forceful presence that exudes an aura of immense power under its glacier-encased heights. For this is more than just a mountain—this is a volcano, a sleeping volcano with the potential to erupt again and blow away its gleaming mantle of snow and ice.

This lofty peak, with its darkly beautiful subalpine forests and flower-covered meadows, can be seen from 100 miles away and is considered to be the most superb landmark of the Pacific Northwest. It comes as no surprise, then, that the 378-square-mile park created around this mountain has become a popular rendezvous for hikers, mountain climbers, nature lovers, campers, and skiers.

The formation of Mount Rainier and its famous glaciers are recent events on the geological calendar. One million years ago successive volcanic eruptions created this rocky spire, followed by massive glaciers that descended on its slopes to sculpture its present shape. The last major volcanic activity occurred a mere two hundred years ago, when pumice was spewed out over the mountain's snow-clad sides.

Mount Rainier's glacier system, the largest "single peak" system in the lower forty-eight states, consists of 35 square miles of ice in twenty-seven named glaciers. Because of these glaciers, the mountain appears higher, more varied than it otherwise would. Because of them too, there are deep valleys separated by high craggy ridges or broad plateaus like those found at such places as Sunrise. From these overlooks, the view drops off into valley depths 1,600 feet below, then abruptly soars up the slopes of Mount Rainier. The mountain's height is thus accentuated by the glacial valleys.

Mount Rainier, as it is enjoyed today, will not last long in terms of geological time. The mountain is quite capable of reawakening any day, perhaps in an eruption violent enough to destroy it. Mount Rainier's identity as a volcano, if not immediately obvious from its size and shape, is betrayed by two craters on its summit. Evidence of the energy still ebbing within the craters is seen at caves along their rims where steam has melted tunnels in the summit ice cap. Exploration parties have crossed the east crater beneath its floor and descended as far as 400 feet below the surface by following these passages. Others have "swum" in a small lake beneath the snows of the west crater. In emergencies, climbers have taken shelter from howling blizzards in the warm steam caves.

The Mount Rainier summit climb is a trip made by more than 2,500 persons each year. Two days are usually needed: the first, to reach base camp; the second, to reach the summit and return to the starting points. Endurance and determination are prerequisites, but the effort is entirely worthwhile. The impression of Mount Rainier as a presence linked in some eternal bond to earth, stars, and infinity is rarely felt, but when it is, the impression comes most often to those on the upper slopes. Author Thomas Hardy wrote of this feeling:

> To persons standing alone on the hill during a clear night such as this, the roll of the world eastward is almost a palpable movement. The sensation may be caused by the panoramic glide of the stars past earthly objects, which is perceptible in a few minutes of stillness, or by the better outlook upon space that the hill affords, or by the wind, or by the solitude; but whatever its origin, the impression of riding along is vivid and abiding.

At 14,410 feet, Mount Rainier reaches into the upper atmosphere to disturb great tides of moist maritime air as they flow eastward from across the Pacific. The resulting encounter creates spectacular cloud halos, wrings out the air, and produces a prodigious amount of snowfall. Paradise Park, located at 5,400 feet on the mountain's south slope, commonly has enough snow to bury the three-story-high Paradise Inn right up to its roof. Even so, the road to Paradise is usually kept open in winter for visitors. When the weather is right, the trip can be most rewarding.

Snowfall is heaviest from Paradise Park up to 9,500 feet. At that height the mountain rears above the wet maritime air masses and the amount of snowfall decreases.

So overwhelming is the presence of Mount Rainier that too little attention is paid to the park's encircling forest. Like all the old-growth forests of the Pacific Northwest, it is a classic of its kind. Douglas fir, red cedars, and western hemlock soar more than 200 feet above mossy, fern-draped valley floors. There is a closeness, a solemnity, in this forest that imparts a feeling of remoteness, particularly in places like Ohanapecosh and Carbon. Tacoma, Seattle, and their urban counterparts are not just a few miles away— they seem not to exist at all.

Ohanapecosh is in the lowland; its forest is like that of many areas in the Puget Sound region. The tall, massive and lush look of this forest provides a pleasant interlude for arriving park visitors and for those campers who stay at such areas at Ohanapecosh or Cougar Rock. In a way, the lowland forest might be considered a dramatic ploy on the part of nature, for it hides Mount Rainier from those entering the park and lowers the curtain for those who are leaving.

Because of the openness of the subalpine landscape, wildlife is easy to find. Deer and mountain goats may be seen in the distance, but marmots are of most interest to the majority of visitors. Nobody who walks through the open meadows just below tree line can escape being noticed by these furry rodents. From beside burrows and among rocks, they watch, they whistle, they pose, and otherwise busy themselves with affairs of animal importance. With patience, one can usually get close enough to marmots to take good pictures.

Paradise is undoubtedly the most popular single area in the national park, though other subalpine areas rival it in beauty. Sunrise, on the northeast flank of Mount Rainier, offers the most sweeping road views of the mountain and the string of volcanic peaks towering above the Cascade Range.

There are 300 miles of fascinating hiking trails to explore. Fishing is permitted (no license required) from the end of May through October. For horseback riding routes, write the superintendent or ask a ranger. Horses can be rented outside the park at nearby stables. Mount Rainier presents a formidable challenge to mountain climbers, and one-day climbing schools, guided summit climbs, and five-day climbing seminars are conducted from Rainier Mountaineering, Inc., at Paradise. For further information, write: Rainier Mountaineering, Inc., 201 St. Helens, Tacoma, WA 98402. Bus tours leaving from the Olympic Hotel are available for a fee from Gray Line Tours, 415 Seneca St., Seattle, WA 98101.

On weekends and holidays from December through April, ski tows operate at Paradise. Inner-tube and platter sliding is permitted on the slopes near the visitor center, and snacks, equipment, and ski lessons are available on weekends and holidays. Private snowmobiles are permitted on designated roads. For winter sports information, write: Paradise Ski Tows, Inc., 11122 Pacific Avenue, Tacoma, WA 98444.

LODGING:Within the park there are Paradise Inn, a convivial hostelry with guest rooms, dining room, gift shop, cocktail lounge, and snack bar; and National Park Inn, a small rustic wooden hostel with dining room and gift shop. Paradise Inn is open from mid-June until early September. National Park Inn is open from early May until mid-October. For reservations and rates, write: Mt. Rainier National Park Hospitality Service, 4820 S. Washington, Tacoma, WA 98409. Other facilities include Paradise Visitor Center, where movies, literature, a cafeteria, gift shop, and church service are available.

The park has seven campgrounds, including Sunshine Point, an all-year location near the Nisqually entrance, and Sunrise, a walk-in site. Stays are limited to fourteen days. Backcountry permits are required and are free. There are no trailer utility hookups in the park, but there is a trailer dumping station at Cougar Rock Campground. Other facilities include piped drinking water, flush toilets, refuse cans, parking and tent pads, fireplaces, tables, and benches. A backcountry camping permit is required.

HOW TO GET THERE: The nearest principal cities are Seattle, 106 miles, and Tacoma, 74 miles, northwest of the park. Yakima, east of the park, is also served by Hughes Airwest. Rental cars are available in all three cities. From Tacoma, on Interstate 5, take State Road 7 to Elbe, where State Road 706 leads to the southwest entrance; State Road 410 leads to the northeast entrance. From Yakima, U.S. Highway 12 and State Road 410 lead to the south and east park entrances respectively. From June to mid-September, daily bus service is available from Tacoma to Seattle. Write to Rainier Hospitality Service, Box 1136, Tacoma, WA 98401.

NORTH CASCADES NATIONAL PARK

WASHINGTON

The Cascade Range of the American Northwest is tangible proof that breathtaking alpine scenery is not solely confined to the European Alps. Within the borders of North Cascades National Park you can gaze on hundreds of majestic mountain peaks, precipitous canyons, more than three hundred glaciers, and countless lakes and streams that flow through lushly forested slopes and ravines.

Established by an act of the 90th Congress in 1968, the North Cascades group has four distinct areas—the North and South units of the park, and the Ross Lake and Lake Chelan national recreations areas. This magnificent park of 1,053 square miles conserves an outstanding part of the extensive North Cascades mountain range near the Canadian border. More than ninety-nine percent of the land in the North Cascades group is federally owned.

Included within the park are two former wilderness study areas—Picket Range Wilderness in the North Unit and Eldorado Peaks Wilderness in the South Unit. Three dams, which impound Ross, Diablo, and Gorge lakes, provide electrical power for Seattle. Diablo and Ross Lakes have minimum drawdown in summer and offer quality recreation.

Ross Lake is 24 miles long, 2 miles across at its greatest width, and covers about 12,000 acres. Diablo Lake is 910 acres and Gorge Lake 210 acres. Lake Chelan is 55 miles long and from 1 to 2 miles wide for most of its length; only the northerly 5 miles and about 2,000 acres are within Lake Chelan National Recreation Area.

The Cascades rank among the world's great mountain ranges. Extending from Canada's Fraser River south beyond Oregon, they are major topographic features, shaping the climate and vegetation over much of the Pacific Northwest.

Formed of weather-resistant rocks, the high stretch of the Cascades intercepts some of the continent's wettest prevailing winds. The resultant heavy precipitation has produced a region of hanging glaciers and icefalls, great ice aprons and ice caps, hanging valleys, waterfalls, alpine lakes nestled in glacial cirques, and glacier-carved canyons such as Stehekin, at the head of Lake Chelan. This lake occupies a glacial trough exceeding 8,500 feet in depth from lake bottom to valley crest—one of the deepest gorges on the continent.

The plant communities show a tremendous variation between the moisture-laden west side of the mountains and the dry east slopes. These plant communities range from rain forest through subalpine coniferous, verdant meadows, and alpine tundra back down to pine forests and sunny, dry shrublands.

Mountain goats, deer, and black bears are common in the wilderness. Less common are the wolverine, marten, fisher, grizzly bear, cougar, and moose. White-tailed ptarmigan and a host of other smaller birds and mammals make their home here. In winter, large numbers of bald eagles can be seen along the Skagit River, where they feed on salmon.

Outdoor recreation can be enjoyed year round. The lower elevations and the big lakes are accessible from early April to mid-October, but at higher elevations the season is from mid-July to mid-September. The western side of the North Cascades gets more rain, has more lakes and streams, and more abundant vegetation. Consequently, it has less sunshine and cooler days than the eastern side of the mountains, where more sunshine, warm rock surfaces, and sparse vegetation offer warm days and cool nights typical of a dry climate.

You will enjoy sightseeing by car on the North Cascades Highway (Wash. 20), Wash. 542, and Cascade River Road; by scheduled boat service on Diablo Lake and Lake Chelan; and by private plane or local charter flights.

Perhaps the most dramatic experience is afforded by views of the high-country glaciers and snowfields contrasting with the greens of open mountain ridges and the heavily forested valleys. Such views are possible only when seen as a panorama from an airplane or from selected vantage points on sites that can be reached only on foot.

Primitive backcountry campsites are accessible by well-defined trails. Colonial Creek and Goodell are developed drive-in campgrounds off Wash. 20 in Ross Lake National Recreation Area.

About 345 miles of hiking and horse trails exist throughout the four areas of the North Cascades group. Permits, required for all backcountry camping, may be obtained at any of the park offices or ranger stations. Horsemen may bring their own animals. Horses and mules are for rent at rural communities on the west, east, and south approaches to the park and recreation areas. Professional guide and packtrain services are available.

Both the North and South units of the park have many high peaks to challenge the mountain climber. For safety, it is recommended that parties have three or more climbers, be equipped with internationally recognized climbing gear, and register names of the party, destination, name of mountain, and approximate days of climb.

Fishing for sport is a principal activity. Besides the two big lakes, there are many small mountain and valley lakes and countless streams. The principal game fish are trout—rainbow, Eastern brook, cutthroat, and Dolly Varden. A Washington State fishing license is required, and state laws apply.

The waters of the lakes and rivers are very cold. Even in August, water activities are mainly confined to boating and fishing.

Hunting is permitted in both the Ross Lake and Lake Chelan national recreation areas. A Washington State hunting license is required, and state laws apply. Hunting is not permitted in the North and South units of North Cascades National Park.

There are no developed ski areas in the North Cascades group, but cross-country skiing is gaining in popularity. Well-developed areas are in national forests to the east, south, and west.

LODGING: For reservations to the limited guest accommodations within or adjacent to the park, write: Diablo Lake Resort, P.O. Box 194, Rockport, WA 98282; or Ross Lake Resort, P.O. Box 194, Rockport, WA 98282; or North Cascades Lodge, Stehekin, WA 98852. Ample tourist accommodations are available within a few hours' drive from the park at Rockport and Stehekin. For reservations, write to the chambers of commerce of these towns.

HOW TO GET THERE: In northwest Washington, the nearest principal city is Seattle. Commuter planes schedule frequent flights from Seattle to Bellingham, west of the park. Rental cars are available in both cities. State Road 20 passes through the park, connecting Interstate 5 on the west and U.S. Highway 97 on the east. From the east, take North Cascades Highway, or boat and floatplane transportation is available into Stehekin Valley from Chelan.

OLYMPIC NATIONAL PARK

WASHINGTON

Witnessing the birth of a mountain range would be an awesome event to experience if it were possible. But since the creation of a mountain range takes millions of years to accomplish, the closest we can come to experiencing such a spectacle is the Olympic National Park in Washington.

The park is located in the heart of the Olympic Mountains, a geologically new mountain range that has not yet lost its pristine freshness to the onslaughts of wind, rain, and snow. Olympic's peaks tower sharp and clear against the sky, crowned by the glorious glacier-capped Mount Olympus, which rises 7,965 feet into the air.

Olympic National park isn't all just bare mountains,

however. Indeed, this park includes one of the rarest features found anywhere on earth—a richly verdant and dense temperate rain forest. In addition, a separate stretch of parkland sweeps right down to the very edge of the Pacific Ocean, where the surf pounds against headland cliffs, sandy beaches, and rocky offshore islands which are sanctuary to a thriving wildlife population of birds, seals, and other marine animals.

Olympic is a veritable gift of the sea—of the sea and its life-giving rains. Clouds borne on the moist sea winds bring rain and snow to the mountain heights, there to join the glacier-fed rivers which return the precious moisture once again to the sea.

This cycle, so compacted in space that it is easily seen from favored vantage points, recalls the ancient wisdom of Ecclesiastes:

All the rivers run into the sea; yet the sea is not full; unto the place whence the rivers come, thither they return again.

But if Olympic is a place given to understanding nature's cycles, it is also a lavish presentment of nature's beauty. Olympic, in a word, in inclusive; it offers much to all.

For those who would understand the natural aspect in terms of its geology, Olympic is a classic example of an area at the cutting edge of continental drift. In the past seventy million years—a mere moment in earth time—these mountains have been squeezed upward along a contact zone between two giant crustal plates. From the west, the Juan de Fuca oceanic plate advances at a rate of no more than two inches per year.

Molten rock, oozing up from the ocean bottom 260 miles west, pushed the crustal segment with inexorable force. At the Olympic Peninsula the moving crust meets the North American continental plate. Ponderously, relentlessly, the eastward-moving crust slides beneath the continent, its top layers separating and piling upward to form the Olympic Range. These top layers, composed primarily of ocean-floor sediments, are the building material for the Olympics. Because of the great temperatures and pressures involved in earth movements, some rocks in the layers have been changed into forms so different from their original appearance that only geologists can recognize them.

Volcanism played a role in the creation of the Olympics too, but here lava welled up through fissures, not from great volcanic cones. Much of the volcanic rock is found along the eastern edge of the park. In most places, emerging lava cooled beneath ancient seas, often forming rounded, pillow-shaped outcroppings now seen on exposed slopes. Where the lava flows were especially thick, they have eroded into jagged peaks like The Needles.

At any time of the year, rains may last for days. Particularly is this true from October through March, when more than three-fourths of Olympic's precipitation falls. Temperatures near sea level remain mild, usually reaching only the low 20s C (low 70s F) in summer and remain between 0 and 10 degrees C (30s and 40s F) during the winter.

Whether flowing seaward or pausing in lakes, water is the delight of Olympic visitors. In its multitude of variations, from sparkling streams to heavy surf, it calls forth the mood of the moment. There is music in a mountain stream that is quite unlike that of surf, yet both become a part of those who hear them, and for those who listen best the music is endless.

In the form of glacial ice, water has been especially active in creating the geography of this region. The Strait of Juan de Fuca is the legacy of a giant continental glacier which pushed down the Puget Sound region. On a lesser scale, alpine glaciers carved many U-shaped valleys in the Olympic Mountains. Sometimes, too, these alpine glaciers left valleys as they melted. When this happened, lakes were created, among them Lakes Quinault and Cushman. Today, small remnant-glaciers continue to wear away at the high country in the Olympics. Perpetuating them is the greatest amount of snowfall in the contiguous forty-eight states—at least 40 feet per year.

Botanists have long delighted in pointing out that Olympic has one of the world's few temperate rain forests. Because of this, a visit to these forests, located chiefly in the westward sloping valleys of the Quinault, Queets, Hoh, and Bogachiel rivers, will be quite instructive. Those who would find inspiration will also profit by such a visit. The rain forest is often compared to a cathedral, the high arching branches and soft light being suggestive of that comparison. The rain forest environment is most conveniently seen at the Hoh Rain Forest Visitor Center. Here, the great stands of western hemlock, Sitka spruce, western red cedar, big-leaf maple, and other species are at their best. Overhanging branches are draped with air-loving club moss and lichens. Everything, in fact, looks green—including the air.

Like the climate and vegetation, the wildlife in Olympic includes just about every category imaginable—as one writer put it, creatures that may be "furry, feathered, segmented, or scaly." Casual summer visitors shouldn't be surprised at seeing deer anywhere in the park. Hurricane Ridge, with its alpine meadows, is probably the easiest place to see deer and to be seen by the dozens of marmots which colonize the slope near Hurricane Ridge Lodge. These large burrowing rodents are adept people-watchers. An animal sharing the marmots' interest in people on a less-frequent basis is the black bear. Curiosity among the bears, however, is motivated by food—in picnic baskets, ice chests, and backpacks. Careless visitors can expect to have their equipment damaged by bears and by rodents. Hikers in the backcountry would do well to hang their packs at least 12 feet above ground overnight or during side trips.

Roosevelt elk, once nearly exterminated by hunting, are also seen frequently, especially along roads and river trails during the winter. The elk usually group together in small bands. With the onset of warm weather, most elk and deer move into the high country. Even higher in the mountains are small bands of goats. Though visitors to the more open high country can expect to see more animals than forest visitors, goats are a rare sight. Along rivers, lakes, and the coast is wildlife of a different sort. Harbor seals, river otters, raccoons, and shorebirds are common. Migrating gray whales may even be seen off the coast in the spring and fall.

All is not biology in Olympic. A park for the people, this mountain-and-sea wilderness promises challenges in whatever form man may wish them. Above the alpine zone, on the sharp-faced crags and jagged peaks, those men and women who have learned the ways of mountaineering find their challenges. Favored by many mountaineers is the climb to Mount Olympus, highest peak in the park. Most often, the venture begins at the Hoh Ranger Station, 16.6 miles away, in the lowland rain forest. Winding upward through thinning forest, the trail crosses Glacier Meadows and then continues above tree line to Blue Glacier. Climbers crossing the glacier must rope up, as they again must do after climbing the Snow Dome to the summit pinnacle. Typically, the climb is challenging and demands considerable technical skill and practical knowledge.

Less technical, but no less demanding in its relationship with the land, is trail hiking. Olympic is a hikers' park, and as any backpacker will acknowledge, you can never know any large national park, much less this one, until you have been afoot in the backcountry. Mountain building, the water cycle, weather, wildlife, and plant life are then best experienced on the personal level. The end result, of course, is the affect the backcountry has on your soul.

For hikers along beaches there are cliffs, sea stacks, tide pools, and countless beachcombers' delights cast upon the shore by the ceaseless surf. During summer and early autumn, the favorite hiking seasons, the rain forest trails lead along springy fern-dappled and moss-draped pathways. In the high country, alpine meadows carpeted with wild flowers and lush with grass invite hikers to marvel in feeling their strength and vigor—their enthusiasm for life—responding to these surroundings.

Motorists at Olympic have the advantages and disadvantages inherent in travel by highway. More places may be seen in a short time, but the chances of in-depth experience increase with the amount of time spent in any one particular place. If your time is limited, spend a few hours in each of a small number of selected places. The decision to see everything is, unfortunately, one that very often leads to superficial park visits.

Parks such as Olympic, when experienced to their fullest, can bring people to an appreciation of man's bond with the wild, and to a realization that no part of life can be completely separated from any other part.

Visitor centers provide audiovisual programs, talks, exhibits, and literature. In summer, self-guiding or ranger-led nature trails and evening campfire programs are conducted. Spur roads lead to scenic points of interest. Swimming and fishing (no license required) are popular, and mountain climbs vary in difficulty. Pack and saddle stock rentals are available in Port Angeles, Quilcene, Amanda Park, and Forks, Washington, for exploring the 600 miles of hiking trails. All-expense bus tours, ranging from three hours to two days, can be arranged through Grayline of the Olympics, 107 East Front Street, Port Angeles, WA 98362. The park also attracts winter sports enthusiasts. Ski rentals and services, food, refreshments, and Indian handicraft displays are available during winter at Hurricane Ridge, a day-use lodge.

LODGING: Within the Sol Duc Hot Springs area, accommodations include motels, housekeeping cabins, trailer park, rental equipment, groceries, and gift shops. Lake Crescent Lodge, at the foot of Storm King Mountain, also provides modern motel and cottage accommodations. For reservations, write: National Park Concessions, Inc., Star Route No. 1, Port

Angeles, WA 98362. Reservations for accommodations at Kalaloch Beach, La Push, and Port Angeles can be made by writing to the park superintendent.

Park campgrounds provide tables, fireplaces, piped water, and toilet facilities, but no showers, laundries, or utility hookups. Of the numerous campgrounds the major ones are Kalaloch, Heart O' the Hills, Mora, Fairholm, Hoh, and Soleduck. Low elevation campgrounds remain open all year, but the higher areas operate from late June to early November. A permit is required for backcountry camping.

HOW TO GET THERE: Seattle, Washington, and Victoria, Canada, are the nearest principal cities. From Victoria, a ferryboat makes connections with Port Angeles, on U.S. Highway 101, just north of the park. From Seattle, buses are available to Port Angeles, where rental cars can be obtained; by car, State Road 104 connects with U.S. Highway 101, which serves the park's north and west entrances and coastal strip.

DENALI NATIONAL PARK

ALASKA

On January 24, 1897, with national attention focused on the Alaska gold rush, a New York newspaper carried a startling story. The author, a gold prospector in Alaska, had traveled inland from Cook Inlet, there to discover a great mountain higher than any he had ever seen before. The experienced mountain man, William A. Dickey, was confident he had gazed upon the highest peak in North America. ". . . It compelled our unbounded admiration," Dickey wrote; ". . . never before had we seen anything to compare with this mountain."

Dickey's article would set others on a course northward, not for gold but to confirm the report of America's grand rival to Mount Everest. The mountain had long been known to the Athabascan Indians by the name *Denali,* "the great one." Soon most of the world would be calling it by the name Dickey gave it after he returned from the wilderness and heard of William McKinley's nomination to the presidency.

Small wonder that the Indians of Alaska called Mount McKinley, Denali. No other mountain in the world, not even in the Himalayas, rises so dramatically above its own base and stands in such lofty isolation over its neighbors. McKinley's summit, crowned by twin peaks, soars to an altitude of 20,320 feet, rising 16,000 feet above the surrounding landscape.

McKinley is by far the most impressive feature of the Alaska Range, a curved chain of mountains that stretches 580 miles across the lower third of Alaska. Though most of the peaks are less than half McKinley's height, the range acts as a natural land barrier between Anchorage, on the coastal lowlands, and Alaska's interior to the north. West of the park the range forms a drainage divide for rivers flowing west to the Bering Sea or south to the Gulf of Alaska.

The park's geology features a portion of the Denali Fault System, the largest crustal break in North America, which stretches for 1,300 miles across the full width of the State of Alaska. Associated with the Alaska Range, the fault passes through the park, separating the most ancient rocks in Alaska from those of much younger age. Events that took place between these extremes have created a beautiful land with contrasting wide, low plains, and dark, somber mountains, brightly colored peaks, and sheer granite domes.

Surprisingly, much of Alaska north of the park was never covered by the last continental ice sheet, which retreated 10,000–14,000 years ago. The park lies at the northern limit of this Ice Age glaciation which covered most of the northern hemisphere. From the park road you can see numerous ice flows still radiating from the high peaks of the Alaska Range, where extreme temperatures keep them from melting. The snout of Muldrow Glacier, 35 miles long, lies within 0.6 mile of the park road. Silt-laden streams that flow from these glaciers form wide gravel bars that serve as natural pathways into the wilderness.

The act creating Mount McKinley National Park was signed by President Wilson in 1917. The name was changed under the Alaska Lands Act of 1980 when the park was merged with the adjacent Denali National Monument to create the Denali National Park and Preserve. With the adjustment in boundaries, the area now totals 5.6 million acres.

Denali's vast wilderness permits a spectacular array of wildlife to live together in a balanced, natural system. Caribou still follow ancient migration patterns as they move in herds of hundreds or more over open tundra and through mountain passes. Sure-footed Dall sheep survey the rugged country from high, rocky slopes, while moose browse below in willow thickets near the spruce forest. In fall or early winter, all three species enter the rut, and the mature males engage in energy-draining battles for the right to breed with adult females.

Wolves roam huge territories in search of weakened caribou, moose, or sheep that may provide their next meal. Ravens, magpies, and gray jays quickly clean up any scraps left over from a kill. The grizzly bear will feed on any carcass it comes across during its ambles along a river bar or over the open tundra, but its dietary staples are grass, roots, blueberries, peavine and ground squirrels that it digs from their burrows.

Beavers cut trees and build dams and lodges. The red squirrel caches spruce cones for the winter. The pika and singing vole carefully lay vegetation in loose piles in the underground nests to which they will retreat once the snow flies. Marsh hawks and short-eared owls swoop low over the tundra in pursuit of voles, ground squirrels, and small birds. The golden eagle soars high overhead looking for small-mammal prey. The lynx hunts the snowshoe hare, its year-round major source of food.

Winter brings severe challenges to subarctic communities. Temperatures become frigid, plant growth ceases, and food is scarce. Grizzly bears meet the problem by fattening up in summer and sleeping most of the winter. Occasionally a grizzly stirs from its deep slumber; but the ground squirrel, a true hibernator, stays curled up, its body functions at a virtual standstill. Beavers and red squirrels subsist on cached foods. The weasel, ptarmigan, and snowshoe hare turn white and continue their struggle for survival above ground under extreme conditions.

Most birds escape the northern winter by flying south. The long-tailed jaeger winters in Japan, the golden plover in Hawaii, the wheatear and arctic warbler in Asia. The arctic tern may travel all the way to Antarctica.

The fragile web of Denali's interdependent wildlife includes 37 mammal species and 130 bird species. Extreme cold prevents most cold-blooded land vertebrates from living in the park; but one amphibian, the wood frog, makes its home here.

During summer, visitors enjoy from sixteen to

twenty-four hours of daylight, which can be used to
tour the park roads; join a wildlife scenic tour, which
departs from the hotel twice daily; arrange for a charter air tour; accept the challenge of a mountain climb;
or fish (no license required) in the lakes and streams.
McKinley Park Hotel provides free conducted nature
walks, husky dog-sled demonstrations, naturalist
talks, hiking, and fishing.

LODGING: The McKinley Park Station Hotel has
ninety-eight rooms and eighty-four railroad sleeping
car accommodations. For reservations, write: Outdoor World, Ltd., McKinley Park, AK 99755. For
three- and four-day "Sourdough Vacations," guided
trips, and a wilderness retreat, write: Camp Denali,
McKinley Park, AK 99755 (June 1 to September 10);
or Box 526, College, AK 99735 (September 11 through
May 31).

Reservations may be made at Igloo, Sanctuary, Tek-
lanika, and Wonder Lake campgrounds by writing to
the superintendent. Wonder Lake (open from June 10
to September 10) has tents only. Riley creek is open all
year, the others from May 25 to October 25. Stays are
for fourteen days. A free backcountry permit is required.

HOW TO GET THERE: From principal airports in Fairbanks and Anchorage, where rental cars are available,
several airlines schedule daily service or charter flights
to the airstrip at McKinley Park, maintained for light
aircraft. From late May to mid-September, the Alaska
Railroad provides daily service from Anchorage and
Fairbanks to the park; twice weekly from September
to May. The train depot and airstrip are near the

visitor center and information stations, where free public transportation is provided. By car, the park is connected with Anchorage and Fairbanks by State Road 3, open all year. From Paxson, Denali Highway (State Road 8) is open during summer only.

GATES OF THE ARCTIC NATIONAL PARK AND PRESERVE

ALASKA

Gates of the Arctic National Park and Preserve is a vast and sometimes hostile region that supports one of the finest remaining unspoiled wildernesses in the world. The park and preserve extend nearly two hundred miles from east to west, covering 8.1 million acres in the central Brooks Range in north central Alaska.

The entire park and preserve area lies north of the Arctic Circle and is about two hundred miles northwest of Fairbanks. It extends from the southern foothills of the Brooks Range, across the mountains' ragged peaks, and down onto the North Slope. Magnificent valleys dissect the range here, many containing clear-water rivers and alpine lakes. A few alpine glaciers occupy the north sides of higher mountains. Most of the park and preserve area, lying north of the tree line, is tundra, vegetated with shrubs and mosses.

Gates of the Arctic is a vast wilderness containing no established National Park Service facilities or trails. The predominant activity here is hiking its long valleys. Excellent hiking terrain is found in the higher elevations' open tundra or sparse shrubs and forest. The Arrigetch Peaks area offers excellent rock and mountain climbing. Hikers, backpackers, and climbers are generally dropped off and picked up by chartered aircraft. These aircraft, variously equipped, can land on either lakes and rivers or river bars.

Many species of wildlife and migratory birds can be found within the park, including grizzlies and black bears, wolves, wolverines, Dall sheep, moose, caribou, marmots, ground squirrels, and eagles. Visitors should remember at all times that these animals are wild and unused to man, and can maim or kill those who fail to respect that fact.

There are also a number of "floatable" rivers in this region, and fishing is generally good. Grayling can be found in clear streams and lakes, lake trout in the larger deep lakes, char in streams on the North Slope, and sheefish and dog salmon in the Kobuk and lower Alatna rivers. Long, cold winters and short, mild summers are the rule in this part of Alaska. On the Brooks Range's southern slopes, mid-summer temperatures may occasionally rise into the upper 20s C (70s and 80s

F) and rarely, the 30s C (80s and 90s F). Highland temperatures are cooler, and on the range's northern flank are between minus 6°C (21°F) and 10°C (50°F); here freezing temperatures occur by early September, sometimes in mid-August. August is also often rainy.

LODGING: There are no established campgrounds, but excellent camping sites are available throughout the park and preserve. Bettles has a lodge, general store, and canoe rentals. Fairbanks has a complete range of retail merchandise and services. A number of guides lead trips through the Brooks Range in summer, and outfitters can supply an array of trip equipment, including boats.

HOW TO GET THERE: Most people approach the central Brooks Range via scheduled flights from Fairbanks to Bettles, and then charter small aircraft in Bettles for flights into the park and preserve. Charter flights into the Brooks Range can also begin in Fairbanks. Air time is generally paid to and from the destination. Additionally, scheduled flights from Bettles to Anaktuvuk Pass, in the center of the park and preserve, are available several times a week.

GLACIER BAY NATIONAL PARK

ALASKA

Two hundred years ago, when Captain George Vancouver sailed up Icy Strait in what is now southeastern Alaska, Glacier Bay virtually did not exist. Its entrance was blocked by a towering wall of ice that marked the seaward outlet of an immense glacier that filled the entire bay basin. So rapidly did this Grand Pacific Glacier recede, however, that today its snout is sixty-five miles farther north and this unique area has been revealed in all its spectacular beauty.

Within the confines of the 3.4-million-acre Glacier Bay National Park you can still see the remnants of a general ice advance which began four thousand years ago. Icebergs, cracked off from near-vertical ice cliffs, dot the waters of the bay against a background of deep fjords and snowcapped mountains with lushly forested slopes.

Sixteen active tidewater glaciers offer a spectacular show of geological forces in action. As water undermines the ice fronts, great blocks of ice up to 200 feet high break loose and crash into the sea, creating huge waves and filling the narrow inlets with massive icebergs.

Muir and Johns Hopkins glaciers discharge such great volumes of ice that it is seldom possible to approach their cliffs closer than two miles. Margerie Glacier, while also very active, is more accessible. From a safe distance of one-half mile, boaters can observe ice falling from the glacier faces.

The snow- and ice-clad mountains of the Fairweather Range are as impressive as the glaciers. The highest peak in the range is 15,320-foot Mount Fairweather. Several other summits, including Mounts Crillon, Quincy Adams, LaPerouse, Lituya, and Salisbury, exceed 10,000 feet. The steepness of their slopes is dramatically visible throughout the upper bay. In Johns Hopkins Inlet, several peaks rise from sea level to 6,500 feet within four miles of the shore. The peaks supply moisture to all glaciers on the peninsula separating Glacier Bay from the Gulf of Alaska.

More than two hundred species of birds have been recorded within Glacier Bay National Park. Many of these are best seen in or near marine environments which supply bountiful and varied food. In Sitakaday Narrows, Adams and Hugh Miller inlets, and the mouth of Glacier Bay, tidal flow is concentrated in narrow and/or shallow portions of the bay, and the resulting water turbulence stirs plankton, shrimp, and fish to the surface. In such locales "feeding frenzies" occur, and large flocks of marbled and Kittlitz's murrelets, black-legged kittiwakes, Bonaparte's gulls, and northern phalaropes gather.

The recent recession of glaciers that once covered Glacier Bay and nearby lowlands has opened a new landscape for pioneering animals as well as plants. Many mammals have shown special means to speed recolonization. Black and brown bears, river otters, and mink are able to swim around ice barricades that prevent access by other land animals. Mountain goats and hoary marmots live in alpine meadows where vegetation receives a head start on ridges exposed first by the waning ice.

Humpback and killer whales, and Dall and harbor porpoises have found open marine corridors to the front of retreating tidewater glaciers. Harbor seals select densely packed icebergs at the face of Muir and Johns Hopkins glaciers for pupping grounds.

Halibut, salmon, Dolly Varden and cutthroat trout occupy Glacier Bay waters. Sport fishing is permitted under regulations established by the Alaska Department of Fish and Game, and fishing licenses are required. Boats for charter may be obtained at Bartlett Cove.

Park naturalists conduct daily hikes, evening programs, and other activities at Glacier Bay Lodge. Hiking trails of various lengths are maintained at the Bartlett Cove area.

LODGING: Glacier Bay Lodge at Bartlett Cove is operated from about mid-May to mid-September. Rooms and meals are available. For reservations, write: Glacier Bay Lodge, Glacier Bay National Park,

Gustavus, AK 99826, during the operating season; and Glacier Bay Lodge, Inc., 312 Park Place Bldg., Seattle, WA 98101, the remainder of the year. Tour boats make daily cruises from the lodge to the glaciers.

Only one campground is maintained in the park, and that is located at Bartlett Cove. However, the park's several hundred miles of shoreline, islands, and alpine meadows offer nearly unlimited camping and hiking opportunities.

HOW TO GET THERE: Glacier Bay is situated at the northwest end of the Alexander Archipelago, in southeastern Alaska. There are no roads to the park, and access is by various types of commercial transport, including regularly scheduled and charter air services, cruise ships and charter boats, private boats, and tours via kayak.

By boat, the distance from Juneau is about one hundred miles. Flying time from Juneau is about thirty minutes. An airfield is at Gustavus, just outside the park. Otherwise, landing is restricted to salt water.

KATMAI NATIONAL PARK

ALASKA

Katmai National Park is an enigmatic land, born of fire and ice, where the hissing steam of sleeping volcanoes seeps up among the icy peaks of the indomitable Aleutian Range. But below this alpine region of contradictions lies still another land—a land of picturesque island-studded lakes, coniferous forests, sharply etched fjords, and surf-pounded beaches—where scores of birds and animals make their homes beside the incomparable Alaska brown bear and the bald eagle.

Katmai National Park is both a recreational retreat and a scientific laboratory; it is a place to study, to explore, and to discover unspoiled nature. It is a home

271

for wildlife, and it is a mecca for the curious, the adventurous, and the seeker of beauty.

Your first foray into Katmai will probably be through Naknek Lake, which is part of a system of rivers, streams, marshes, ponds, and elongate lakes formed in valleys eroded by glacial ice. Naknek, largest of the lakes, is bordered by mountains that rise three thousand feet above its pumice beaches. The lower slopes of these and other mountains of the lake country are blanketed with dense stands of spruce and birch. The forests merge into the tundra of the higher slopes, where wild flowers abound in summer.

Beyond the lake region is the backbone of the peninsula, the ice-shrouded Aleutian Range. Glaciers carve the slopes and valleys of these volcanic mountains, some of which emit smoke and steam. Major eruptions can be expected at any time on the Aleutian Peninsula. Mt. Mageik, Mt. Martin, and Mt. Trident have erupted in recent time. The ash-filled Valley of Ten Thousand Smokes is evidence of the forces at work in this dynamic land.

The mountains of the Aleutians rise seven thousand feet above the seas of the Shelikof Coast. Deep bays, rock shoals, wide beaches, sheer cliffs, narrow fjords, and intricate coves are part of the one-hundred-mile coastline. Beyond the beaches and the bays, the land opens into wide valleys separated by the rugged mountains. Sea lions, sea otters, seals, moose, brown bears, bald eagles, and many other animal species live along the coast.

In the lower elevations of Katmai, forests of white spruce, balsam, poplar, and birch are mixed with thickets of alder and willow, and grasslands dominated by bluejoint and bluegrass. Many hills and knolls are covered with blueberry, crowberry, and dwarf birch. At higher elevations, only low-growing plants typical of the Arctic tundra survive the cold climate, strong winds, and short growing season.

Where thick ash deposits occur, as in the Valley of Ten Thousand Smokes, plants are scarce. Lichens and other pioneer plants are beginning to appear where soil and moisture are present.

The varied plant life and Katmai's great diversity of habitats provide food, protection, and breeding grounds for many animal species, including more than thirty species of land mammals. The Alaska brown bear is the most prominent mammal at Katmai. Most brown bears weigh between five hundred and one thousand pounds; larger animals are occasionally seen. In this natural system they may be observed in most of the park from early spring until late fall.

Moose live in most parts of the coastal lake regions, while the forest and pond areas are inhabited by river otter, mink, marten, weasel, and beaver. Red fox, arctic fox, wolf, lynx, and wolverine are predators that help control the rodent population.

Coastal waters abound with marine life, including sea lions, hair seals, and sea otters.

Whistling swans, ducks, loons, grebes, and terns nest on lake edges and in marshes. Grouse and ptarmigan are plentiful in the upland areas. More than forty species of songbirds spend their summers at Katmai. Seabirds are abundant on the coast, along with bald eagles, hawks, falcons, and owls which nest on rock pinnacles and treetops.

The freshwater lakes and streams at Katmai are important spawning grounds for several salmon species. Each summer nearly a million salmon return to the

Naknek system after spending several years in ocean waters. These salmon complete their life cycles by laying eggs for new generations.

You can travel by small boat to many parts of the park. Concessioner boats will take you on fishing and scenic tours to any part of Naknek Lake. You may wish to go ashore to explore the beach, forest, or tundra.

A four-wheel-drive "bus" travels daily over a winding trail from Brooks River to the Valley of Ten Thousand Smokes. The trail ends on a hill overlooking the valley. A foot trail descends into the valley and to the edge of volcanic deposits. Ranger-naturalists accompany the tour groups.

Charter aircraft are available at King Salmon for scenic flights when the weather is favorable. You will see the bays, fjords, and waterfalls of the rugged coastal section; and in the mountain region, glacier-clad mountains, smoking volcanic peaks, and the jade-green crater lake of Mount Katmai. Your flight passes over the Valley of Ten Thousand Smokes and deep, narrow gorges that have been eroded in the volcanic deposits. In the lake region, you will see island-studded bays, alpine lakes, and the great expanse of Naknek Lake.

LODGING: Wien Air Alaska (4100 International Airport Road, Anchorage, AK 99502) provides accommodations and services at Brooks River and Lake Grosvenor. Package tours from Anchorage are available from June 1 until Labor Day. Facilities at Brooks River Lodge on Naknek Lake include a modern lodge and cabins with plumbing. Meals are provided at the lodge. The bus tour to the Valley of Ten Thousand

Smokes begins here. Facilities at Lake Grosvenor
Camp include a dining room and cabins without
plumbing. Fishing equipment and guide-operated
boats can be rented at both Brooks River and Lake
Grosvenor.

You may camp anywhere in the park. You should
become familiar with the precautions to be taken when
camping in bear country. Fire permits, required for
backcountry camping, are available at the Brooks
River Ranger Station or at headquarters in King Salmon.

A National Park Service campground with tables,
water, wood, firepits, shelters, and a food cache is
located at Brooks River. A fire permit is not required.
Camping supplies and groceries should be obtained
before visiting the park. Camper tents and stoves can
be rented from the concessioner. Fuel is available.

HOW TO GET THERE: Katmai is 290 air miles southwest of Anchorage. Daily commercial jet flights connect Anchorage with King Salmon. Travel from King
Salmon to Brooks River is by amphibious bush aircraft.

KENAI FJORDS NATIONAL PARK

ALASKA

The tempestuous Gulf of Alaska and steeply rugged Kenai Mountain Range combine to create a region of stark contrast and wild beauty in south central Alaska. The Kenai Peninsula, site of the 587,000-acre Kenai Fjords National Park, is bathed year round in moist sea air that blows in off the gulf and presses up against the rocky slopes of these englaciated promontories.

So much precipitation falls in this cool climate that the 800-square-mile Harding Icefield buries all but the tops of the central mountain range. This nearly flat icefield stands almost one mile above the Gulf of Alaska, radiating glaciers out in all directions. To the southeast they reach down to the Kenai Fjords, where several tidewater glaciers calve directly into salt water.

Mountain ridges extend into the Gulf of Alaska, their seaward ends depressed by tectonic forces so that only mountaintops remain above sea level. Glaciers carved the submerged valleys between these jagged ridges. When the glaciers receded and were replaced by the ocean, the valleys became fjords.

The ends of peninsulas, free of ice for at least several hundred years, support mature rain forests. Along the shoreline, bald eagles nest in the spruce and hemlock trees. Mountain goats inhabit the rocky slopes above tree line, while sea otters live in the shallow an protected bays and lagoons.

Harbor seals summer in the waters and on icebergs calved from tidewater glaciers. Steller's sea lions live on the rocky offshore islands at the entrances to Aialik Bay and Nuka Bay. Thousands of seabirds seasonally rear their young on the steep cliffs and offshore islands of the Kenai Fjords.

Entering the Kenai Fjords by boat is a popular and rewarding experience. Seabirds, sea lions, seals, porpoise, and whales are frequently sighted along this rugged coastline. Here, too, you can watch tidewater glaciers in Aialik Bay, Northwestern Lagoon, and Nuka Bay actively calve huge blocks of ice. Fishing for salmon and bottom fish is usually productive, but the steep terrain throughout Kenai Fjords limits camping and hiking.

The Harding Icefield that blankets the mountaintops is awesome and beautiful. Air charters out of Seward, Homer, and Anchorage provide spectacular views of the icefield, glaciers, and coastline.

Crossing the icefield or glaciers on foot or skis is

recommended only for experienced and well-equipped mountaineers. Crevasses and foul weather pose the main dangers here. Experience, skill, good equipment, and stamina are required for successful icefield and glacial travel.

The Kenai Fjords are rugged, remote, and exposed to the tempestuous Gulf of Alaska. Strong currents flow past them and few landing sites exist. You are strongly advised to employ an experienced guide and seaworthy craft. Boaters entering the fjords without a guide should be very experienced and first seek information on landing sites, weather conditions, and navigational hazards from the National Park Service or the U.S. Coast Guard.

LODGING: Seward and Homer have hotels, motels, campgrounds, food, and most supplies. Contact their chambers of commerce for more information. There are no campgrounds in the park.

HOW TO GET THERE: Seward and Homer are within a few hours' drive of Anchorage, where air transport, both scheduled and charter, is available. Seward has bus service from Anchorage. Charter boats and aircraft are available in both communities. The state ferry system connects Seward, Homer, Kodiak, and Prince William Sound, and passes along the coast of Kenai Fjords. Seward, closest to the park, is the usual starting point for trips into the park area.

KOBUK VALLEY NATIONAL PARK

ALASKA

Some 25 miles north of the Arctic Circle lies an isolated, forested valley nestled in a natural semi-enclosed bowl formed by the Baird Mountains on the north and the Waring Mountains to the south. This is Kobuk Valley National Park, a 1,710,000-acre wilderness that transects the central portion of the Kobuk River approximately 350 miles west-northwest of Fairbanks. Although the park is flanked by the villages of Kiana and Ambler, the nearest town of any size is the regional center of Kotzebue, 75 miles to the west on Kotzebue Sound.

The boreal (northern) forest reaches its northern limit in the park, resulting in an open woodland of small trees in a mat of mosses and stunted shrubs. The

Great Kobuk Sand Dunes and the Little Kobuk Sand Dunes extend over some 25 square mile south of the Kobuk River. Relict plants, remnants of the flora that existed during the Pleistocene epoch, still survive in the valley, where the climate approximates Ice Age conditions. The Salmon River flows out of the Baird Mountains and runs clear and swift to the Kobuk River. Inland Eskimos still live off the resources of the lands and waters in the valley, continuing the pattern of subsistence that has existed for thousands of years.

The park is a large expanse of wild land in which the National Park Service has no facilities, trails, or services. Visitors will be interested in backpacking in the Baird and Waring mountains and along their foothills and valleys. Most areas present good terrain for hiking, although stands of willows will be encountered occasionally. The Great Kobuk Sand Dunes are an unusual and interesting phenomenon which can be reached by an easy hike from the river.

The Kobuk River flows placidly through the park, and interesting river trips are possible in both motorized and non-motorized craft. The Salmon River is a fine river for canoeing and kayaking. Wildlife in the park includes grizzly bear, black bear, caribou, moose, wolves, and lynx. Grayling, arctic char, sheefish, and several species of salmon inhabit the waters within the park.

Long, cold winters and warm, brief summers characterize the park. Temperatures within the park during June, July, and August range from 40°F to 90°F, with daytime highs often in the 80s. June and July are usually the clearest months, with rain increasing in August and September. Winter temperatures can drop to -60°F, and -20°F is common.

LODGING: There are no campgrounds within the park. Camping is permitted throughout most of the park; however it is not permitted in sensitive archeological zones where it would interrupt subsistence activities, or upon private inholdings along the Kobuk River without the consent of the owners. A hotel is located in Kotzebue and some lodgings are available in Kiana, but there are no commercial lodgings at present in Ambler.

HOW TO GET THERE: Northwestern Alaska cannot be reached by road. There are daily commercial flights to Kotzebue from both Anchorage and Fairbanks, and there are connecting flights to Kiana and Ambler. From Kotzebue, direct access to the park can be gained by light charter aircraft. Aircraft can also be chartered in Ambler and Kiana, though arrangements should be made in advance. Aircraft charters cost approximately $130 to $200 per hour for two to four passengers. Aircraft landings occur on primitive airstrips and gravel bars, and float-equipped planes can land on the river. Boats can also at times be chartered in Kiana and Ambler. Backpackers can walk into the park from either Ambler or Kiana.

LAKE CLARK NATIONAL PARK AND PRESERVE

ALASKA

Steaming volcanoes, craggy peaks, blue-green glaciers, and sparkling lakes—these are just some of the natural wonders to be found in Lake Clark National Park and Preserve. This 3.6-million-acre park, which straddles the convergence of the Alaska and Aleutian mountain ranges, is located about one hundred miles southwest of Anchorage, across Cook Inlet from the Kenai Peninsula. It encompasses an extremely beautiful yet rugged wilderness where eagles, hawks, waterfowl, seabirds, bear, moose, caribou, and Dall sheep roam at will.

The park and preserve bear few marks of human activity. Opportunities to see, photograph, and experience nature as it has evolved are many. Predominantly wilderness in character, the park and preserve particularly appeal to hikers, backpackers, and climbers seeking relatively low but challenging mountains. You can camp out in solitude, observe abundant wildlife, run numerous rivers, sport fish in both park and preserve, and sport hunt in the preserve.

These activities can be arduous and require both stamina and wilderness skills, depending on the area. But lakeshore and coastal areas, game trails, river bars, and ridges provide less demanding opportunities to enjoy magnificent natural resources. Those with limited time may fly over the area, seeing majestic panoramas of mountains, volcanoes, glaciers, forests, waterfalls, rivers, and lakes. An overflight can be rewarding and memorable, reflecting the vast, awesome, and beautiful nature of Alaska.

Sport fishing is good in many waters of the park and preserve. Grayling, northern pike, and several trout and salmon species can be caught throughout most of the season of open water. Sport hunting, chiefly for caribou and moose, is permitted in the preserve in season with licenses, fees, and bag limits set by the Alaska Department of Fish and Game.

Local residents carry on the subsistence way of life within the national park and preserve. Their camps, fishnets, and other equipment are critical to their well-being. Please observe the usual courtesies respecting their property and their privacy.

Winter travel is recommended only to those experienced in cold-weather camping and survival techniques. Temperatures can plummet to −40°F or lower. Conditions for cross-country skiing and similar activities are best in March and early April, before the thawing lakes and streams make all travel difficult.

Many attractions and resources here are far from modern conveniences, so you should arrive self-sufficient. Quality clothing, camping and rain gear, and good insect repellent are essential.

LODGING: There is no lodging in the park. Stores in Iliamna and Nondalton, somewhat convenient to the area, provide limited food, equipment, and clothing selections. Kenai, Homer, and Anchorage stores offer wider selections. Some merchants in Nondalton, Iliamna, and on Lake Clark offer rooms and cabins, meals, and guiding and outfitting services. Air and boat charter operators may also provide guides and rental equipment.

HOW TO GET THERE: Because of Alaska's size, traditions, and lack of ground transportation, the National Park Service has generally adopted relaxed rules for aircraft, snowmobile, and motorboat access to Alaska parklands. Access to the Lake Clark region is almost exclusively by small aircraft, wheeled or float equipped. There is no highway access. Scheduled commercial flights between Anchorage and Iliamna, thirty miles outside the boundary, provide near access. Charter flights out of Anchorage, Kenai, and Homer can land within the park boundary.

WRANGELL– ST. ELIAS NATIONAL PARK AND PRESERVE

ALASKA

Southeastern Alaska is a land of great diversity highlighted by gently rolling foothills and lofty mountains, scenic coastal beaches and churning glacier-fed rivers. Within this region can be found the 12.4-million-acre Wrangell–St. Elias National Park and Preserve, an area so huge that it stretches from the Tetlin lowlands north of the Alaska Range to the Malaspina Glacier along Yakutat Bay nearly 250 miles to the south. In between it crosses over both the Wrangell and St. Elias mountain chains as well as the broad Chitina River valley down to the Gulf of Alaska. The eastern edge of the park borders the Yukon Territory and Canada's Kluane National Park.

The park and preserve contain some of North America's highest mountains, including eight peaks over 14,500 feet. Mt. St. Elias, at 18,008 feet, is the fourth highest in North America. The mountains, glaciers, and snowfields dominate the landscape. There are well over a hundred major glaciers here, and some, such as the Nabesna and Malaspina, are among the world's largest. Several dozen major river systems emanate within the park and preserve. Most are heavily silt-laden and flow in the ribboned patterns characteristic of glacially derived rivers.

Opportunities abound for wilderness backpacking, lake fishing, car camping, river running, cross-country skiing, and mountain climbing. Principal hiking routes include the scenic Chitistone Canyon (the historic goat trail), which is quite demanding; the Beaver Creek drainage; the Hanagita River valley; Nikolai Pass; the Jacksina Creek drainage; and the Kuskulana and Kotsina drainages. Only the latter is accessible by ground transportation. Mounts Drum, Sanford, Blackburn, and St. Elias are all popular with climbers. The Bremner, Chitina, and Copper rivers offer excellent rafting possibilities in all classes of water. Sightseeing tours by air should emphasize the Nabesna Glacier and Icy Bay.

This is a vast and sometimes hostile region. Animals are wild and should be respected because they can kill or maim those who are careless. You should know your gear and possess both wilderness travel and wilderness survival skills. Winter travel is recommended only to those experienced in cold-weather camping and survival techniques.

LODGING: Rustic overnight accommodations (no electricity, plumbing, etc.) are available in Kennicott, McCarthy, Ptarmigan Lake Lodge, Chisana, Solo Creek, and Sportsman's Paradise Lodge. Scattered fish camps and guide cabins throughout the region can also accommodate backcountry parties. The major ones are located on Tanada and Copper lakes in the north, Ptarmigan and Rock lakes in the northeast, and Tebay and Hanagita lakes in the south central part of the park.

More standard accommodations are available in motels and cabins in and around the community of Glennallen, on the Glenn and Richardson highways, and along the Tok cutoff. Bureau of Land Management campgrounds are found at Liberty Falls, near Chitina, and Sourdough and Dry Creek, near Gulkana.

To visit the backcountry you must be self-sufficient, carring enough food to cover unexpected delays in getting picked up. Rain gear and wool clothing are musts. Glennallen has a good supermarket.

HOW TO GET THERE: There is road access into the park and preserve from the community of Chitina via the Chitina-McCarthy road. This is a four-wheel-drive route part of the year, but it is generally passable in summer. It extends some sixty-five miles up the Chitina River valley, following the historic route of the Copper River and Northwestern Railroad to the town of McCarthy. Road access into the northern section of the park/preserve is from Slana (on the Tok cutoff) along a secondary state route which extends some forty-five miles to the abandoned mining community of Nabesna. All other access is by air. Charter aircraft services are available in most Alaskan communities, including Anchorage, Fairbanks, Northway, Gulkana, Glennallen, Cordova, Valdez, McCarthy, Yakutat, and Talsona Lake. Costs vary according to type of aircraft and flight time.

QUICK REFERENCE GUIDE

In addition to the forty-eight great national parks described in the preceding pages, the U.S.A. can boast of an almost unlimited number of other spectacular national historical parks, national monuments and other affiliated recreation areas.

In the following pages you will find a brief description and a mailing address for each of these areas, including the forty-eight great national parks, listed by state.

To obtain the most up-to-date information about accommodations, campgrounds, and reservation requirements, write to the appropriate park.

ALABAMA

Horseshoe Bend National Military Park
Route 1, Box 103
Daviston, AL 36256

Gen. Andrew Jackson's forces broke the power of the Creek Indian Confederacy and opened Alabama and other parts of the Old Southwest to settlement after fierce fighting here Mar. 27, 1814, in the battle on the Tallapoosa River.

Russell Cave National Monument
Route 1, Box 175
Bridgeport, AL 35740

An almost continuous archeological record of human habitation from at least 7000 B.C. to about A.D. 1650 is revealed in this cave.

Tuskegee Institute National Historic Site
P.O. Box 1246
Tuskegee Institute, AL 36088

Booker T. Washington founded this college for black Americans in 1881. Preserved here are the brick buildings the students constructed themselves, Washington's home, and the George Washington Carver Museum. An antebellum mansion serves as park headquarters and visitor center.

ALASKA

Aniakchak National Monument
540 West 5th Avenue
Room 202
Anchorage, AK 99501

The Aniakchak Caldera, covering some 30 square miles, is one of the great dry calderas in the world. Located in the volcanically active Aleutian Mountains, the Aniakchak last erupted in 1933. The crater includes lava flows, cinder cones, and explosion pits, as well as the aptly named Surprise Lake, which cascades through a 1500-foot gash in the crater wall.

Bering Land Bridge National Monument 540 West 5th Avenue Room 202 Anchorage, AK 99501	Located on the Seward Peninsula in northwest Alaska, the monument is a remnant of the land bridge that once connected Asia with North America more than 13,000 years ago. Paleontological and archeological resources abound; large populations of migrating birds nest here. Ash explosion craters and lava flows, rare in the Arctic, are also present.
Cape Krusenstern National Monument 540 West 5th Avenue Room 202 Anchorage, AK 99501	Archeological sites located along a succession of 114 lateral beach ridges illustrate Eskimo communities of every known cultural period in Alaska, dating back some 4,000 years. Older sites are located inland, along the foothills. The monument includes a representative example of the arctic coastline along the Chukchi Sea.
Denali National Park P.O. Box 9 McKinley Park, AK 99755	Mount McKinley, at 20,320 feet, is the highest mountain in North America. Large glaciers of the Alaska Range, caribou, Dall sheep, moose, grizzly bears, timber wolves, and other wildlife are highlights of this national park.
Gates of the Arctic National Park 540 West 5th Avenue Room 202 Anchorage, AK 99501	Lying entirely north of the Arctic Circle, the park includes a portion of the Central Brooks Range, the northernmost extension of the Rocky Mountains. Often referred to as the greatest remaining wilderness in North America.

Glacier Bay National Park
P.O. Box 1089
Juneau, AK 99802

Great tidewater glaciers, a dramatic range of plant communities from rocky terrain recently covered by ice to lush temperate rain forest, and a large variety of animals, including brown and black bear, mountain goats, whales, seals, and eagles can be found within the park.

Katmai National Park
P.O. Box 7
King Salmon, AK 99613

Variety marks this vast land: lakes, forests, mountains, and marshlands all abound in wildlife. The Alaska brown bear, the world's largest carnivore, thrives here, feeding upon red salmon which spawn in the park's lakes and streams.

Kenai Fjords National Park
540 West 5th Avenue
Room 202
Anchorage, AK 99501

The park, within 20 miles of Seward, includes one of the four major ice caps in the U.S., the Harding Icefield. Glaciers radiating from the 700-square-mile icefield continue to cut deep glacial valleys, many ending at tidewater.

Klondike Gold Rush National Historical Park
P.O. Box 517
Skagway, AK 99840

Historic buildings in Skagway and portions of Chilkoot and White Pass Trails, all prominent in the 1897–98 gold rush, are included in the park.

Kobuk Valley National Park
540 West 5th Avenue
Room 202
Anchorage, AK 99501

Embracing the central valley of the Kobuk River, the park, located entirely north of the Arctic Circle, includes a blend of biological, geological, and cultural resources.

Lake Clark National Park
540 West 5th Avenue
Room 202
Anchorage, AK 99501

Located in the heart of the Chigmit Mountains along the western shore of Cook inlet, the park contains great geologic diversity, including jagged peaks, granite spires, glaciers, and two symmetrical active volcanoes.

Noatak National Preserve
540 West 5th Avenue
Room 202
Anchorage, AK 99501

The Noatak River basin is the largest mountain-ringed river basin in the nation still virtually unaffected by man. The preserve includes landforms of great scientific interest, including the 65-mile-long Grand Canyon of the Noatak, a transition zone and migration route for plants and animals between subarctic and arctic environments, and an array of flora which is among the most diverse anywhere in the earth's northern latitudes. Hundreds of archeological sites and rich wildlife populations add to the significance of the area.

Sitka National Historical Park
P.O. Box 738
Sitka, AK 99835

The site of the 1804 fort and battle which marked the last major Tlingit Indian resistance to Russian colonization is preserved here. Tlingit totem poles are exhibited.

Wrangell–St. Elias National Park
540 West 5th Avenue
Room 202
Anchorage, AK 99501

The Chugach, Wrangell, and St. Elias mountain ranges converge here in what is often referred to as the "mountain kingdom of North America."

Yukon-Charley National Preserve
540 West 5th Avenue
Room 202
Anchorage, AK 99501

Located along the Canadian border in central Alaska, the preserve includes 115 miles of the 1800-mile Yukon River and the entire 88-mile Charley River basin. Numerous old cabins and relics are reminders of the importance of the Yukon River during the 1897–98 gold rush. Paleontological and archeological sites here add much to our knowledge of man and his environment thousands of years ago. Peregrine falcons nest in the high bluffs overlooking the river, while the rolling hills that make up the preserve are home to a rich array of wildlife. The Charley, clean and clear, is considered by many to be the best whitewater river in Alaska.

ARIZONA

Canyon de Chelly National Monument
P.O. Box 588
Chinle, AZ 86503

At the base of sheer red cliffs and in caves in canyon walls are ruins of Indian villages built between A.D. 350 and 1300. Modern Navajo Indians live and farm here.

Casa Grande National Monument
P.O. Box 518
Coolidge, AZ 85228

Perplexing ruins of a massive four-story building, constructed of high-lime desert soil by Indians who farmed the Gila Valley 600 years ago, raise many unanswered questions for modern man.

Chiricahua National Monument
Dos Cabezas Star Route
Willcox, AZ 85643

The varied rock formations here were created millions of years ago by volcanic activity, aided by erosion.

Coronado National Memorial
Route 1, Box 126
Hereford, AZ 85615

Our Hispanic heritage and the first European exploration of the Southwest, by Francisco Vasquez de Coronado in 1540–42, are commemorated here, near the point where Coronado's expedition entered what is now the United States.

Fort Bowie National Historic Site
P.O. Box 158
Bowie, AZ 85605

Established in 1862, this fort was the focal point of military operations against Geronimo and his band of Apaches. The ruins can be reached only by trail.

Grand Canyon National Park
P. O. Box 129
Grand Canyon, AZ 86023

The park, focusing on the world-famous Grand Canyon of the Colorado River, encompasses the course of the river and adjacent uplands from the southern terminus of Glen Canyon National Recreation Area to the eastern boundary of Lake Mead National Recreation Area.

Hohokam Pima National Monument
P.O. Box 518
Coolidge, AZ 85228

Preserved here are the archeological remains of the Hohokam culture. Hohokam is a Pima Indian word meaning "those who have gone." *Not open to the public.*

Hubbell Trading Post National Historic Site
P.O. Box 150
Ganado, AZ 86505

This still-active trading post illustrates the influence of reservation traders on the Indians' way of life.

Lake Mead National Recreation Area
601 Nevada Hwy.
Boulder City, NV 89005

Lake Mead, formed by Hoover Dam, and Lake Mohave, by Davis Dam, on the Colorado River comprise this first national recreation area established by an act of Congress.

Montezuma Castle National Monument P.O. Box 68 Clarkdale, AZ 86324	One of the best-preserved cliff dwellings in the U.S., this five-story, 20-room castle is 90 percent intact. Montezuma Well is also of archeological and geological interest.
Navajo National Monument Tonalea, AZ 86044	Betatakin, Keet Seel, and Inscription House are three of the largest and most elaborate cliff dwellings known.
Organ Pipe Cactus National Monument Route 1, Box 100 Ajo, AZ 85321	Sonoran Desert plants and animals found nowhere else in the U.S. are protected here, alongside traces of a historic trail, Camino del Diablo.
Petrified Forest National Park AZ 86028	Trees that have petrified, or changed to multicolored stone, Indian ruins and petroglyphs, and portions of the colorful Painted Desert are features of the park.
Pipe Spring National Monument Moccasin, AZ 86022	The historic fort and other structures, built here by Mormon pioneers, memorialize the struggle for exploration and settlement of the Southwest.
Saguaro National Monument P.O. Box 17210 Tucson, AZ 85731	Giant saguaro cactus, unique to the Sonoran Desert of southern Arizona and northwestern Mexico, sometimes reach a height of 50 feet in this cactus forest.
Sunset Crater National Monument Route 3, Box 149 Flagstaff, AZ 86001	Its upper part colored as if by sunset glow, this volcanic cinder cone with summit crater was formed just before A.D. 1100.

300

Tonto National Monument
P.O. Box 67
Tumacacori, AZ 85640

These well-preserved cliff dwellings were occupied during the 13th and 14th centuries by Salado Indians who farmed in the Salt River valley.

Tumacacori National Monument
P.O. Box 67
Roosevelt, AZ 85545

This historic Spanish Catholic mission building stands near the site first visited by Jesuit Father Kino in 1691.

Tuzigoot National Monument
P.O. Box 68
Clarkdale, AZ 86324

Ruins of a large Indian pueblo which flourished in the Verde Valley between A.D. 1100 and 1450 have been excavated here.

Walnut Canyon National Monument
Route 1, Box 25
Flagstaff, AZ 86001

These cliff dwellings were built in shallow caves under ledges of limestone by Pueblo Indians about 800 years ago.

Wupatki National Monument
Tuba Star Route
Flagstaff, AZ 86001

Ruins of red sandstone pueblos built by farming Indians about A.D. 1065 are preserved here. The modern Hopi Indians are believed to be partly descended from these people.

ARKANSAS

Arkansas Post National Memorial
Route 1, Box 16
Gillett, AR 72055

On this site the first permanent French settlement in the lower Mississippi valley was founded in 1686.

Buffalo National River
P.O. Box 1173
Harrison, AR 72601

Offering both swift-running and placid stretches, the Buffalo is one of the few remaining unpolluted, free-flowing rivers in the lower 48 states. It courses through multicolored bluffs and past numerous caves and springs along its 132-mile length.

Fort Smith National Historic Site
P.O. Box 1406
Fort Smith, AR 72902

One of the first U.S. military posts in the Louisiana Territory, the fort was a center of authority for the untamed region to the west from 1817 to 1890.

Hot Springs National Park
P.O. Box 1860
Hot Springs National Park, AR 71901

More than a million gallons of water a day flow from 47 hot springs here, unaffected by climate or seasonal temperatures. Persons suffering from illness or injury often seek relief in the ancient tradition of thermal bathing.

Pea Ridge National Military Park
Pea Ridge, AR 72751

The Union victory here on Mar. 7-8, 1862, in one of the major engagements of the Civil War west of the Mississippi, led to the Union's total control of Missouri.

CALIFORNIA

Cabrillo National Monument
P.O. Box 6175
San Diego, CA 92106

Juan Rodriguez Cabrillo, Portuguese explorer who claimed the west coast of the U.S. for Spain in 1542, is memorialized here. Gray whales migrate offshore during the winter.

Channel Islands National Park
1699 Anchors Way Dr.
Ventura, CA 93003

The park, with large rookeries of sea lions, nesting seabirds and unique plants and animals, consists of Anacapa and Santa Barbara islands. San Miguel Island, owned by the U.S. Navy, is managed jointly by the Navy and the National Park Service (permit required to visit San Miguel).

Death Valley National Monument
Death Valley, CA 92328

This large desert, nearly surrounded by high mountains, contains the lowest point in the Western Hemisphere. The area includes Scotty's Castle, the grandiose home of a famous prospector, and other remnants of gold and borax mining activity.

Devils Postpile National Monument
Three Rivers, CA 93271

Hot lava cooled and cracked some 900,000 years ago to form basalt columns 40 to 60 feet high resembling a giant pipe organ. The John Muir Trail between Yosemite and Kings Canyon national parks crosses the monument.

Fort Point National Historic Site
P.O. Box 29333
Presidio of San Francisco, CA 94129

This classic brick and granite mid-19th-century coastal fortification is the largest on the west coast of North America.

Golden Gate National Recreation Area
Fort Mason
San Francisco, CA 94123

The park encompasses shoreline areas of San Francisco and Marin counties, including ocean beaches, redwood forests, lagoons, marshes, ships of the National Maritime Museum, historic military properties, a cultural center at Fort Mason, and Alcatraz Island, site of a famous penitentiary.

John Muir National Historic Site 4202 Alhambra Ave. Martinez, CA 94553	The home of John Muir and adjacent Martinez Adobe commemorate Muir's contribution to conservation and literature.
Joshua Tree National Monument 74485 National Monument Dr. Twentynine Palms, CA 92277	A representative stand of Joshua trees and a great variety of plants and animals, including the desert bighorn, exist in this desert region.
Kings Canyon National Park Three Rivers, CA 93271	Two enormous canyons of the Kings River and the summit peaks of the High Sierra dominate this mountain wilderness. General Grant Grove, with its giant sequoias, is a detached section of the park.
Lassen Volcanic National Park Mineral, CA 96063	Lassen Peak, the only recently active volcano in the coterminous U.S. until the eruption of Mt. St. Helens, erupted intermittently from 1914 to 1921.
Lava Beds National Monument P.O. Box 867 Tulelake, CA 96134	Volcanic activity spewed forth molten rock and lava here, creating an incredibly rugged landscape—a natural fortress used by the Indians in the Modoc Indian War, 1872–73.
Muir Woods National Monument Mill Valley, CA 94941	The virgin stand of coastal redwoods was named for John Muir, writer and conservationist.
Pinnacles National Monument Paicines, CA 95043	Spirelike rock formations 500 to 1,200 feet high, with caves and a variety of volcanic features, rise above the smooth contours of the surrounding countryside.

Point Reyes National Seashore
Point Reyes, CA 94956

This peninsula near San Francisco is noted for its long beaches backed by tall cliffs, lagoons and esteros, forested ridges, and offshore bird and sea lion colonies. Part of the area remains a private pastoral zone.

Redwood National Park
Drawer N
Crescent City, CA 95531

Coastal redwood forests with virgin groves of ancient trees, including the world's tallest, live in a mixture of sun and fog. The park includes 40 miles of scenic Pacific coastline.

Santa Monica Mountains National
Recreation Area
23018 Ventura Blvd.
Woodland Hills, CA 91364

This park is a large, rugged landscape, covered with chaparral, fronting on the sandy beaches north of Los Angeles. The area will provide recreational opportunities within easy reach of millions in southern California.

Sequois National Park
Three Rivers, CA 93271

Great groves of giant sequoias, the world's largest living things, Mineral King Valley, and Mount Whitney, the highest mountain in the U.S. outside of Alaska, are spectacular attractions here in the High Sierra.

Whiskeytown-Shasta-Trinity National
Recreation Area
P.O. Box 188
Whiskeytown, CA 96095

Whiskeytown Unit, with its mountainous backcountry and large reservoir, provides a multitude of outdoor recreation opportunities. Shasta and Clair Engle units are administered by the Forest Service, U.S. Dept. of Agriculture.

Yosemite National Park
P.O. Box 577
Yosemite National Park, CA 95389

Granite peaks and domes rise high above broad meadows in the heart of the Sierra Nevada; groves of giant sequoias dwarf other trees and tiny wild flowers; and mountains, lakes and waterfalls, including the nation's highest, are found here.

COLORADO

Bent's Old Fort National Historic Site
P.O. Box 581
La Junta, CO 81050

As a principal outpost of civilization on the Southern Plains in the early 1800s and rendezvous for Indians, the post became the center of a vast fur-trading empire in the West.

Black Canyon of the Gunnison National Monument
P.O. Box 1648
Montrose, CO 81401

Shadowed depths of this sheer-walled canyon accentuate the darkness of ancient rocks of obscure origin.

Colorado National Monument
Fruita, CO 81521

Sheer-walled canyons, towering monoliths, weird formations, dinosaur fossils, and remains of prehistoric Indian cultures reflect the environment and history of this colorful sandstone country.

Curecanti National Recreation Area
P.O. Box 1040
Gunnison, CO 81230

Three lakes—Blue Mesa, Morrow Point, and Crystal—extend for 40 miles along the Gunnison River. When full, Blue Mesa Lake, with a surface area of 14 square miles, is the largest lake in Colorado.

Dinosaur National Monument
P.O. Box 210
Dinosaur, CO 81610

Spectacular canyons were cut by the Green and Yampa rivers through upfolded mountains. A quarry contains fossil remains of dinosaurs and other ancient animals.

Florissant Fossil Beds National Monument P.O. Box 185 Florissant, CO 80816	A wealth of fossil insects, seeds, and leaves of the Oligocene period are preserved here in remarkable detail. Here, too, is an unusual display of standing petrified sequoia stumps.
Great Sand Dunes National Monument P.O. Box 60 Alamosa, CO 81101	Among the largest and highest in the U.S., these dunes were deposited over thousands of years by southwesterly winds blowing through the passes of the lofty Sangre de Cristo Mountains.
Hovenweep National Monument McElmo Route Cortez, CO 81321	Pre-Columbian Indians built these six groups of towers, pueblos, and cliff dwellings.
Mesa Verde National Park Mesa Verda National Park, CO 81330	These pre-Columbian cliff dwellings and other works of early man are the most notable and best preserved in the U.S.
Rocky Mountain National Park Estes Park, CO 80517	The park's rich scenery, typifying the massive grandeur of the Rocky Mountains, is accessible by Trail Ridge Road, which crosses the Continental Divide. Peaks towering over 14,000 feet shadow wildlife and wild flowers in these 412 square miles of the Rockies' Front Range.
Yucca House National Monument c/o Mesa Verde National Park Mesa Verde National Park, CO 81330	Ruins of these large prehistoric Indian pueblos are as yet unexcavated.

CONNECTICUT

Appalachian
National Scenic Trail
P.O. Box 236
Harpers Ferry, WV 25425

Approximately 2,000 miles of this scenic trail follow the Appalachian Mountains from Mount Katahdin, Maine, through N.H., Vt., Mass., Conn., N.Y., N.J., Pa., Md., W.Va., Va., Tenn., and N.C., to Springer Mountain, Ga. The trail is one of the two initial units of the National Trail System.

DISTRICT OF COLUMBIA

Ford's Theatre National Historic Site
511 Tenth St., NW
Washington, DC 20004

On Apr. 14, 1865, President Lincoln was shot while attending a show here. He was carried across the street to the Petersen house, where he died the next morning. The theatre contains the Olroyd Collection of Lincolniana.

Frederick Douglass Home
1411 W St., SE
Washington, DC 20020

From 1877 to 1895, this was the home of the nation's leading 19th-century black spokesman. He was U.S. minister to Haiti, 1889.

John F. Kennedy Center for the Performing Arts
National Park Service
2700 F St., NW
Washington, DC 20566

Cultural events are presented in this structure designed by Edward Durell Stone. The building contains the Eisenhower Theater, a concert hall, an opera house, and the Terrace Theater.

Lincoln Memorial
1100 Ohio Dr., SW
Washington, DC 20242

This classical structure of great beauty contains a marble seated statue 19 feet high of the Great Emancipator by sculptor Daniel Chester French. Architect of the building was Henry Bacon.

Lyndon Baines Johnson Memorial Grove
on the Potomac
1100 Ohio Dr., SW
Washington, DC 20242

A living memorial to the 36th president, the park overlooks the Potomac River vista of the Capital. The design features 500 white pines and engravings on Texas granite.

National Mall
1100 Ohio Dr., SW
Washington, DC 20242

This landscaped park, extending from the Capitol to the Washington Monument, was envisioned as a formal park in the L'Enfant Plan for the city of Washington.

National Visitor Center
Union Station
Washington, DC 20002

The National Visitor Center encompasses a diverse complex of programs and facilities to welcome visitors to the nation's capital.

Rock Creek Park
5000 Glover Rd., NW
Washington, DC 20015

One of the largest urban parks in the world, this wooded preserve contains a wide range of natural, historical, and recreational resources in the midst of metropolitan Washington, D.C.

Sewall-Belmont House National Historic Site
144 Constitution Ave., NE
Washington, DC 20002

Rebuilt after fire damage from the War of 1812, this red-brick house is one of the oldest on Capitol Hill. It has been the National Women's Party headquarters since 1929 and commemorates the party's founder and women's suffrage leader, Alice Paul, and associates.

Theodore Roosevelt Island
c/o George Washington
Memorial Parkway
Turkey Run Park
McLean, VA 22101

On this wooded island sanctuary in the Potomac River, trails lead to an imposing statue of Roosevelt, the conservation-minded 26th president. His tenets on nature, manhood, youth, and the state are inscribed on tablets.

Thomas Jefferson Memorial
1100 Ohio Dr., SW
Washington, DC 20242

This circular, colonnaded structure, in the classic style introduced in this country by Jefferson, memorializes the author of the Declaration of Independence and president from 1801 to 1809. The interior walls present inscriptions from his writings. The heroic statue was sculptured by Rudulph Evans; architects were John Russell Pope and associates, Otto Eggers and Daniel Higgins.

Washington Monument
1100 Ohio Dr., SW
Washington, DC 20242

A dominating feature of the nation's capital, this 555-foot obelisk honors the country's first president, George Washington. The architect-designer was Robert Mills.

White House
1100 Ohio Dr., SW
Washington, DC 20242

The White House has been the residence and office of the presidents of the U.S. since Nov. 1800. The cornerstone was laid Oct. 13, 1792, on the site selected by George Washington and included in the L'Enfant Plan; renovations were made 1949–52.

FLORIDA

Big Cypress National Preserve
P.O. Box 1247
Naples, FL 33939

Adjoining the northwest section of Everglades National Park, this large area provides a freshwater supply crucial to the park's survival. Subtropical plant and animal life abounds in this ancestral home of the Seminole and Miccosukee Indians.

Biscayne National Park
P.O. Box 1369
Homestead, FL 33030

Most of the park is reef and water, but within its boundaries about 25 keys, or islands, form a north-south chain, with Biscayne Bay on the west and the Atlantic Ocean on the east.

Canaveral National Seashore
P.O. Box 2583
Titusville, FL 32780

Immediately north of the famed Kennedy Space Center, the seashore offers a great variety of wildlife, including many species of birds, on a segment of largely undeveloped wild lands. The area includes a portion of 140,393-acre Merrit Island National Wildlife Refuge, administered by the Fish and Wildlife Service, U.S. Dept. of the Interior.

Castillo de San Marcos National Monument
1 Castillo Dr.
St. Augustine, FL 32084

Construction of this oldest masonry fort in the continental U.S. was started in 1672 by the Spanish to protect St. Augustine, first permanent settlement by Europeans in the continental U.S. (1565). The floor plan is the result of "modernization" work done in the 18th century.

De Soto National Memorial
75th St., NW
Bradenton, FL 33505

The landing of Spanish explorer Hernando de Soto in Florida in 1539 and the first extensive organized exploration of what is now the southern U.S. by Europeans are commemorated here.

311

Everglades National Park
P.O. Box 279
Homestead, FL 33030

This largest remaining subtropical wilderness in the coterminous U.S. has extensive fresh- and saltwater areas, open Everglades prairies, and mangrove forests. Abundant wildlife includes rare and colorful birds.

Fort Caroline National Memorial
12713 Fort Caroline Rd.
Jacksonville, FL 32225

The fort overlooks the site of a French Huguenot colony of 1564–65, the second French attempt at settlement within the present U.S. Here, the French and Spanish began two centuries of European colonial rivalry in North America.

Fort Jefferson National Monument
c/o U.S. Coast Guard Base
Key West, FL 33040

Built in 1856 to help control the Florida Straits, this is the largest all-masonry fortification in the Western world; it served as a Federal military prison during and after the Civil War. The bird refuge and marine life here are features.

Fort Matanzas National Monument
Route 1, Box 105
St. Augustine, FL 32084

This Spanish fort was built 1740–42 to protect St. Augustine from the British.

Gulf Islands National Seashore
P.O. Box 100
Gulf Breeze, FL 32561

Offshore islands and keys have both sparkling white sand beaches and historic ruins. Mainland features of this unit, which is located near Pensacola, Florida, include the Naval Live Oaks Reservation, beaches, and ruins of military forts. All areas are accessible by car.

GEORGIA

Andersonville National Historic Site
Andersonville, GA 31711

This Civil War prisoner-of-war camp commemorates the sacrifices borne by American prisoners not only in the 1861–65 conflict but in all wars. Site includes Andersonville National Cemetery, which has 15,591 interments, 1,041 unidentified.

Chattahoochee River National Recreation Area
P.O. Box 1396
Smyrna, GA 30080

A series of sites along a 48-mile stretch of the Chattahoochee River, extending into Atlanta, will be preserved for public enjoyment of scenic, recreational, and historic values.

Chickamauga & Chattanooga National Military Park
P.O. Box 2126
Fort Oglethorpe, GA 30742

This park includes the Civil War battlefields of Chickamauga, Orchard Knob, Lookout Mountain, and Missionary Ridge.

Cumberland Island National Seashore
P.O. Box 806
St. Marys, GA 31558

Magnificent and unspoiled beaches and dunes, marshes, and freshwater lakes make up this largest of Georgia's Golden Isles. Accessible by tour boat only.

Fort Frederica National Monument
Route 4, Box 286-C
St. Simons Island, GA 31522

Gen. James E. Oglethorpe built this British fort in 1736–48, during the Anglo-Spanish struggle for control of what is now the southeastern U.S.

Fort Pulaski National Monument
P.O. Box 98
Tybee Island, GA 31328

Bombardment of this early 19th-century fort by federal rifled cannon in 1862 first demonstrated the ineffectiveness of old-style masonry fortifications.

Kennesaw Mountain National Battlefield Park
P.O. Box 1167
Marietta, GA 30061

Two engagements took place here between Union and Confederate forces during the Atlanta Campaign, June 20–July 2, 1864.

Martin Luther King, Jr. National Historic Site
522 Auburn Ave. N.E.
Atlanta, GA 30312

Atlanta birthplace and gravesite of the Civil Rights leader with King Memorial and Center for Social Change, Ebenezer Baptist Church, and other structures.

Ocmulgee National Monument
1207 Emery Hwy.
Macon, GA 31201

The evolution of the Indian mound-builder civilization in the southern U.S. is represented in the remains of mounds and villages.

GUAM

War in the Pacific National Historical Park
P.O. Box 3441
Agana, GU 96910

This park will provide an opportunity to interpret events in the Pacific Theater of World War II. It includes major historic sites associated with the 1944 battle for Guam, an example of the island-hopping military campaign against the Japanese.

HAWAII

Haleakala National Park
P.O. Box 537
Makawao, HI 96768

The park preserves the outstanding features of Haleakala Crater, on the island of Maui, and protects the unique and fragile ecosystems of Kipahulu Valley, the scenic pools along Oheo gulch, and many rare and endangered species.

Hawaii Volcanoes National Park
Hawaii National Park, HI 96718

Active volcanism continues here, on the island of Hawaii, where at lower elevations luxuriant and often rare vegetation provides food and shelter for a variety of animals.

Kalaupapa National Historical Park
c/o Pacific Area Director
300 Ala Moana Blvd.
P.O. Box 50165
Honolulu, HI 96850

Preserves Molokai Island leper colony site (1886–1969); areas relating to early Hawaiian occupation; scenic, geologic, biotic resources, including habitat for rare and endangered species.

Kaloko-Honokohau National Historical Park
Box 50165
Honolulu, HI 96850

Park is intended to preserve native culture of Hawaii. This was the site of important Hawaiian settlements before arrival of European explorers. It includes three large fishponds, house sites, and other archeological remnants.

Pu'uhonua o Honaunau National Historical Park
P.O. Box 128
Honaunau, Kona, HI 96726

Until 1819, vanquished Hawaiian warriors, noncombatants, and kapu breakers could escape death by reaching this sacred ground. Prehistoric house sites, royal fishponds, coconut groves, and spectacular shore scenery comprise the park.

315

Puukohola Heiau National Historic Site
P.O. Box 4963
Kawaihae, HI 96743

Ruins of Puukohola Heiau ("Temple on the Hill of the Whale"), built by King Kamehameha the Great during his rise to power, are preserved.

USS Arizona Memorial
c/o Pacific Area Office
Box 50165
Honolulu, HI 96850

Floating memorial over the battleship sunk in Pearl Harbor Dec. 7, 1941, by the Japanese.

IDAHO

**Craters of the Moon
National Monument**
P.O. Box 29
Arco, ID 83213

Volcanic cones, craters, lava flows, and caves make this an astonishing landscape.

**Nez Perce
National Historical Park**
P.O. Box 93
Spalding, ID 83551

The history and culture of the Nez Perce Indian country are preserved, commemorated, and interpreted here. Four federally owned sites are administered by the National Park Service, and 20 sites through cooperative agreements.

Yellowstone National Park
(see Wyoming)

ILLINOIS

Lincoln Home
National Historic Site
526 S. Seventh St.
Springfield, IL 62703

Abraham Lincoln left his house here in 1861 to accept the presidency. It was the only home he ever owned.

INDIANA

George Rogers Clark National Historical
Park
401 S. Second St.
Vincennes, IN 47591

This classic memorial, near the site of old Fort Sackville, commemorates the seizure of the fort from the British by Lt. Col. George Rogers Clark on Feb. 25, 1779.

Indiana Dunes National Lakeshore
1100 N. Mineral Springs Rd.
Porter, IN 46304

Magnificent dunes rise as high as 180 feet above Lake Michigan's southern shore. Other natural features include beaches, bogs, marshes, swamps, and prairie remnants; historic sites include an 1822 homestead and 1900 family farm, both restored.

Lincoln Boyhood National Memorial
Lincoln City, IN 47552

On this southern Indiana farm, Abraham Lincoln grew from youth into manhood.

IOWA

Effigy Mounds National Monument
P.O. Box K
McGregor, IA 52157

The monument contains outstanding examples of prehistoric burial mounds, some in the shapes of birds and bears.

Herbert Hoover National Historic Site
P.O. Box 607
West Branch, IA 52358

The birthplace, home, and boyhood neighborhood of the 31st president, 1929–33; the gravesites of President and Mrs. Hoover; and the Hoover Presidential Library and Museum, which is administered by the National Archives and Records Service, General Services Administration, are within the park.

KANSAS

For Larned National Historic Site
Route 3
Larned, KS 67550

The fort protected traffic along the Santa Fe Trail, was the key military base in the Indian War of 1868–69, and served as an Indian agency.

Fort Scott National Historic Site
Old Fort Blvd.
Fort Scott, KS 66701

The reconstructed 19th-century fort commemorates historic events of the Civil War period.

KENTUCKY

Abraham Lincoln Birthplace National Historic Site
R.F.D. 1
Hodgenville, KY 42748

An early 19th-century Kentucky cabin, symbolic of the one in which Lincoln was born, is preserved in a memorial building at the site of his birth.

Cumberland Gap National Historical Park
P.O. Box 840
Middlesboro, KY 40965
(also in Virginia and Tennessee)

This mountain pass on the Wilderness Road, explored by Daniel Boone, developed into a main artery of the great trans-Allegheny migration for settlement of "the Old West" and an important military objective in the Revolutionary and Civil wars.

Mammoth Cave National Park
Mammoth Cave, KY 42259

This series of underground passages—with beautiful limestone gypsum, and travertine formations, deep pits and high domes, and an underground river—has been explored and mapped for 194 miles, making this the longest recorded cave system in the world.

LOUISIANA

Jean Lafitte National Historical Park and Preserve
400 Royal St., Room 200
New Orleans, LA 70130

The park preserves significant examples of natural and historical resources of the Mississippi Delta. It includes the Chalmette Unit, where American forces were victorious in the Battle of New Orleans in the War of 1812. Chalmette Unit includes Chalmette National Cemetery, 15.219 interments. 6.773 unidentified. Grave sites are not available.

319

MAINE

Acadia National Park
Route 1, Box 1
Bar Harbor, ME 04609

The sea sets the mood here, uniting the rugged coastal area of Mount Desert Island (highest elevation on the eastern seaboard), picturesque Schoodic Peninsula on the mainland, and the spectacular cliffs of Isle au Haut.

Appalachian National Scenic Trail
P.O. Box 236
Harpers Ferry, WV 25425

Approximately 2,000 miles of this scenic trail follow the Appalachian Mountains from Mount Katahdin, Maine, through N.H., Vt., Mass., Conn., N.Y., N.J., Pa., Md., W.Va., Va., Tenn., and N.C., to Springer Mountain, Ga. The trail is one of the two initial units of the National Trail System.

Saint Croix Island National Monument
c/o Acadia National Park
Route 1, Box 1
Bar Harbor, ME 04609

The attempted French settlement of 1604, which led to the founding of New France, is commemorated on Saint Croix Island in the Saint Croix River on the Canadian border.

MARYLAND

Antietam National Battlefield
Box 158
Sharpsburg, MD 21782

Gen. Robert E. Lee's first invasion of the North was ended on this battlefield in 1862. Antietam (Sharpsburg) National Cemetery—5,032 interments, 1,836 unidentified—adjoins the park. Grave sites are not available.

Assateague Island National Seashore
Route 2, Box 294
Berlin, MD 21811

This 37-mile barrier island, with sandy beach, migratory waterfowl, and wild ponies, includes 9,021-acre Chincoteague National Wildlife Refuge, administered by the Fish and Wildlife Service, U.S. Dept. of the Interior.

Catoctin Mountain Park
Thurmont, MD 21788

Part of the forested ridge that forms the eastern rampart of the Appalachian Mountains in Maryland, this mountain park has sparkling streams and panoramic vistas of the Monocacy Valley.

Chesapeake and Ohio Canal National Historical Park
Box 158
Sharpsburg, MD 21782

The park follows the route of the 184-mile canal along the Potomac River between Washington, D.C., and Cumberland, Md. The canal was built between 1828 and 1850.

Clara Barton National Historic Site
5801 Osford Rd.
Glen Echo, MD 20768

This 38-room home of the founder of the American Red Cross was for seven years headquarters of that organization.

Fort McHenry National Monument and Historic Shrine
Baltimore, MD 21230

Successful defense of this fort (Sept. 13–14, 1814) in the War of 1812 inspired Francis Scott Key to write "The Star Spangled Banner."

Fort Washington Park
National Capital Parks, East
5210 Indian Head Hwy.
Oxon Hill, MD 20021

This fort across the Potomac from Mt. Vernon, built to protect Washington, D.C., was begun in 1814 to replace an 1809 fort destroyed by the British. Recreational facilities are included in the park.

Greenbelt Park
6501 Greenbelt Rd.
Greenbelt, MD 20770

Just 12 miles from Washington, D.C., this woodland park offers urban dwellers access to many forms of outdoor recreation.

Hampton National Historic Site
535 Hampton Lane
Towson, MD 21204

This is a fine example of the lavish Georgian mansions built in America during the latter part of the 18th century.

Monocacy National Battlefield
c/o C & O Canal National
Historical Park, Box 158
Sharpsburg, MD 21782

In a battle here July 9, 1864, Confederate Gen. Jubal T. Early defeated Union forces commanded by Brig. Gen. Lew Wallace. Wallace's troops delayed Early, however, enabling Union forces to marshal a successful defense of Washington, D.C.

Piscataway Park
National Capital Parks, East
5210 Indian Head Hwy.
Oxon Hill, MD 20021

The tranquil view from Mount Vernon of the Maryland shore of the Potomac is preserved as a pilot project in the use of easements to protect parklands from obtrusive urban expansion.

Thomas Stone National Historic Site
c/o George Washington
Birthplace National Monument,
Washington's Birthplace, VA 22575

"Habre-de-Venture," a Georgian mansion built in 1771 near Port Tobacco, Md., was the home of Thomas Stone, 1771–87. A signer of the Declaration of Independence, Stone was delegate to the Continental Congress, 1775–78 and 1783–84. *Not open to the public.*

MASSACHUSETTS

Adams National Historic Site
P.O. Box 531
Quincy, MA 02269

The home of Presidents John Adams and John Quincy Adams, of U.S. Minister to Great Britain Charles Francis Adams, and of the writers and historians Henry Adams and Brooks Adams, this house at 135 Adams Street reflects the influence of each of these distinguished men. The park also includes (at 133 and 141 Franklin Street) two other houses, the birthplaces of the two presidents.

Boston National Historical Park
Charlestown Navy Yard
Boston, MA 02129

This park includes Faneuil Hall, Old North Church, Old State House, Bunker Hill, Old South Meeting House, Charlestown Navy Yard, berth for USS *Constitution*, Paul Revere House, and Dorchester Heights.

Cape Cod National Seashore
South Wellfleet, MA 02663

Ocean beaches, dunes, woodlands, freshwater ponds, and marshes make up this park on outer Cape Cod. The area preserves notable examples of Cape Cod homes, an architectural style founded in America.

John Fitzgerald Kennedy National Historic Site
83 Beals St.
Brookline, MA 02146

This house is the birthplace and early boyhood home of the 35th president.

Longfellow National Historic Site
105 Brattle St.
Cambridge, MA 02138

Poet Henry Wadsworth Longfellow lived here from 1837 to 1882 while teaching at Harvard. The house had been General Washington's headquarters during the siege of Boston, 1775–76.

Lowell National Historical Park P.O. Box 1098 Lowell, MA 01853	America's first planned industrial community is commemorated by this park at the heart of the city. Elements of Lowell's factories, canal system, and the life-style of its people will be preserved and interpreted here.
Minute Man National Historical Park P.O. Box 160 Concord, MA 01742	Scene of the fighting on Apr. 19, 1775, that opened the American Revolution, the park includes North Bridge, Minute Man statue, four miles of Battle Road between Lexington and Concord, and "The Wayside," Nathaniel Hawthorne's home.
Salem Maritime National Historic Site Custom House 174 Derby St. Salem, MA 01970	During the Revolution, this was the only major port never occupied by the British. Later, it was one of the nation's great mercantile centers. Structures of maritime significance include the Custom House, where Nathaniel Hawthorne worked; Derby Wharf; the Bonded Warehouse; and the West India Goods Store.
Saugus Iron Works National Historic Site 244 Central St. Saugus, MA 01906	This reconstruction of the first integrated iron works in North America, begun in 1646, includes the ironmaster's house, furnace, forge, and rolling and slitting mill.
Springfield Armory National Historic Site 1 Armory Square Springfield, MA 01105	Over a span of 200 years this small-arms manufacturing center produced such weapons as the 1795 flintlock and the 1883, 1903, M-1, and M-14 rifles. The largest collection of Confederate and other small arms is maintained here.

MICHIGAN

Isle Royale National Park
87 North Ripley St.
Houghton, MI 49931

The largest in Lake Superior, this forested island is also distinguished for its wilderness character, timber wolves and moose herd, and pre-Columbian copper mines.

Pictured Rocks National Lakeshore
P.O. Box 40
Munising, MI 49862

Multicolored sandstone cliffs, broad beaches, sand bars, dunes, waterfalls, inland lakes, ponds, marshes, hardwood and coniferous forests, and numerous birds and animals comprise this scenic area on Lake Superior. This was the first national lakeshore.

Sleeping Bear Dunes National Lakeshore
400 Main St.
Frankfort, MI 49635

Beaches, massive sand dunes, forests, and lakes are outstanding characteristics of the Lake Michigan shoreline and two offshore islands.

MINNESOTA

Grand Portage National Monument
P.O. Box 666
Grand Marais, MN 55604

This nine-mile portage was a rendezvous for traders and trappers on a principal route of Indians, explorers, missionaries, and fur traders into the Northwest. The Grand Portage post of the North West Company has been reconstructed here.

Lower St. Croix National Scenic River
(see Wisconsin)

Pipestone National Monument
P.O. Box 727
Pipestone, MN 56164

From this quarry, Indians obtained materials for making pipes used in ceremonies.

Voyageurs National Park
P.O. Box 50
International Falls, MN 56649

Beautiful northern lakes, once the route of the French-Canadian voyageurs, are surrounded by forest in this land where geology and history capture your imagination.

MISSISSIPPI

Brices Cross Roads National Battlefield Site
c/o Natchez Trace Parkway
R.R. 1, NT-143
Tupelo, MS 38801

The Confederate cavalry was employed with extraordinary skill here during the battle of June 10, 1864.

Gulf Islands National Seashore
4000 Hanley Rd.
Ocean Springs, MS 39564
(see also Florida)

Sparkling beaches, historic ruins, and wildlife sanctuaries, accessible only by boat, can be found on the offshore islands of this unit, located near Pascagoula and Biloxi, Miss. On the mainland there's an urban park with a nature trail, picnic area, and a campground at Ocean Springs.

Natchez Trace Parkway
R.R. 1, NT-143
Tupelo, MS 38801
(also in Alabama and
Tennessee

This historic route generally follows the old Indian trace, or trail, between Nashville, Tenn. and Natchez, Miss. (Of the estimated 448 miles, 333 are completed.)

Tupelo National Battlefield
c/o Natchez Trace Parkway
R.R. 1, NT-143
Tupelo, MS 38801

Here, on July 13–14, 1864, Lt. Gen. Nathan Bedford Forrest's cavalry battled a Union force of 14,000 sent to keep Forrest from cutting off the railroad supplying Maj. Gen. William T. Sherman's march on Atlanta.

Vicksburg National Military Park
P.O. Box 349
Vicksburg, MS 39180

Fortifications of the 47-day siege of Vicksburg, which ended July 3, 1863, are remarkably well preserved here. Victory gave the North control of the Mississippi River and cut the Confederacy in two. Vicksburg National Cemetery—18,207 interments, 12,954 unidentified—adjoins the park. Grave sites are not available.

MISSOURI

George Washington Carver National
  Monument
P.O. Box 38
Diamond, MO 64804

Existing landmarks at the birthplace and childhood home of the famous black agronomist include a spring, a grove of trees, and the graves of the Moses Carver family.

Jefferson National Expansion Memorial National Historic Site
11 North 4th St.
St. Louis, MO 63102

This park on St. Louis' Mississippi riverfront memorializes Thomas Jefferson and others who directed territorial expansion of the U.S. Eero Saarinen's prize-winning, stainless-steel gateway arch commemorates westward pioneers. Visitors may ascend the 630-foot-high arch. In the nearby courthouse, Dred Scott sued for freedom in the historic slavery case.

Ozark National Scenic Riverways
P.O. Box 490
Van Buren, MO 63965

For about 140 miles the Current and Jacks Fork rivers flow through a quiet world of nature. Notable features include huge freshwater springs and numerous caves.

Wilson's Creek National Battlefield
521 N. Highway 60
Republic, MO 67538

The Confederate victory here on Aug. 10, 1861, was the first major engagement west of the Mississippi. It culminated in severe losses on both sides, yet Union troops were able to retreat and regroup.

MONTANA

Big Hole National Battlefield
P.O. Box 237
Wisdom, MT 59761

Nez Perce Indians and U.S. Army troops fought here in 1877—a dramatic episode in the long struggle to confine the Nez Perce, and other Indians, to reservations.

Bighorn Canyon National Recreation Area
P.O. Box 458
Fort Smith, MT 59035
(also in Wyoming)

Bighorn Lake, formed by Yellowtail Dam on the Bighorn River, extends 71 miles, including 47 miles through spectacular Bighorn Canyon. The Crow Indian Reservation borders a large part of the area.

Custer Battlefield National Monument P.O. Box 39 Crow Agency, MT 59022	The famous Battle of the Little Bighorn between 12 companies of the 7th U.S Cavalry and the Sioux and Northern Cheyenne Indians was fought here on June 25–26, 1876. Lt. Col. George A. Custer and about 268 of his force were killed. Custer Battlefield National Cemetery—with 4,487 interments, 277 unidentified—is included within the park.
Fort Benton P.O. Box 25287 Denver, CO 80225	Founded in 1846, this American Fur Company trading post was an important river port from 1859 through the Montana gold rush of 1862 until rail service surpassed river cargo transport.
Glacier National Park West Glacier, MT 59936	With precipitous peaks ranging about 10,000 feet, this ruggedly beautiful land includes nearly 50 glaciers, many lakes and streams, a wide variety of wild flowers, and wildlife such as bighorn sheep, bald eagles, and grizzly bears.
Grant-Kohrs Ranch National Historic Site P.O Box 790 Deer Lodge, MT 59722	This was the home ranch area of one of the largest and best-known 19th-century range ranches in the country.
Yellowstone National Park (see Wyoming)	

NEBRASKA

Agate Fossil Beds National Monument
P.O. Box 427
Gering, NE 69341

These renowned quarries contain numerous, well-preserved Miocene mammal fossils and represent an important chapter in the evolution of mammals.

Homestead National Monument of America
Route 3
Beatrice, NE 68310

One of the first claims under the Homestead Act of 1862 was filed for this land; includes Freeman School.

Scotts Bluff National Monument
P.O. Box 427
Gering, NE 69341

Rising 800 feet above the valley floor, this massive promontory was a landmark on the Oregon Trail, associated with overland migration between 1843 and 1869 across the Great Plains.

NEVADA

Lake Mead National Recreation Area
601 Nevada Hwy.
Boulder City, NV 89005

Lake Mead, formed by Hoover Dam, and Lake Mohave, by Davis Dam, on the Colorado River comprise this first national recreation area established by an act of Congress.

Lehman Caves National Monument
Baker, NV 89311

Tunnels and galleries decorated by stalactites and stalagmites honeycomb these caverns of light-gray and white marble.

NEW HAMPSHIRE

Saint-Gaudens National Historic Site
R.D. 2
Windsor, VT 05089

This memorial to sculptor Augustus Saint-Gaudens contains his home, "Aspet," and his studios and gardens.

NEW JERSEY

Edison National Historic Site
Main St. and Lakeside Ave.
West Orange, NJ 07052

Buildings and equipment used by Thomas A. Edison for many of his experiments are here, as are his library, papers, and models of some of his inventions. The site also includes Glenmont, Edison's 23-room home, with original furnishings.

Gateway National Recreation Area
P.O. Box 437
Highlands, NJ 07732
(see also New York)

The narrow Sandy Hook peninsula offers bathing beaches, interesting plant and animal life, and historic structures, including the Sandy Hook Lighthouse, reputed to be the oldest in the U.S. (1764).

Morristown National Historical Park
230 Morris St.
Morristown, NJ 07960

For two winters during the Revolution—1777 and 1779–80—the Continental Army established winter headquarters here. Washington's headquarters, Ford Mansion, is included in the park.

State of Liberty National Monument
(see New York)

NEW MEXICO

Aztec Ruins National Monument
P.O. Box U
Aztec, NM 87410

Ruins of this large Pueblo Indian community of 12th-century masonry and timber buildings have been excavated and stabilized. The ruins, misnamed by settlers, are unrelated to the Aztecs of Mexico.

Bandelier National Monument
Los Alamos, NM 87544

On the canyon-slashed slopes of the Pajarito Plateau are the ruins of many cliff houses of 15th-century Pueblo Indians.

Capulin Mountain National Monument
Capulin, NM 88414

This symmetrical cinder cone is an interesting example of a geologically recent, extinct volcano.

Carlsbad Caverns National Park
3225 National Parks Hwy.
Carlsbad, NM 88220

This series of connected caverns, the largest underground chambers yet discovered, has countless magnificent and curious formations.

Chaco Culture National Historical Park
Star Route 4
Box 6500
Bloomfield, NM 87413

The canyon, with hundreds of smaller ruins, contains 13 major Indian ruins unsurpassed in the U.S., representing the highest point of Pueblo pre-Columbian civilization.

El Morro National Monument
Ramah, NM 87321

"Inscription Rock" is a soft sandstone monolith on which are carved hundreds of inscriptions, including those of 17th-century Spanish explorers and 19th-century American emigrants and settlers. The monument also includes pre-Columbian petroglyphs.

Fort Union National Monument
Watrous, NM 87753

Three U.S. Army forts were built on this site—a key defensive point on the Santa Fe Trail—and were occupied from 1851 to 1891. Ruins of the last fort, which was the largest military post in the Southwest, have been stabilized.

Gila Cliff Dwellings National Monument
Gila Hot Springs
Rte. 11, Box 100
Silver City, NM 88061

These well-preserved cliff dwellings in natural cavities on the face of an overhanging cliff were inhabited from about A.D. 100 to 1300.

Georgia O'Keeffe National Historic Site
Southwest Regional Office
P.O. Box 728
Santa Fe, NM 87501

Home and studio of the artist in Abiquiu.

Pecos National Monument
P.O. Drawer 11
Pecos, NM 87552

Foundations of a 17th-century mission, ruins of an 18th-century church, ancient pueblo structural remains, and restored kivas comprise the park. This site was once a landmark on the Santa Fe Trail, ruts of which are still in existence.

Salinas National Monument
Rte. 1
Mountain Air, NM 87036

Perched high atop a limestone ridge, Pueblo de las Humanas was occupied from about A.D. 900 through the 1670s. Two 17th-century Franciscan mission churches, 21 Pueblo Indian apartment complexes, and 16 kivas are elements of the massive archeological remains of a settlement which once housed 2,000 Pueblo Indians.

White Sands National Monument
P.O. Box 458
Alamogordo, NM 88310

The park contains the world's largest gypsum dune field, covering nearly 230 square miles. The glistening white dunes rise 60 feet high. Small animals have adapted to this harsh environment by developing light, protective coloration. Plants also have adapted, extending root systems to remain atop the ever-shifting dunes.

NEW YORK

Castle Clinton National Monument
National Park Service
26 Wall St.
New York, NY 10005

Built 1808–11, this structure served successively as a defense for New York harbor, a promenade and entertainment center, and an immigration depot through which more than 8 million people entered the U.S. from 1855 to 1890. It is located in Battery Park, Manhattan.

Eleanor Roosevelt National Historic Site
Hyde Park, NY 12538

Mrs. Roosevelt used her "Val-Kill" estate as a personal retreat from her busy life. The pastoral setting of the cottage, built for her by her husband in 1925, includes fields, trees, swamps, and ponds. She also used the estate to entertain friends and dignitaries and to promote the many causes which interested her.

Federal Hall National Memorial
National Park Service
26 Wall St.
New York, NY 10005

This graceful building is on the site of the original Federal Hall where the trial of John Peter Zenger, involving freedom of the press, was held in 1735; the Stamp Act Congress convened, 1765; the Second Continental Congress met, 1785; Washington took the oath as first U.S. president, and the Bill of Rights was adopted, 1789. Present building was completed in 1842 as a federal customs house.

Fire Island National Seashore
120 Laurel St.
Patchogue, NY 11772

This barrier island off the south shore of Long Island possesses opportunities for beach-oriented recreation and ecological observations.

Fort Stanwix National Monument
112 E. Park St.
Rome, NY 13440

The American stand here in August 1777 was a major factor in repulsing the British invasion from Canada. The fort was also the site of the treaty of Fort Stanwix with the Iroquois, Nov. 5, 1768.

Gateway National Recreation Area
Floyd Bennett Field
Bldg. 69
Brooklyn, NY 11234

With beaches, marshes, islands, and adjacent waters in the New York Harbor area, this park offers urban residents a wide range of recreational opportunities.

General Grant National Memorial
National Park Service
26 Wall St.
New York, NY 10005

This memorial to Ulysses S. Grant, the Union commander who brought the Civil War to an end, includes the tombs of General and Mrs. Grant. As president of the U.S. (1869–77), Grant signed the act establishing the first national park, Yellowstone, Mar. 1, 1872. The memorial is on Riverside Drive near West 122d St.

Hamilton Grange National Memorial
287 Convent Ave.
New York, NY 10031

"The Grange," named after his grandfather's estate in Scotland, was the home of Alexander Hamilton, American statesman and first secretary of the Treasury.

335

Home of Franklin D. Roosevelt National Historic Site Hyde Park, NY 12538	This was the birthplace, lifetime residence, and "Summer White House" of the 32d president. He entertained many distinguished visitors here. The grave sites of President and Mrs. Roosevelt are in the Rose Garden. Designated Jan. 15, 1944.
Martin Van Buren National Historic Site P.O. Box 545 Kinderhook, NY 12106	Lindenwald Estate, south of Albany, was the home of the eighth president—a leader in the emergence of Jacksonian Democracy—for 21 years, until his death in 1862. Being Restored. *Not open to the public.*
Sagamore Hill National Historic Site Cove Neck Rd., Box 304 Oyster Bay, NY 11771	This estate was the home of Theodore Roosevelt from 1885 until his death in 1919. Used as the "Summer White House" 1901–08, it contains original furnishings. The Old Orchard Museum is on the grounds.
Saratoga National Historical Park R.D. 1, Box 113-C Stillwater, NY 12170	The American victory here over the British in 1777 was the turning point of the Revolution and one of the decisive battles in world history. Maj. Gen. Philip Schuyler's country home is nearby.
Statue of Liberty National Monument Liberty Island New York, NY 10004	The famous 152-foot copper statue bearing the torch of freedom was a gift of the French people in 1886 to commemorate the alliance of the two nations in the American Revolution. The monument includes the American Museum of Immigration, in the base of the statue, and Ellis Island, an immigration port from 1892 to 1954.

Theodore Roosevelt Birthplace National Historic Site
28 E. 20th St.
New York, NY 10003

The 26th president was born in a four-story brownstone house here on Oct. 27, 1858. Demolished in 1910, it was reconstructed 1921–23, following T.R.'s death.

Theodore Roosevelt Inaugural National Historic Site
641 Delaware Ave.
Buffalo, NY 14209

Theodore Roosevelt took the oath of office as president of the U.S. on Sept. 14, 1901, here in the Ansley Wilcox House, after the assassination of President William McKinley.

Upper Delaware Scenic and Recreational River
Cochecton, NY 12726

The National Park Service will acquire numerous access sites along 100 miles of this free-flowing fishing stream between Hancock and Sparrow Bush.

Vanderbilt Mansion National Historic Site
Hyde Park, NY 12538

This palatial mansion is a fine example of homes built by 19th-century millionaires.

Women's Rights National Historical Park
c/o North Atlantic Regional Office
15 State St.
Boston, MA 02109

Commemorates the 1848 birth of the women's rights movement at Seneca Falls and action by Susan B. Anthony, Elizabeth Cady Stanton, and others.

NORTH CAROLINA

Blue Ridge Parkway
700 Northwestern Bank Building
Asheville, NC 28801

Following the crest of the Blue Ridge Mountains, this scenic parkway averages 3,000 feet above sea level, embracing several large recreational areas, and preserving mountain folk culture and scenic resources. First national parkway.

Cape Hatteras National Seashore
Route 1, Box 675
Manteo, NC 27954

Beaches, migratory waterfowl, fishing, and points of historical interest, including the Cape Hatteras Lighthouse overlooking the "graveyard of the Atlantic," are special features of the first national seashore.

Cape Lookout National Seashore
P.O. Box 690
Beaufort, NC 28516

This series of barrier islands extends for 58 miles along the lower Outer Banks, embracing beaches, dunes, salt marshes, and historic Portsmouth Village.

Carl Sandburg Home National Historic Site
P.O. Box 395
Flat Rock, NC 28731

"Connemara" was the farm home of the noted poet-author for the last 22 years of his life. During his residence here, several of his books were published.

Fort Raleigh National Historic Site
c/o Cape Hatteras
National Seashore, Route 1, Box 675
Manteo, NC 27954

The first English settlement in North America was attempted here (1585–87). The fate of Sir Walter Raleigh's "Lost Colony" remains a mystery.

Guilford Courthouse National Military Park
P.O. Box 9806
Greensboro, NC 27408

The battle fought here on Mar. 15, 1781, opened the campaign that led to Yorktown and the end of the Revolution.

Moores Creek National Battlefield
P.O. Box 69
Currie, NC 28435

The battle on Feb. 27, 1776, between North Carolina Patriots and Loyalists, is commemorated here. The Patriot victory notably advanced the revolutionary cause in the South.

Wright Brothers National Memorial
c/o Cape Hatteras National Seashore,
Route 1, Box 675
Manteo, NC 27954

The first sustained flight in a heavier-than-air machine was made here by Wilbur and Orville Wright on Dec. 17, 1903.

NORTH DAKOTA

Fort Union Trading Post National Historic Site
Buford Route
Williston, ND 58801
(also in Montana)

The trading post that stood here was the principal fur-trading depot in the Upper Missouri River region from 1829 to 1867. Located at the confluence of the Missouri and Yellowstone rivers, Ft. Union served the Dakotas, Montana, and the Prairie Provinces.

Knife River Indian Villages National Historic Site
P.O. Box 175
Stanton, ND 58571

Remnants of historic and prehistoric Indian villages, last occupied in 1845 by the Hidatsa, contain an array of artifacts of Plains Indian culture.

Theodore Roosevelt National Park
P.O. Box 7
Medora, ND 58645

The park includes scenic badlands along the Little Missouri River and part of Theodore Roosevelt's Elkhorn Ranch.

OHIO

Cuyahoga Valley National Recreation Area
P.O. Box 158
Peninsula, OH 44264

This recreation area links the urban centers of Cleveland and Akron, preserving the rural character of the Cuyahoga River valley and such historic resources as the century-old Ohio and Erie Canal system.

Mound City Group National Monument
16062 State Route 104
Chillicothe, OH 45601

Twenty-three burial mounds of Hopewell Indians (200 B.C.–A.D. 500) yielded copper breastplates, tools, obsidian blades, shells, ornaments of grizzly bear teeth, and stone pipes carved as birds and animals. These provide insights into the ceremonial customs of these prehistoric people.

Perry's Victory and International Peace Memorial
P.O. Box 78
Put-in-Bay, OH 43456

Commodore Oliver H. Perry won the greatest naval battle of the War of 1812 on Lake Erie. The memorial—the world's most massive Doric column—was constructed in 1912–15 "to inculcate the lessons of international peace by arbitration and disarmament."

William Howard Taft National Historic Site
2038 Auburn Ave.
Cincinnati, OH 45219

This house was the birthplace and boyhood home of the only man to serve both as president and chief justice of the U.S.—27th president, 1909–13; U.S. chief justice, 1921–30.

OKLAHOMA

Chickasaw National Recreation Area
P.O. Box 201
Sulphur, OK 73086

The man-made Lake of the Arbuckles provides water recreation for an extensive Midwest area, and numerous cold mineral and freshwater springs, including bromide waters, surface here.

OREGON

Crater Lake National Park
P.O. Box 7
Crater Lake, OR 97604

This unique, deep blue lake lies in the heart of Mount Mazama, an ancient volcanic peak that collapsed centuries ago. The lake is encircled by multicolored lava walls reaching 500 to 2,000 feet above the lake waters.

Fort Clatsop National Memorial
Route 3, Box 604-FC
Astoria, OR 97103

The Lewis and Clark Expedition camped here in the winter of 1805–06.

John Day Fossil Beds National Monument
420 W. Main St.
John Day, OR 97845

Plant and animal fossils show five epochs, from Eocene to end of Pleistocene.

Oregon Caves National Monument
19000 Caves Highway
Cave Junction, OR 97523

Groundwater dissolving marble bedrock formed these cave passages and intricate flowstone formations.

PENNSYLVANIA

Allegheny Portage Railroad National
    Historic Site
P.O. Box 247
Cresson, PA 16630

Traces of the first railroad crossing of the Allegheny Mountains can still be seen here. An inclined plane railroad, it permitted transportation of passengers and freight over the mountains, providing a critical link in the Pennsylvania Mainline Canal system and with the West. Built between 1831 and 1834, it was abandoned by 1857.

Delaware National Scenic River
c/o Delaware Water Gap
National Recreation Area
Bushkill, PA 18324
(also in New Jersey)

This park contains the portion of the Delaware River which lies within the boundaries of Delaware Water Gap National Recreation Area. The free-flowing stream offers swimming, canoeing, and fishing opportunities.

Delaware Water Gap National
    Recreation Area
Bushkill, PA 18324
(also in New Jersey)

This scenic area preserves relatively unspoiled land on both the New Jersey and Pennsylvania sides of the Middle Delaware River. The river segment flows through the famous gap in the Appalachian Mountains. The park sponsors an "Artist-in-Residence" program, and three environmental education centers.

Edgar Allen Poe National Historic Site
c/o Independence
National Historical Park
313 Walnut Street
Philadelphia, PA 19106

The life and work of this gifted American author are described in exhibits in this house at 530 N. Seventh Street, where Poe lived 1844–45.

Eisenhower National Historic Site
c/o Gettysburg National Military Park
Gettysburg, PA 17325

This was the home and farm of President and Mrs. Dwight D. Eisenhower. *Not open to the public.*

Fort Necessity National Battlefield
The National Pike
Farmington, PA 15437

Colonial troops commanded by Lt. Col. George Washington, then 22 years old, were defeated here in the opening battle of the French and Indian War on July 3, 1754. The park includes the nearby monument to Maj. Gen. Edward Braddock and the early 19th-century Mount Washington Tavern, and Jumonville Glenn, site of the first skirmish of the French and Indian War, May. 28, 1754. Established as national battlefield site Mar. 4, 1931.

Friendship Hill National Historic Site
c/o Fort Necessity National Battlefield
The National Pike
Farmington, PA 15437

Stone and brick home on the Monongahela River, near Point Marion, Pa., belonged to Albert Gallatin, secretary of the Treasury, 1801–13, under Presidents Jefferson and Madison. *Not open to the public.*

Gettysburg National Military Park
Gettysburg, PA 17325

The great Civil War battle fought here July 1–3, 1863, repulsed the second Confederate invasion of the North. Gettysburg National Cemetery—7,036 interments, 1,668 unidentified—adjoins the park. President Lincoln delivered his Gettysburg address here in dedicating the cemetery Nov. 19, 1863.

Hopewell Village National Historic Site
R.D. 1, Box 345
Elverson, PA 19520

This is one of the finest examples of a rural American 19th-century ironmaking village. The buildings include the blast furnace and auxiliary structures.

Independence National Historical Park
313 Walnut Street
Philadelphia, PA 19106

The park includes structures and properties in old Philadelphia associated with the American Revolution and the founding and growth of the U.S.—Independence Hall, the Liberty Bell, Congress Hall, old City Hall, the First and Second Banks of the United States, Franklin Court, and Deshler-Morris House in Germantown.

Johnstown Flood National Memorial
c/o Allegheny Portage
Railroad National Historic Site
P.O. Box 247
Cresson, PA 16630

The tragic Johnstown Flood of 1889, caused by a break in the South Fork Dam, is memorialized here.

Thaddeus Kosciusko National Memorial
c/o Independence
National Historical Park
313 Walnut St.
Philadelphia, PA 19106

The life and work of this Polish-born patriot and hero of the American Revolution are commemorated at 301 Pine St., Philadelphia.

Upper Delaware Scenic and Recreational River
(see New York)

Valley Forge National Historical Park
Valley Forge, PA 19481

Site of the Continental Army's bitter winter encampment, 1777–78, the park contains General Washington's headquarters, a variety of monuments and markers, and re-creations of log buildings and cannons used by colonial troops.

PUERTO RICO

San Juan
National Historic Site
P.O. Box 712
Old San Juan, PR 00902

These massive masonry fortifications, oldest in the territorial limits of the U.S., were begun by the Spanish in the 16th century to protect a strategic harbor guarding the sea lanes to the New World.

RHODE ISLAND

Roger Williams National Memorial
P.O. Box 367, Annex Station
Providence, RI 02901

This memorial is in honor of the founder of the Rhode Island Colony and a pioneer in religious freedom.

SOUTH CAROLINA

Congaree Swamp National Monument
P.O. Box 11938
Columbia, SC 29211

Located on an alluvial floodplain 20 miles southeast of Columbia, the park contains the last significant tract of virgin southern bottomland hardwoods in the southeastern U.S.

Cowpens National Battlefield
c/o Kings Mountain National Military
  Park
P.O. Box 31
Kings Mountain, NC 28086

Brig. Gen. Daniel Morgan won a decisive Revolutionary War victory here over British Lt. Col. Banastre Tarleton on Jan. 17, 1781.

Fort Sumter National Monument
Drawer R
Sullivans Island, SC 29482

The first engagement of the Civil War took place here on Apr. 12, 1861. The park also embraces Fort Moultrie, scene of the patriot victory of June 28, 1776——one of the early defeats of the British in the Revolutionary War. The fort has been restored to reflect 171 years of seacoast defense.

Kings Mountain National Military Park P.O. Box 31 Kings Mountain NC 28086	American frontiersmen defeated the British here on Oct. 7, 1780, at a critical point during the Revolution.
Ninety Six National Historic Site P.O. Box 496 Ninety Six, SC 29666	The important colonial backcountry trading village and government seat after 1769 was held briefly by the British during the Revolutionary War and is the scene of Nathanael Greene's siege in 1781. The site contains earthwork embankments of a 1759 fortification, the remains of two historic villages, a colonial plantation complex, and numerous prehistoric sites.
SOUTH DAKOTA Badlands National Park P.O. Box 6 Interior, SD 57750	Carved by erosion, this scenic landscape contains animal fossils of 40 million years ago. Prairie grasslands support bison, bighorn sheep, deer, and antelope.
Jewel Cave National Monument Custer, SD 57730	Caverns, in limestone formation, consist of a series of chambers connected by narrow passages, with many side galleries and fine calcite crystal encrustations.
Mount Rushmore National Memorial	Colossal heads of Presidents George Washington, Thomas Jefferson, Abraham Lincoln, and Theodore Roosevelt were sculptured by Gutzon Borglum on the face of a granite mountain.

347

Wind Cave National Park
Hot Springs, SD 57747

These limestone caverns in the scenic Black Hills are decorated by beautiful boxwork and calcite crystal formations. Elk, deer, pronghorn, prairie dogs, and bison live in the park.

TENNESSEE

Andrew Johnson National Historic Site
Depot St.
Greeneville, TN 37743

The site includes two homes and the tailor shop of the 17th president, who served from 1865 to 1869, and the Andrew Johnson National Cemetery, where the president's burial site is one of 741 interments.

Appalachian National Scenic Trail
(see Maine)

Big South Fork National River and
Recreation Area
P.O. Drawer 630
Oneida, TN 37841
(also in Kentucky)

The free-flowing Big South Fork of the Cumberland River and its tributaries pass through scenic gorges and valleys containing a wide range of natural and historical features. The U.S. Army Corps of Engineers is coordinating planning and development of the area.

Chickamauga & Chattanooga National
Military Park
(see Georgia)

Cumberland Gap National Historical
Park
(see Kentucky)

**Fort Donelson
National Military Park**
P.O. Box F
Dover, TN 37058

The first major victory for the Union Army in the Civil War occurred here in February 1862 under the leadership of Ulysses S. Grant. Fort Donelson (Dover) National Cemetery—1,197 interments, 512 unidentified—adjoins the park.

Great Smoky Mountains National Park
Gatlinburg, TN 37738
(also in North Carolina)

Loftiest range east of the Black Hills, and one of the oldest uplands on earth; the Smokies have a diversified and luxuriant plant life, often of extraordinary size. The park has been selected for international Biosphere Reserve status.

Natchez Trace Parkway
(see Mississippi)

Obed Wild & Scenic River
P.O. Drawer 630
Oneida, TN 37841

The Obed River and its two main tributaries, Clear Creek and Daddy's Creek, cut into the Cumberland Plateau of eastern Tennessee, providing some of the most rugged scenery in the southeast. Elevations range from 900 to 2,900 feet above sea level.

Shiloh National Military Park
Shiloh, TN 38376

The bitter battle fought here Apr. 6–7, 1862, prepared the way for Maj. Gen. U.S. Grant's successful siege of Vicksburg. Well-preserved prehistoric Indian mounds overlook the river. Shiloh (Pittsburg Landing) National Cemetery—3,761 interments, 2,370 unidentified—adjoins the park.

Stones River National Battlefield
Route 10, Box 401
Old Nashville Hwy.
Murfreesboro, TN 37130

The fierce midwinter battle, which began the Federal offensive to trisect the Confederacy, took place here Dec. 31, 1862–Jan. 2, 1863. Stones River (Murfreesboro) National Cemetery—6,831 interments, 2,562 unidentified—adjoins the park. Grave sites are not available.

TEXAS

Alibates Flint Quarries National Monument
c/o Lake Meredith NRA
P.O. Box 1438
Fritch, TX 79036

For more than 10,000 years, pre-Columbian Indians dug agatized dolomite from quarries here to make projectile points, knives, scrapers, and other tools.

Amistad National Recreation Area
P.O. Box 1463
Del Rio, TX 78840

Boating and watersports highlight activities in the U.S. section of Amistad Reservoir on the Rio Grande. Administered under cooperative agreement with United States section, International Boundary and Water Commission, United States and Mexico, Nov. 11, 1965.

Big Bend National Park
Big Bend National Park, TX 79834

Mountains contrast with desert in this great bend of the Rio Grande, where a variety of unusual geological formations are found.

Big Thicket National Preserve
P.O. Box 7408
Beaumont, TX 77706

This unique ecosystem is a mingling of diverse plant associations resulting in a large variety of plant species found in close proximity. Study and research opportunities are excellent.

Chamizal National Memorial
800 S. San Marcial St.
El Paso, TX 79905

The peaceful settlement of a 99-year boundary dispute between the U.S. and Mexico is memorialized here. The Chamizal Treaty, ending the dispute, was signed in 1963. An amphitheater and 500-seat auditorium are used by theatrical groups from both nations.

Fort Davis National Historic Site
P.O. Box 1456
Fort Davis, TX 79734

A key post in the West Texas defensive system, the fort guarded emigrants on the San Antonio–El Paso road from 1854 to 1891.

Guadalupe Mountains National Park
3225 National Pks Hwy.
Carlsbad, NM 88220

Rising from the desert, this mountain mass contains portions of the world's most extensive and significant Permian limestone fossil reef. Also featured are a tremendous earth fault, lofty peaks, unusual flora and fauna, and a colorful record of the past.

Lake Meredith National Recreation Area
P.O. Box 1438
Fritch, TX 79036

Man-made Lake Meredith on the Canadian River is a popular water-activity center in the Southwest. Administered under cooperative agreement with Bureau of Reclamation, U.S. Dept. of the Interior, Mar. 15, 1965. Name changed from Sanford National Recreation Area on Oct. 16, 1972.

Lyndon B. Johnson National Historic Site
P.O. Box 329
Johnson City, TX 78636

The birthplace, boyhood home, and ranch of the 36th president, 1963–69, and his grandparents' old ranch make up the park.

Padre Island National Seashore
9405 S. Padre Island Dr.
Corpus Christi, TX 78418

Noted for its wide sand beaches, excellent fishing, and abundant bird and marine life, this barrier island stretches along the Gulf Coast for 80.5 miles.

Palo Alto Battlefield National Historic Site
P.O. Box 191
Brownsville, TX 78520

The park contains the site of the first of two important Mexican War battles fought on American soil. Gen. Zachary Taylor's victory here made invasion of Mexico possible.

Rio Grande Wild and Scenic River
c/o Big Bend National Park
Big Bend National Park, TX 79834

A 191.2-mile strip on the American shore of the Rio Grande in the Chihuahuan Desert protects the river. It begins in Big Bend National Park and continues downstream to the Terrell–Val Verde County Line.

San Antonio Missions National Historical Park
c/o Southwest Regional Office–National Park Service
P.O. Box 728
Sante Fe, NM 87501

Four Catholic frontier missions, part of a system that stretched across the Spanish Southwest in the 18th century, are commemorated here. Included in the park are a related historic dam and aqueduct system.

UTAH

Arches National Park
446 S. Main St.
Moab, UT 84532

Extraordinary products of erosion in the form of giant arches, windows, pinnacles, and pedestals change color here constantly as the sun moves overhead.

Bryce Canyon National Park
Bryce Canyon, UT 84717

In horseshoe-shaped amphitheaters along the edge of the Paunsaugunt Plateau in southern Utah stand innumerable highly colored and bizarre pinnacles, walls, and spires, perhaps the most colorful and unusual erosional forms in the world.

Canyonlands National Park
446 S. Main St.
Moab, UT 84532

In this geological wonderland, rocks, spires, and mesas rise more than 7,800 feet. Here, too, are petroglyphs left by Indians about 1,000 years ago.

Capitol Reef National Park
Torrey, UT 84775

Narrow high-walled gorges cut through a 60-mile uplift of sandstone cliffs with highly colored sedimentary formations. Dome-shaped white-cap rock along the Fremont River accounts for the name.

Cedar Breaks National Monument
P.O. Box 749
Cedar City, UT 84720

A huge natural amphitheater has eroded into the variegated Pink Cliffs (Wasatch Formation), which are 2,000 feet thick at this point.

Glen Canyon National Recreation Area
P.O. Box 1507
Page, AZ 86040
(also in Arizona)

Lake Powell, formed by the Colorado River, stretches for 186 miles behind one of the highest dams in the world.

Golden Spike National Historic Site
P.O. Box 394
Brigham City, UT 84302

Completion of the first transcontinental railroad in the U.S. was celebrated here where the Central Pacific and Union Pacific railroads met in 1869.

Natural Bridges National Monument
446 S. Main St.
Moab, UT 84532

Three natural bridges, carved out of sandstone, are protected here. The highest is 220 feet above the stream bed, with a span of 268 feet.

Rainbow Bridge National Monument
P.O. Box 1507
Page, AZ 86040

Greatest of the world's known natural bridges, this symmetrical arch of salmon-pink sandstone rises 290 feet above the floor of Bridge Canyon.

Timpanogos Cave National Monument
R.R. 3, Box 200
American Fork, UT 84003

This colorful limestone cavern on the side of Mount Timpanogos is noted for helictites—water-created formations that grow in all directions and shapes, regardless of the pull of gravity.

Zion National Park
Springdale, UT 84767

Colorful canyon and mesa scenery includes erosion and rock-fault patterns that create phenomenal shapes and landscapes. Evidence of former volcanic activity is here, too.

VERMONT

Appalachian National Scenic Trail
(see Maine)

VIRGINIA

Appalachian National Scenic Trail
(see Maine)

Appomattox Court House National Historical Park
P.O. Box 218
Appomattox, VA 24522

Here on Apr. 9, 1865, Gen. Robert E. Lee surrendered the Confederacy's largest field army to Lt. Gen. Ulysses S. Grant.

Arlington House, The Robert E. Lee Memorial
c/o George Washington Memorial Parkway
Turkey Run Park
McLean, VA 22101

This antebellum home of the Custis and Lee families overlooks the Potomac River and Washington, D.C.

Assateague Island National Seashore
(see Maryland)

Blue Ridge Parkway
(see North Carolina)

Booker T. Washington National Monument
Route 1, Box 195
Hardy, VA 24101

This site was the birthplace and early childhood home of the famous black leader and educator.

Colonial National Historical Park
P.O. Box 210
Yorktown, VA 23690

This park encompasses most of Jamestown Island, site of the first permanent English settlement; Yorktown, scene of the culminating battle of the American Revolution in 1781; a 23-mile parkway connecting these and other colonial sites with Williamsburg; and Cape Henry Memorial, which marks the approximate site of the first landing of Jamestown's colonists in 1607. Yorktown National Cemetery, containing Civil War grave sites—2,183 interments, 1,434 unidentified—adjoins the park. Grave sites are not available.

Fredericksburg and Spotsylvania County Battlefields Memorial National Military Park
P.O. Box 679
Fredericksburg, VA 22401

Portions of four major Civil War battlefields—Fredericksburg, Chancelorsville, the Wilderness, Spotsylvania Court House—Chatham Manor, and several smaller historic sites comprise the park. The battles occurred between 1862 and 1864. Fredericksburg National Cemetery—15,333 interments, 12,746 unidentified—is near the park. Grave sites are not available.

George Washington Birthplace National Monument
Washington's Birthplace, VA 22575

Birthplace of the first U.S. president, the park includes a memorial mansion and gardens, and the tombs of his father, grandfather, and great-grandfather.

George Washington Memorial Parkway
Turkey Run Park,
McLean, VA 22101
(also in Maryland)

This landscaped riverfront parkway links many landmarks in the life of George Washington. It connects Mount Vernon and Great Falls on the Virginia side of the Potomac and Great Falls with Chain Bridge on the Maryland side. The parkway includes natural, historical, and recreational areas.

Maggie L. Walker National Historic Site
c/o Richmond National Battlefield Park
3215 E. Broad St.
Richmond, VA 23223

The brick house at 110-A E. Leigh St., Richmond, was the home of the daughter of an ex-house slave who became the first woman president of an American financial institution.

Manassas National Battlefield Park
P.O. Box 1830
Manassas, VA 22110

The Battles of First and Second Manassas were fought here July 21, 1861, and Aug. 28–30, 1862. The 1861 battle was the first test of Northern and Southern military prowess. Here, Confederate Brig. Gen. Thomas J. Jackson acquired his nickname "Stonewall."

Petersburg National Battlefield
P.O. Box 549
Petersburg, VA 23803

The Union Army waged a 10-month campaign here 1864–65 to seize Petersburg, center of the railroads supplying Richmond and Gen. Robert E. Lee's army. Also includes City Point in Hopewell, Va., where Ulysses S. Grant made his headquarters at Appomattox Manor for the final 10 months of the war.

Prince William Forest Park
P.O. Box 208
Triangle, VA 22172

In this forested watershed of Quantico Creek, pines and hardwoods have replaced worn-out farmland.

Richmond National Battlefield Park
3215 East Broad St.
Richmond, VA 23223

The park commemorates several battles to capture Richmond, the Confederate capital, during the Civil War.

Shenandoah National Park
Rt. 4, Box 292
Luray, VA 22835

Skyline Drive winds through hardwood forests along the crest of this outstanding portion of the Blue Ridge Mountains, with spectacular vistas of historic Shenandoah Valley and the Piedmont.

Wolf Trap Farm Park for the Performing Arts
1551 Trap Rd.
Vienna, VA 22180

At this first national park for the performing arts, Filene Center can accommodate an audience of 6,500, including 3,000 on the sloping lawn, in a setting of rolling hills and woods. The stagehouse is 10 stories high and the stage 100 feet wide by 64 feet deep.

VIRGIN ISLANDS

Buck Island Reef National Monument
Box 160, Christiansted,
St. Croix, VI 00820

Coral grottoes, sea fans, gorgonias, and tropical fishes—along an underwater trail—make this one of the finest marine gardens in the Caribbean. The island is a rookery for frigate birds and pelicans, and the habitat of green turtles.

Christiansted National Historic Site
P.O. Box 160, Christiansted
St. Croix, VI 00820

Colonial development of the Virgin Islands is commemorated by 18th- and 19th-century structures in the capital of the former Danish West Indies on St. Croix Island. Discovered by Columbus in 1493, St. Croix was purchased by the U.S. in 1917.

Virgin Islands National Park
P.O. Box 806
Charlotte Amalie,
St. Thomas, VI 00801

The park covers about three-fourths of St. John Island and Hassel Island in St. Thomas harbor and includes quiet coves, blue-green waters, and white sandy beaches fringed by lush green hills. Here, too, are early Carib Indian relics and the remains of Danish colonial sugar plantations.

WASHINGTON

Coulee Dam National Recreation Area
P.O. Box 37
Coulee Dam, WA 99116

Formed by Grand Coulee Dam (part of the Columbia River Basin project) 130-mile long Franklin D. Roosevelt Lake is the principal recreation feature here.

Fort Vancouver National Historic Site
E. Evergreen Blvd.
Vancouver, WA 98661

As the western headquarters of Hudson's Bay Company, 1825 to 1849, this was the hub of political and fur-trading activities. A U.S. military reservation—Vancouver Barracks established in 1849—took over the fort in 1860, remaining active until 1949.

Klondike Gold Rush National Historical Park
117 S. Main St.
Seattle, WA 98104
(see also Alaska)

The park orientation center is at 117 S. Main St. in Seattle's Pioneer Square area.

Lake Chelan National Recreation Area
800 State St.
Sedro Woolley, WA 98284

Here the beautiful Stehekin Valley, with a portion of fjordlike Lake Chelan, adjoins the southern unit of North Cascades National Park.

Mount Rainier National Park
Tahoma Woods, Star Route
Ashford, WA 98304

This greatest single-peak glacial system in the U.S. radiates from the summit and slopes of an ancient volcano, with dense forests and subalpine flowered meadows below.

North Cascades National Park
800 State St.
Sedro Woolley, WA 98284

High jagged peaks intercept moisture-laden winds, producing glaciers, icefalls, waterfalls, and other water phenomena in this wild alpine region, where lush forests and meadows, plant and animal communities thrive in the valleys.

Olympic National Park
600 East Park Ave.
Port Angeles, WA 98362

This mountain wilderness contains the finest remnant of Pacific Northwest rain forest, active glaciers, rare Roosevelt elk, and 50 miles of wild, scenic ocean shore.

Ross Lake National Recreation Area
800 State St.
Sedro Woolley, WA 98284

Ringed by mountains, this reservoir in the Skagit River drainage separates the North and South units of North Cascades National Park.

San Juan Island National Historical Park
300 Battle Point Road
Friday Harbor, WA 98250

This park marks the historic events on the island from 1853 to 1871 in connection with final settlement of the Oregon Territory's northern boundary, including the so-called Pig War of 1859.

Whitman Mission National Historic Site
Route 2
Walla Walla, WA 99362

Dr. and Mrs. Marcus Whitman ministered to spiritual and physical needs of the Indians here until slain by a few of them in 1847. The mission was a landmark on the Oregon Trail.

WEST VIRGINIA

Appalachian National Scenic Trail
(see Maine)

Chesapeake and Ohio Canal National Historical Park
(see in Maryland)

Harpers Ferry National Historical Park
P.O. Box 65
Harpers Ferry, WV 24525
(also in Maryland)

Because of its strategic location at the confluence of the Shenandoah and Potomac rivers, this town changed hands many times during the Civil War. John Brown's raid took place here in 1859.

New River Gorge National River
National Park Service
143 S. Third St.
Philadelphia, PA 19106

A rugged, whitewater river, flowing northward through deep canyons, the New is among the oldest rivers on the continent. The free-flowing, 66-mile section from Hinton to Fayetteville is abundant in natural, scenic, historic, and recreational values.

WISCONSIN

Apostle Islands National Lakeshore
Old Courthouse Building
Bayfield, WI 54814

Twenty picturesque islands and on an 11-mile strip of adjacent Bayfield Peninsula along the south shore of Lake Superior comprise the northern park.

Lower St. Croix
National Scenic River
P.O. Box 708
St. Croix Falls, WI 54024

Recreational opportunities for much of the upper Midwest are provided here along this 27-mile segment of the St. Croix River, a component of the Wild and Scenic Rivers System.

St. Croix National Scenic River
P.O. Box 708
St. Croix, Falls, WI 54024

About 200 miles of the beautiful St. Croix River and its Namekagon tributary make up this area, an initial component of the National Wild and Scenic Rivers System.

WYOMING

Devils Tower National Monument
Devils Tower, WY 82714

This 865-foot tower of columnar rock, the remains of a volcanic intrusion, was the nation's first national monument.

Fort Laramie National Historic Site
Fort Laramie, WY 82212

A fur-trade post once stood here, but the surviving buildings are those of a major military post that guarded covered-wagon trails to the West, 1849–90.

Fossil Butte National Monument
P.O. Box 527
Kemmerer, WY 83101

An abundance of rare fish fossils, 40–65 million years old, is evidence of former habitation of this now semiarid region.

Grand Teton National Park
P.O. Drawer 170
Moose, WY 83012

The most impressive part of the Teton Range, this series of blue-gray peaks rising more than a mile above the sagebrush flats was once a noted landmark of Indians and "Mountain Men." The park includes part of Jackson Hole, winter feeding ground of the largest American elk herd.

**John D. Rockefeller, Jr.
Memorial Parkway**
c/o Grand Teton
National Park
P.O. Drawer 170
Moose, WY 83012

Linking West Thumb in Yellowstone with the south entrance of Grand Teton National Park, this scenic 82-mile corridor commemorates Rockefeller's role in aiding establishment of many parks, including Grand Teton.

Yellowstone National Park
P.O. Box 168
Yellowstone National
Park, WY 82190
(also in Montana and Idaho)

Old Faithful and some 10,000 other geysers and hot springs make this the earth's greatest geyser area. Here, too, are lakes, waterfalls, high mountains, and the Grand Canyon of the Yellowstone—all set apart in 1872 as the world's first national park. It is the third largest park in the National Park System.

TRAVEL TIPS

More than half of the parks charge no entrance fee, while the rest charge a very small fee. If you plan to make several trips to the parks, it is worthwhile obtaining a Golden Eagle Passport for ten dollars, which gives you free access to all parks for one year. Senior citizens are entitled to the Golden Age Passport, issued free, which is a lifetime entrance permit, and the handicapped can get the similar Golden Access Passport. All of these passports are available at any national park which charges an entrance fee.

In addition, some parks may also charge minimal fees for special recreational facilities or services such as boat ramps, guided tours, or campsites.

Since each park is unqiue, some offer more in the way of visitor amenities than others. This is the result of many factors, the most important being the desire to keep these havens of nature as unspoiled as possible. Only those improvements which are necessary for the protection, convenience, and comfort of visitors have been permitted, and those improvements vary widely from park to park.

Reservations should be made well in advance if you are planning to stay in one of the hotels or lodges located within the park grounds. Not all parks have such accommodations, but where they don't exist within the park itself, plenty of hotel and motel space usually can be found a short distance away in nearby communities.

Camping is especially encouraged throughout the park system, with some parks even offering camping equipment for rent. And while quite a few have special areas set aside for recreational vehicles, not all are fully equipped with hookups for water, electricity, and sewage.

Although camping sites are usually operated on a first-come, first-served basis, the increasing popularity of this pastime has forced a number of parks to take reservations, particularly during peak visitor seasons. Many parks accept mailed-in reservations, although more and more are being added each year to the National Park Service's computerized reservation system. For additional information on the reservation program, you can write to: Office of Public Affairs, National Park Service, Interior Building, Washington, D.C. 20240.

If you are hoping to get in some backcountry camping, you'd also be wise to check the current listings to determine which parks require backcountry-use permits. These permits, issued free of charge, are intended to control the number of people camping at one time in areas where the ecology is especially fragile.

Home delivery from Pocket Books

Here's your opportunity to have fabulous bestsellers delivered right to you. Our free catalog is filled to the brim with the newest titles plus the finest in mysteries, science fiction, westerns, cookbooks, romances, biographies, health, psychology, humor—every subject under the sun. Order this today and a world of pleasure will arrive at your door.

368